Project Management Using Microsoft® Project 2016

A Training and Reference Guide for Project Managers Using
Standard, Professional, Server, Web Application and
Project Online for Office 365

by Gus Cicala

project assistants

Wilmington, Delaware

Project Management Using Microsoft Project 2016

Author: Gus Cicala
Content Contributor
 & Microsoft MVP: Jeremy Cottino
Technical Content Editor: Bill Gundrum
Development Editor: Jan Goodman

Copy Editor: Daniel Cicala
Product Manager: Noreen Hackman
Cover Design: Asha Hossain

Printed in the United States of America

First Edition

ISBN-13: 978-0692869154
ISBN-10: 0692869158

Library of Congress Control Number: 2017935279

For permission requests, and any other inquiries related to Project Assistants Publishing, contact us:

E-mail: info@projectassistants.com
Web: www.projectassistants.com
Tel: 800-642-9259
Fax: 302-358-2992
Mail: 1521 Concord Pike, Suite 301
Wilmington, DE 19803

Notice

Dedication

To all the Zen masters of project management who strive for the promise of "Delivering the future into the present" one day at a time through your mastery of the arts and science of our profession:

ॐ *May your patience with the reality of the present enable you to craft the expected project outcomes through a skillful re-synching of the revised plan with the passionless and relentless unfolding of reality.*

ॐ *May you always have a keen awareness and unconditional acceptance of what "is."*

ॐ *May the winds of unfavorable variances be always at your back, propelling your project to deliver the transformational benefits for our species and the wider universe.*

ॐ *May you be bestowed with a wealth of resilience and an abundance of composure that inspires your stakeholders to consistently accept the new realities of the present.*

ॐ *May you prevail despite the ongoing resistance from those who desperately grasp for the unwelcome and unexpected past to be controlled and maybe even attempt to re-write that unforgiving history to align to the ever-elusive and now long lost original baseline.*

...Namaste!

Gus Cicala

April 2017

Acknowledgements

I would like to acknowledge and thank everyone who played an important role in the development and publication of this book:

- ❏ Jeremy Cottino, a very talented Microsoft Project MVP, who came to my rescue on short notice, to add the new Microsoft Project 2016 content for Resource Engagements

- ❏ Noreen Hackman, a true leader who aggressively attacks every challenge with gusto, for her instrumental role in unknotting the mysteries of turning a corporate training guide into a successful commercial publication

- ❏ Daniel Cicala, for bringing his command of the English language to tame and herd the expertise of technical people into a clear and coherent text

- ❏ Asha Hossain, for providing her fantastic graphical art support for the Project Assistants brand over the past 20 years, including the cover of this book

- ❏ Bill Gundrum, a powerhouse of Microsoft Project expertise and experience, who again has fine-tuned the technical content to make for a clean, accurate, and complete product

I would be remiss in not mentioning many of the past team members who were so instrumental in developing an indispensable portion of the original content that has survived through to this edition: Jan Goodman, Alex Ovecka, Fred Oettle, Denise Cicala, Ira Brown, Michael Steinberg, Graham McHardy, John Godley, and Laurie Van Dusen.

I am grateful and blessed for your dedication, commitment and valuable contributions to our success.

Table of Contents

part I

Introduction to Project Management

chapter 1

Introduction

- Using This Guide

- High-Level Overview of Microsoft Project 2016

Learning Objectives for this Chapter

At the end of the chapter, the reader should be able to:

- Know how to navigate this text and download the exercise files
- Describe the key components of the Microsoft Project 2016 solution

This guide will introduce you to the project manager's perspective on the latest version of Microsoft Project, Microsoft Project 2016. This set of software tools supports the management of all projects across an organization, or enterprise project management (EPM).

EPM requires that accurate planning and scheduling information flow from the project manager to the technical experts doing the actual work of the projects, as well as the executives making resource commitments and strategic decisions for the organization. Effective EPM allows organizations to better meet portfolio commitments and achieve their goals. The process begins with the project manager, using a variety of tools described in this manual.

Project Assistants has been providing project management theory and Microsoft Project training material for our training courses since the release of Microsoft Project version 3 in 1993. Prior to the release of Microsoft Project 2013, we were surprised that we could not find a work for purchase that provided hands-on training exercises for Microsoft Project on the desktop as well as the enterprise features used in Microsoft Project Professional and Project Web Application. We had a responsibility to provide this content to our clients, so we decided to convert our own content into a formal, cohesive guide.

This text was created to serve as that comprehensive reference and training guide, assembling content and best practices honed over many years of Microsoft Project and general project management training.

Our debut was *Project Management Using Microsoft Project 2013* and we have updated the material for Microsoft Project 2016. We have improved the exercises with new features, we have re-captured the screen images in larger, improved quality. We also added the new features in Microsoft Project 2016, especially the new resource engagement feature, covered in thorough detail in Section 13.4: *Resource Engagements*.

1.1 Using This Guide

Many training guides on technology are primarily manuals on features and functions of the software. The goal of this book is to show why those features and functions are important from a project management theory standpoint, and then demonstrate how to effectively leverage that value. When used cover-to-cover, this text serves as a comprehensive guide to running a project from initiation to closeout with guides along the way for how to use Microsoft Project to facilitate that. This guide can also be used as preparatory material for Microsoft Exam 74-343.

The information in this book was selected based on our 20+ years of project management and Microsoft Project consulting experience. In selecting the features and functions to be covered, we selected a middle-of-the-road approach that deliberately glosses over simple topics that are assumed to be known by the reader. A more difficult decision was faced when determining which advanced features (such as earned value management) to cover in a book of this nature. The features chosen for coverage in this book represent the interests of most organizations with which we have interacted.

There is no need to follow the order in which the material is presented. For example, you may want to start with the overview on Navigating in Microsoft Project 2016 Views, since knowing where to find information is the foundation to unlocking the powerful potential of the tool.

If you are skipping around the book, note that the features are demonstrated in great detail the first time through to take out any guesswork, so if you get stuck, you can always refer back to the first section that covers that feature. Also, many of the exercises build on each other, so you may have to start back on earlier chapters if you'd like your exercise files to be up-to-date.

This text covers Microsoft Project 2016 Standard, Microsoft Project 2016 Professional, Microsoft Project Server 2016, Microsoft Project Web Application 2016 (PWA) and Microsoft Project Online 2016 for Office 365. This text is presented in the context of what a project manager needs to know. As a result, features not relevant to a project manager, such as the Project Server administrator functions, are not covered. Everything in this book is usable in Microsoft Project Professional, and all but Part IV "Enterprise Project Management" applies to Microsoft Project Standard as well.

With the release of Microsoft Project 2016, Microsoft now offers an off-premises hosted version of Microsoft Project that is referred to as Microsoft Project Online. This tool is part of the Microsoft Office 365 hosted solution family of products that is intended for organizations that wish to reap the benefits of using this technology in a software-as-a-service (SaaS) environment. From the perspective of a project manager using Microsoft Project, the vast majority of the features and functions remain unchanged. When the Microsoft Project Professional and PWA features are covered, nuances related to the use of these features in Project Online will be pointed out. Similarly, there are limited differences between Project Server hosted on premises and Project Online hosted off premises, so they are also highlighted in Part IV chapters as they come up, rather than in a standalone chapter.

The exercise files use a standardized style to explain how to navigate the ribbon. The ribbon is what we call the tabulated menu bar that Microsoft has been using since the release of Microsoft Project 2010. All commands are in bold and italics, and subcategories of the ribbon are separated by colons. When it says, for example, *Task:View:Resource Usage View*, that means, "Go to the Task tab in the ribbon, then under the subcategory labeled View, you will find the Resource Usage View."

Downloading Exercise Files Used in This Book

To use the exercise files in this book, you will need to download and potentially unzip them, depending on your browser and method of download.

These files are available for free on Project Assistants' website and can be re-downloaded at any time. To download them:

❑ Go to our updates and materials webpage:

http://projectassistants.projestic.com/updates-materials-project-2016/

❑ Click "Register" and fill in the appropriate information.

❑ You will receive an email with a download link for the compressed exercise file.

❑ Once the file is downloaded, unzip the exercise files to a location of your choice.

Our updates and materials webpage will also host any news regarding significant corrections, updates to the text, or modifications to the supporting exercise files:

http://projectassistants.projestic.com/updates-materials-project-2016/

If you have any questions about downloading and using the exercise files, please contact Project Assistants at info@projectassistants.com.

If you are an instructor who needs access to the answer key for the end of chapter quizzes, please email your request with a copy of your proof of purchase and a copy of your teaching credentials to the author: GusCicala@projectassistants.com.

Note: The hands-on exercise files that you download were designed to show month-day format without the year. Before you begin, you may want to change the default date to drop the year from the display. To do so, navigate to *File: Options*, choose *General*, then choose the *Date Format* dropdown. Choose "1/28."

If you prefer to see the year in schedule dates, you may have to widen the date columns to include the year in the display.

NOTE

Project Assistants offers a full spectrum of Microsoft Project training solutions that can be customized to reflect your organization's unique needs. Please visit our website to learn more about our training offerings:

http://projectassistants.com/solutions-type/training

Additionally, we offer the ability to license a Microsoft Word version of this volume that can be modified, by you or us, for your specific training needs.

Please contact us to learn more about our training solutions and material licensing options:

Project Assistants, Inc.
1.800.642.9259
302.477.9711
info@projectassistants.com

1.2 High-Level Overview of Microsoft Project 2016

Microsoft Project 2016 is a set of integrated software applications that together provide the tools needed for enterprise project management (EPM). The three basic components are presented in the following figure:

Figure 1.

Microsoft
Project 2016
components

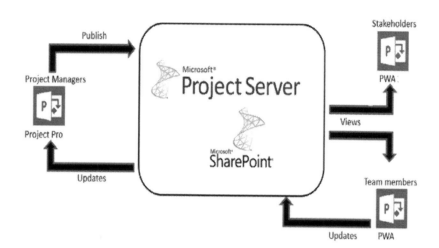

Notes:

- If you are using Microsoft Project 2016 Standard (instead of Microsoft Project 2016 Professional) this diagram does not apply, as Microsoft Project standard cannot connect to Microsoft Project Server.

- If you are using Office 365, the Microsoft Project Server/SharePoint environment is collectively referred to as Project Online.

If using Microsoft Project Server/Project Online, the EPM process begins with a project manager developing a project plan using Microsoft Project 2016 Professional. This version supports EPM by optionally connecting with Project Server 2016 when starting Microsoft Project 2016 Professional.

The project is sent to a server running Microsoft Project Server 2016, in a process called "publishing" the project. Once the project is published, it becomes available to other parts of the organization.

Assignments for team members are sent to team members who may receive an automatic email notification that they have new or changed assignments to view.

Team members can view their assignments and report progress on those tasks using a web-based tool called Microsoft Project Web App. When they update the task status, the project manager can view those updates using Web App and approve or reject them. Once approved, the information automatically updates the project plan itself, freeing the project manager to focus on the effects of those updates.

The potential weak link in any such system is, of course, the quality and usefulness of the actual project plans that are shared with the rest of the project and management teams.

As with all Microsoft applications, there are multiple ways to do many tasks. Rather than cover every possible method, we will recommend the best practice in each area and list alternatives with brief directions for their use.

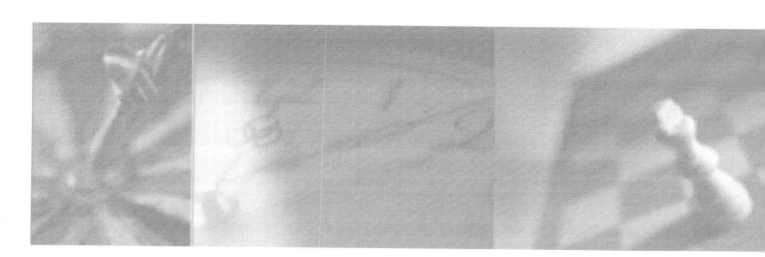

chapter 2

Understanding Project Management Concepts

- What is Project Management?

- The Importance of Methodology

- Project Phases and the Project Lifecycle

- Project Stakeholders and Organizational Influences

- Project Processes

Learning Objectives for this Chapter

At the end of the chapter, the reader should be able to:

- Define the basic definition of Project Management and how project management fits into the environment in which projects typically occur.
- Describe the common attributes of a successful project.
- Describe the most common type of projects and the typical lifecycle methodologies that are employed to deliverer project results.
- Understand the importance of the role of project stakeholders and how organizational influences impact the success or failure of projects
- Describe the five (5) major process groups that comprise the overall project management process flow

2.1 What is Project Management?

Project management is an organized set of people, processes, and procedures working together to provide on-time, on-budget delivery of stated objectives with high quality and satisfied sponsors. It achieves this while still taking into consideration that any successful team effort relies on treating people with respect.

Project management as we know it first appeared in World War II as a tool for construction and logistics. The need for enormous amounts of materiel for the invasion of Europe and the vast distances of the Pacific Ocean fostered the development of new ways of planning and scheduling military operations. These approaches were clearly successful, but required practitioners to manage enormous amounts of data—with no electronic help, no less.

After the success of these methods in the war, companies such as DuPont and Remington Arms (which was owned by DuPont) experimented with using them in the civilian sector. Since then, the tools and philosophy of project management have been widely used in both the public and private sectors of our global economy.

Reasons for adopting project management tools and techniques usually include some or all of the following:

- ❑ Internal and external competition
- ❑ Pervasiveness of multi-discipline projects
- ❑ Increasingly complex projects
- ❑ Customer demands
- ❑ Technological change

Basically, organizations see project management as a way to do things better, faster, and cheaper. It's an incredibly powerful tool—when it's used well. So how do you use it well?

The Project Management Institute (PMI) was founded in 1969 to promote professionalism in project management. They've collected and constantly updated project management best practices—what works and what doesn't—over many thousands of projects into a record called the "Guide to the Project Management Body of Knowledge" (PMBOK Guide). This guide has been accepted by the American National Standards Institute (ANSI) as the U.S. standard for project management.

Modern project management includes adapting the general principles in the PMBOK Guide to fit an organization's specific situation. No single approach could possibly fit all industries and organizations on our diverse planet.

What Makes a Project a Project?

Textbook definitions of projects vary, but they all include the following features:

- A project is goal-oriented, producing a unique deliverable or set of deliverables.
- A project consists of connected, related activities.
- A project has limited duration, which means projects are typified by a predefined schedule and usually tied to a specific end date.
- A project has elements of uniqueness.
- Projects are defined by three constraints which must be managed: time, cost, and scope (work content) of the project.

The modern philosophy of project management includes:

- An emphasis on the organizational support needed for project management (both philosophical and systems support).
- The artistic and scientific aspects of management which project managers have to bring to the table.
 - Art: Team management, reward/punishment, and management style
 - Science: Scope, risk, quality, cost, and time management systems
 - Both: Communication, resource, integration, and contract management
- Specific knowledge, skills, tools, and techniques that are useful for managing projects.
- A focus on meeting the needs of the client/customer (internal and external).

What Defines a Successful Project?

A project is deemed successful when the objectives of the sponsor are met. It is important to meet with the sponsor very early in the project to understand their goals and objectives, which should be documented in a project definition document (for example: project charter or statement of work). Some characteristics of a successful project are:

❑ On-time

❑ On-budget

❑ High-quality

❑ Fulfilled objectives

❑ Satisfied customers

❑ Achieved outcomes

To achieve these characteristics, project management must follow a process, be supported by a methodology, and have quality assurance to continue improving the process and the methodology.

The Project Management Process

There are three major stages in the project management process, each stage including several individual processes:

Figure 2.

The Project
Management
Process

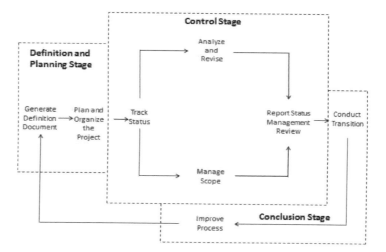

❑ **Definition and Planning**

 o **Definition** – Documents the overall project objectives, scope, approach, schedule, budget, resources, deliverables, and completion criteria

 o **Planning and Organization** – Provides the detailed roadmap that will be used to guide the project team when constructing the final deliverables

❑ **Control**

- o **Tracking** – Collects information from the team to assist the project manager in assessing actual progress
- o **Analysis** – Highlights any deviations from the original plan against current progress
- o **Revision** – Makes any necessary plan modifications to steer the project back on course
- o **Scope Management** – Provides an orderly means of modifying the original project definition
- o **Status Reporting and Management Reviews** – Ensures that all relevant project stakeholders are kept apprised of all key project information

❑ **Conclusion**

- o **Providing Feedback/Continuous Improvement** – Instills quality in the process of project management

Though we've focused on the technical aspects of project management up to this point, the last few processes emphasize another aspect crucial to being successful: the people.

Since the project manager is responsible for client satisfaction, clearly stating expectations and constantly managing those expectations is an important skill in avoiding disappointment and dissatisfaction, from both project team members and customers.

Effective project managers are often blessed with a broad range of competencies from intellectual to interpersonal to technical and judgmental. It is this unique package of skills that provides the effective project manager with an integrated, situational approach to successful management that cannot be readily documented and shared in a text on the topic.

The Four Principles of Effective Project Managers

Effective project managers recognize four essential truths which are found in all projects. These key project principles are:

❑ **Principle 1:** If you don't know where you're going, you probably won't get there.

Application: Set an effective project objective, developed with the input of the client(s) and project team members.

❑ **Principle 2:** If you fail to plan, you plan to fail.

Application: Learn and use the available planning techniques developed by previous project managers and thinkers about project management.

❑ **Principle 3:** If you catch problems early, they are easier to solve.

Application: Proactively look for trouble, with an eye toward managing problems, rather than being victimized by them.

❑ **Principle 4:** People and politics are the biggest variables in every project.

Application: Remember to make time to focus attention on people issues, both internal to the team and external.

Effective project managers are comfortable operating in the "gray area," even if they have come from a technical environment where hard and fast answers may be considered the norm.

Project Management Tools

"A computer will not make a good manager out of a bad manager. It makes a good manager better faster and a bad manager worse faster."

Edward M. Esber
Former CEO, Ashton-Tate

Advantages and Disadvantages of Using Project Management Software Tools

One of the obvious advantages of project management tools is that computers make your project plan easy to update and the quality of the output is high, which can save you time. Computers are excellent for handling the extensive calculations required to keep a plan up to date. Their use may even be mandatory when project or resource scheduling information needs to be shared across the enterprise. You can also conveniently and dynamically select the information you want from a large amount of data.

Project management software, however, tends to be fairly complicated relative to other types of personal computer software. This reality makes for a longer learning curve for training and on-the-job experience. It is not uncommon for a project manager to need upwards of a year to become comfortable with a new tool. These complications are compounded by the fact that project management terminology is not necessarily intuitive. Whereas the terminology required to use a word processing or spreadsheet application is generally acquired in grammar and high school, many project managers need training in the fundamentals of project management theory to begin to be productive with a tool.

Another consideration is the effort it takes to load all of the information into the tool. Once the project manager makes the commitment of time, it is important to reap the return on that investment by using the tool to run the project.

Conclusion

Based upon these advantages and disadvantages, the investment required to use a tool should only be made for larger projects with higher budgets. A two-month project with 2 or 3 people assigned will not require the same rigor as a two-year project with 25 people assigned who are geographically dispersed. As in any business decision, the benefits should outweigh the cost. Based on these concepts, sound judgment is required to decide how deep to go with using a tool.

2.2 The Importance of Methodology to Project Management

A methodology is an integrated, cohesive, and well-documented set of repeatable processes that provide for quality deliverables through the consistent execution of practices that have been proven to work.

Methodologies are usually developed in organizations that are tired of "reinventing the wheel," opting instead to document successful processes and share them across the organization. Methodologies include document templates (such as sample design reports), procedures (such as detailed approaches for producing a data model), forms (such as requests for system enhancements), and work plans (such as Microsoft Project work plan templates).

An effective methodology:

- ❑ Defines repeatable processes
- ❑ Instills quality into service-based processes
- ❑ Removes creativity from processes that should not be creative
- ❑ Provides a floor—not a ceiling
- ❑ Organizes the project tasks for the work plan
- ❑ Forms the foundation for continuous improvement

Methodology is the project manager's primary means of ensuring quality in a project. It supplies the project manager and the entire project team with a "cookbook" for performing the tasks in the project plan.

Project management is consistent from project to project, but methodologies tend to vary. The project manager needs to determine if the organization already has a methodology for the specific type of project they will manage.

Many methodologies contain detailed procedures to provide a consistent means of performing a process. A procedure for data modeling might look something like this:

Figure 3.

Data Modeling Procedures
1. Determine all business entities *Detailed paragraph explaining how to determine business entities*
2. Determine cardinality between entities *Detailed paragraph explaining how to determine cardinality between business entities*
3. Normalize the data model *Detailed paragraph explaining how to normalize a data model*
4. Migrate the data model to third normal form *Detailed paragraph explaining how to migrate a data model*
5. Convert the normalized data model to a physical data model *Detailed paragraph explaining how to convert the normalized data model to the physical data model*

2.3 Project Phases and the Project Lifecycle

Although earlier we referred to "the project lifecycle," there are a variety of approaches used to define a project from start to finish and to break it down into phases. In this section, we'll look at some alternate approaches to project lifecycles. For more examples and detail on this subject visit PMI.org and download a copy of the most recent PMBOK Guide.

Project Phase Deliverables

Each project phase is marked by completion of one or more *deliverables*. A deliverable is a product, such as a feasibility study, a design, or a prototype. The deliverables, like the phases, are part of a logical, usually chronological, approach designed to ensure proper completion of the project's desired product.

The conclusion of a project phase generally includes a review of both the desired deliverables and the project performance, in order to detect and correct errors as early as possible and to decide if the project should continue into its next phase. These phase-end reviews are often called *phase exits, stage gates,* or *kill points.*

Characteristics of the Project Lifecycle

The project lifecycle defines a project from beginning to end. Of course, lifecycles vary from industry to industry and even from organization to organization. For example, when an organization identifies an opportunity that it would like to look into, it will often authorize a feasibility study to decide if it should undertake the project. The project lifecycle definition will determine whether the feasibility study is treated as the first project phase or as a separate, stand-alone project.

The project lifecycle definition will also determine which transitional actions at the end of the project are included and which are not. In this manner, the project lifecycle definition can be used to link the project to the ongoing operations of the performing organization.

The phase sequence defined by most project lifecycles generally involves some form of technology transfer or handoff, such as requirements to design, construction to operations, or design to manufacturing. Deliverables from the preceding phase are usually approved before work starts on the next phase. However, a subsequent phase is sometimes begun prior to approval of the previous phase deliverables when the risks involved are deemed acceptable. This practice of overlapping phases is often called *fast tracking.*

Project lifecycles generally define:

❑ What technical work should be done in each phase (e.g. is the work of the architect part of the definition phase or part of the execution phase).

❑ Who should be involved in each phase (e.g. concurrent engineering requires that the implementers be involved with requirements and design).

Project lifecycle descriptions may be very general or very detailed. Highly detailed descriptions may have numerous forms, charts, and checklists to provide structure and consistency. Such detailed approaches are the project management methodologies, as we discussed above.

Most project lifecycle descriptions share a number of common characteristics:

❑ Cost and staffing levels are low at the start, higher towards the end, and drop rapidly as the project draws to a conclusion.

❑ The probability of successfully completing the project is lowest, and hence risk and uncertainty are highest, at the start of the project. The probability of successful completion generally increases as the project continues.

❑ The ability of stakeholders to influence the final characteristics of the project product and the final cost of the project is highest at the start and gets progressively lower as the project continues. A major contributor to this phenomenon is that the cost of change and error correction generally increases as the project continues.

Care should be taken to distinguish the *project* lifecycle from the *product* lifecycle. For example, a project undertaken to bring a new desktop computer to market is just one phase or stage of the product lifecycle.

Although many project lifecycles have similar phase names with similar work resources required, few are identical. Most have four or five phases, but some have nine or more. Even within a single application area, there can be significant variations—one organization's software development lifecycle may have a single design phase while another's has separate phases for functional and detail design.

Sub-projects within projects may also have distinct project lifecycles. For example, an architectural firm hired to design a new office building is first involved in the owner's definition phase when doing the design, and then in the owner's implementation phase when supporting the construction effort. The architect's design project, however, will have its own series of phases from conceptual development through definition and implementation to closure. The architect may even treat designing the facility and supporting the construction as separate projects with their own distinct phases.

Representative Project Lifecycles

Figure 4.

The above illustration provides a perspective of how project management fits into the environment in which projects typically occur. The three major process areas in which projects occur are:

- ❏ Portfolio management
- ❏ Project management
- ❏ Project lifecycle management

Ideally, projects are planned, selected, measured and responded to through a *portfolio management* process in which the right projects are chosen against factors such as business objectives, budgets, and available resources.

Project management provides a set of *business control* processes that enable the project manager to deliver a project to completion on-time and on-budget. The project management process tends to be fairly similar in a broad variety of project types, regardless of the project lifecycle management methods that are used to deliver the project.

The deliverables of a project are conceived, designed, developed and tested through project lifecycle management processes that typically vary widely across many different industries. These project lifecycles document the processes that ultimately become the project tasks that need to be performed to complete the project with high quality (i.e. on specification).

The following illustration shows some project lifecycles that are common in the world of project management. This illustration is provided to show how these lifecycles conceptually fit into the overall environment in which projects typically occur.

Figure 5.

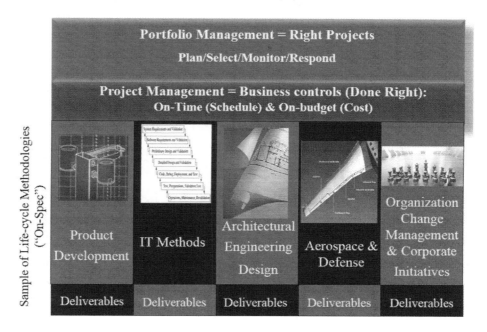

2.4 Project Stakeholders and Organizational Influences

Project stakeholders are individuals and organizations who are actively involved in the project or whose interests may be affected as a result of project execution or successful project completion. The project management team must identify the stakeholders, determine what their needs and expectations are, and then manage and influence those expectations to ensure a successful project. Stakeholder identification is often especially difficult. For example, is an assembly line worker—whose future employment depends on the outcome of a new product design project—a stakeholder?

Key stakeholders on every project include a:

❑ Project manager – The individual responsible for managing the project

❑ Customer – The individual or organization who will use the project product

 Note: There may be multiple layers of customers. For example, the customers for a new pharmaceutical product may include the doctors who prescribe it, the patients who take it, and the insurers who pay for it.

❑ Performing organization – The enterprise whose employees are most directly involved in doing the work of the project

❑ Sponsor – The individual or group within the performing organization who provides the financial resources for the project

There are many other ways to define project stakeholders: internal and external; owners and funders; suppliers and contractors; team members and their families; government agencies and media outlets; and finally individual citizens, temporary or permanent lobbying organizations, and society at large. The naming of stakeholders helps the project manager and team consider which individuals and organizations may require attention. Stakeholder roles and responsibilities may overlap, as when an engineering firm provides financing for a plant it is designing.

Managing stakeholder expectations may be difficult because stakeholders often have different objectives that may come into conflict. Some examples include:

❑ The manager of a department that has requested a new management information system may desire low cost, while the System Architect may emphasize technical excellence, and then the programming contractor may be most interested in maximizing its profit.

❑ The Vice President of Research at an electronics firm may define new product success as state-of-the-art technology, while the Vice President of Manufacturing may define it as world-class practices, and then the Vice President of Marketing may be primarily concerned with the number of new features.

❑ The owner of a real estate development project may be focused on timely performance, while the local governing body may desire to maximize tax revenue, an environmental group may want to minimize adverse environmental impacts, and nearby residents may hope to relocate the project.

In general, differences among stakeholders should be resolved in favor of the customer; however, this does not mean that the needs and expectations of other stakeholders can be disregarded. Finding appropriate resolutions to such differences can be one of the major challenges of project management.

Organizational Influences

Projects are typically part of a larger organization, such as a corporation or a government agency. The project will be influenced by the organization or organizations that set it up, especially by their structure.

Project-based organizations are those whose operations consist primarily of projects. These organizations fall into two categories:

❑ Organizations that primarily perform projects for others; for example architectural firms, engineering firms, consultants, construction contractors, government contractors

❑ Organizations that use *management by projects* because of the nature of their business, primarily involving non-repetitive or time-limited activities.

Project-based organizations usually have management systems in place to support project management, such as financial systems designed for accounting, tracking, and reporting on multiple simultaneous projects.

Non-project-based organizations seldom have management systems designed to support project work efficiently and effectively. This can make project management more difficult, so non-project-based organizations often have sub-units that operate as project-based organizations with systems to match.

The project management team should be acutely aware of how the organization's systems affect the project. For example, if the organization rewards its functional managers for charging staff time to projects, the project management team should be careful that assigned staff members are being used effectively on the project.

2.5 Project Processes

Projects involve processes which are performed by people and generally fall into one of two major categories:

❑ Project management processes are concerned with describing and organizing the work of the project. The project management processes that are applicable to most projects, most of the time, are described in detail in the PMBOK Guide.

❑ Product-oriented processes are concerned with specifying and creating the project product. Product-oriented processes are typically defined by the project lifecycle and vary by application area.

Project management processes and product-oriented processes overlap and interact throughout the project. The scope of the project cannot be defined in the absence of some basic understanding of how to create the product.

Process Groups

Project management processes can be organized into five groups of one or more processes each:

❑ **Initiating processes** – Recognizing that a project or phase should begin and committing to do so

❑ **Planning processes** – Devising and maintaining a workable scheme to accomplish the business need that the project was undertaken to address

❑ **Executing processes** – Coordinating people and other resources to carry out the plan

❑ **Controlling processes** – Ensuring that project objectives are met by monitoring and measuring progress and taking corrective action when necessary

❑ **Closing processes** – Formalizing acceptance of the project or phase and bringing it to an orderly end

The process groups are linked by the results they produce; the result or outcome of one becomes an input to another. Among these process groups, the links are iterated; planning provides executing with a documented project plan early on, and then provides documented updates to the plan as the project progresses. Also, these project management process groups are not one-time events, but instead are overlapping activities that occur throughout each phase of the project.

The process group interactions also cross phases; closing one phase provides an input to initiating the next. For example, closing a design phase requires customer acceptance of the design document. Simultaneously, the design document defines the product description for the ensuing implementation phase.

The PMBOK Guide focuses on these interactions and describes each individual process in terms of its:

- ❑ **Inputs** – Documents or documentable items that will be acted upon

- ❑ **Tools and techniques** – Mechanisms applied to the inputs to create the output

- ❑ **Outputs** – Documents or documentable items that are a result of the process

This process approach can be very useful to the project manager, and we encourage you to become familiar with the processes common to most projects in most areas as described in the PMBOK Guide. An understanding of these detailed processes will also be necessary if you decide to pursue the PMP certification sponsored by PMI.

End of Chapter Quiz Questions

1. Fill in the blanks: Project management consists of an organized set of _____, _____, and _____ working together.

2. True or False: A single approach to project management could fit all industries and organizations.

3. List at least 3 features of a project (what makes a project a project):

 1. _____
 2. _____
 3. _____

4. What are the three constraints of a project that must be managed?

 1. _____
 2. _____
 3. _____

5. Describe what is meant by the art and science of project management.

6. Fill in the blank: A project is deemed successful when the objectives of the _____ are met.

7. What are at least four (4) characteristics of a successful project?

 1. _____
 2. _____
 3. _____
 4. _____

8. To achieve a successful project, project management must follow a _____, be supported by a _____, and have _____ _____ to continue improving.

9. What are the three (3) major stages in the project management process?

 1. _____
 2. _____
 3. _____

10 - 17. Match the Process listed in the left column of the table below, to the correct description from the right column, by entering the letter that the process corresponds to in the blank line.

10. Definition _____	A. Provides an orderly means of modifying the original project definition
11. Planning and Organization _____	B. Makes any necessary plan modifications to steer the project back on course
12. Tracking _____	C. Instills quality in the process of project management
13. Analysis _____	D. Ensures that all relevant project stakeholders are kept apprised of all key project information
14. Revision _____	E. Provides the detailed roadmap that will be used to guide the project team when constructing the final deliverables
15. Scope Management _____	F. Collects information from the team to assist the project manager in assessing actual progress
16. Status Reporting and Management Reviews _____	G. Documents the overall project objectives, scope, approach schedule, budget, resources, deliverables, and completion criteria
17. Providing Feedback/Continuous Improvement _____	H. Highlights any deviations from the original plan against current progress

18. What are the four (4) principles of effective project managers?

 1. _____

 2. _____

 3. _____

 4. _____

19. Why is it important to catch problems early?

20. Fill in the blank: _____ and _____ are the biggest variables in every project. Remember to make time to focus attention on _____ issues, both internal to the team and external.

21. What are at least four (4) advantages of using project management software tools?

 1. _____

 2. _____

 3. _____

 4. _____

22. Provide an example to show when it is appropriate or cost effective to use a project management tool, versus, another example to show when it is not cost effective to use one; describe why you gave those examples.

23. What are the properties of an effective methodology:

24. What is a deliverable?

```
┌─────────────────────────────────────────────────────────────────┐
│                                                                   │
│                                                                   │
│                                                                   │
│                                                                   │
└─────────────────────────────────────────────────────────────────┘
```

25. What two things do project lifecycles generally define?

 1. _____

 2. _____

26. What are the common characteristics that most project lifecycle descriptions share?

```
┌─────────────────────────────────────────────────────────────────┐
│                                                                   │
│                                                                   │
│                                                                   │
└─────────────────────────────────────────────────────────────────┘
```

27. What are the three major process areas in which projects occur?

 1. _____

 2. _____

 3. _____

28. Fill in the blank: _____ are individuals and organizations who are actively involved in the project or whose interests may be affected as a result of project execution or successful project completion.

29. What are the five (5) project management process groups?

 1. _____

 2. _____

 3. _____

 4. _____

 5. _____

chapter 3

Introduction to Microsoft Project 2016

- How Microsoft Project 2016 Handles Data

- The Ribbon in Microsoft Project 2016

- Navigating in Microsoft Project 2016 Views

- Help Options in Microsoft Project 2016

- Finding the Right Information

 Learning Objectives for this Chapter

At the end of the chapter, the reader should be able to:

- Understand the basic information structure in Microsoft Project 2016
- Become familiar with the ribbon in Microsoft Project 2016
- Effectively navigate through the most common Microsoft Project 2016 Views
- Find the Help options in Microsoft Project 2016
- Know how to navigate to and change Microsoft Project options
- Develop a comprehensive approach to finding the right information in Microsoft Project 2016

3.1 How Microsoft Project 2016 Handles Data

Microsoft Project 2016 is a powerful tool that allows you to plan, track, analyze, and report on the progress of one or many related projects. In the process of doing so, however, an enormous amount of data is generated. To avoid overwhelming the user, Microsoft Project uses a clever data management approach that simplifies the project manager's job.

A project consists of activities that have a distinct beginning and end (known as tasks) and the people, equipment, and supplies used to complete those activities (known as resources).

Once you have entered the tasks and resources into a project, you will want to specify which resources will be made available to work on each task. A connection between a resource and a task is known as an assignment. Each time a resource is scheduled to work on a task, a new resource assignment is created in your project.

Figure 6.

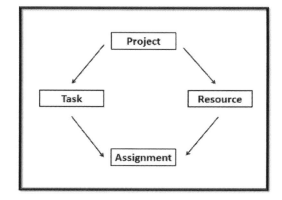

Note: Microsoft Project also saves modified objects with the Microsoft Project plan.

Figure 7.

Sample **Organizer** dialog box displaying a list of objects that are saved in Microsoft Project files

We mentioned earlier that project managers have to manage time, cost and scope. Microsoft Project creates hidden storage areas that contain the necessary data. The Tasks area (above) contains details about each task—how long it should be (duration) and its relationship to any other tasks (dependencies). This is organized in a database format, with each row representing an individual task and each column a field associated with that task, as creating a task generates a large number of related fields. The Resources area contains details about each resource, including how much it costs to use that resource and availability data, such as how much time each person can devote to project work each day.

In theory, one could create a project schedule from the scope-related information (duration and dependency) for each task, but clearly resource availability affects when a task can be done. For that reason, connecting a task with a resource generates a resource assignment stored in the Assignment area. This combined information is used by Microsoft Project to create the actual schedule.

In addition to Tasks, Resources, and Assignments, there will be higher-level data related to the project itself, rather than its detailed components. Examples might include the geographic location of the project, the business unit that owns or requested the project, or the name of the project manager. The Project area gives us a place to store that type of data and is especially important for published projects, as we will see later.

Microsoft Project 2016 provides many different ways to enter, view, and report information about the tasks, resources, and resource assignments in a project. As with all Microsoft applications, these can be menu-driven or controlled by icons on toolbars.

3.2 The Ribbon in Microsoft Project 2016

Users of previous versions of Microsoft Project will notice a ribbon, as shown in the following figure (similar to other Microsoft Office products), rather than the traditional pull-down menus. Commands are placed on the ribbon and organized in tabs – *File, Task, Resource, Project, View,* and *Format*. Within each tab, related commands are in groups.

Figure 8.

The Microsoft
Project 2016
Ribbon

The groups and tabs on the ribbon are customizable; commands may be placed in groups and tabs as desired. To customize groups and tabs on the ribbon:

1 Click the *File* tab and then select *Options* (going forward we will document this functionality as *File:Options*) at the bottom of the left sidebar. The **Project Options** dialog box will appear.

2 In the left sidepane of this box select *Customize Ribbon*.

Figure 9.

Project Options
dialog box with
*Customize
Ribbon* selected

3 Click the *Add* and *Remove* buttons as required to move commands to and from various tabs in the ribbon.

You can also customize the Quick Access Toolbar at the top-left corner of your screen to include various commands as shortcuts:

1 Click *File:Options* to open the **Project Options** dialog box.

2 In the left sidepane of this box, select *Quick Access Toolbar.*

3	Click the *Add* and *Remove* buttons as required to move commands to and from the Quick Access Toolbar. In the following figure, the command "Link the Selected Tasks" has been selected for addition to the Quick Access Toolbar.

Figure 10.

Project Options dialog box with *Quick Access Toolbar* selected

4	Click *OK* to save your change. You will now see the *Link the Selected Tasks* icon in the Quick Access Toolbar.

Figure 11.

Link the Selected Tasks icon

You can also access the Quick Access Toolbar or ribbon customization options by right clicking a tab (*Task* in the following example) and then selecting the option desired to access the **Project Options** dialog box.

Figure 12.

Right clicking on a tab

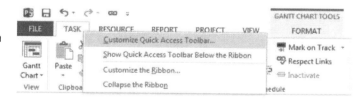

3.3 Navigating in Microsoft Project 2016 Views

Familiarizing Yourself with the Microsoft Project 2016 Screen

Once the desired view has been selected, finding the correct information within that view is fairly easy—that is, if you know the shortcuts and navigation tools available.

 This exercise uses the file **Navigation.mpp**. Launch Microsoft Project 2016 without connecting to Project Server and open this project from the Exercise Directory as follows:

1 In the left sidebar you will see a list of recently opened projects, as shown in the following figure. Note: your screen may differ as it will reflect projects you have recently opened.

Figure 13.

Initial screen

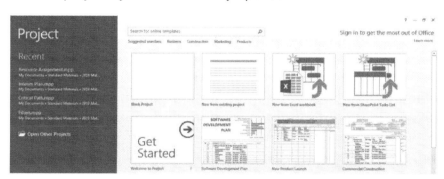

2 Assuming **Navigation.mpp** does not appear in the list of recently opened projects, select *Computer* and then click *Browse* to see the **Open** dialog box. From the **Open** dialog box navigate to and select the file **Navigation.mpp**, and click *Open*.

Figure 14.

Open dialog box

3 Click the right arrow button at the bottom of the task list section of the screen to scroll through the columns that are hidden behind the Gantt Chart. Your screen will resemble the following as you scroll through the various columns:

Figure 15.

Scrolling
through columns

4 The vertical line that divides the data fields on the left from the chart on the right is the *divider bar*. Place the cursor on the divider bar to see a double vertical line with horizontal arrows. Click and drag to the right to show more data fields, or to the left to show more of the Gantt Chart.

5 Move your mouse over the cell just above Task ID 0. The following text box will appear to inform you of which view and table is currently applied to your project:

Figure 16.

Display of Table
and View

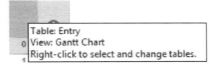

5 Click the cell above Task ID 0 to Select All. Your screen will resemble the following:

Figure 17.

Select all

7 Press Ctrl + End on the keyboard. Your view will jump to the last column in the task list.

8 Press *Ctrl + Home*. Your view will return to the first row and column of the task list:

9 Press *Alt + End*. Your view will jump to the end of the project's Gantt bars.

10 Press *Alt + Home*. Your view will shift to the start of the project's
 Gantt bars.

You can expand and collapse tasks hierarchically using the + or - on tasks.
Alternatively, you can navigate to *View:Data* and then select the desired
outline level from the *Outline* dropdown list.

Figure 18.

Outline level
options

11 Select *View:Data:Outline:Outline Level 1*. This collapses the list of
 tasks so that your screen will resemble the following:

Figure 19.

Screen after
collapsing list of
tasks

You may want to adjust the timescale on the right side of the Task Usage,
Resource Usage, or Gantt Chart views (for example, if the default timescale
is daily and you need a weekly or monthly summary). There are several
ways to do this.

12 From *View:Zoom* adjust the timescale by clicking on the *Zoom* icon
 [🔍] and selecting *Zoom In*, *Zoom Out*, or *Zoom*. *Zoom* brings you to
 the **Zoom** dialog box where you can specify the desired Zoom level.

Figure 20.

Adjusting the
timescale

13 In the *Zoom* group, the *Timescale* dropdown allows you to adjust the
 Units (for example, from Days to Weeks or Months), along with any
 other items you want to change.

14 The *Entire Project* or *Selected Tasks* icons in the *Zoom* group will
 resize to automatically fit the entire project or any selected tasks.

15 At the bottom right of the screen is a Zoom Slider that can be moved left or right to increase or decrease the Timescale.

16 Move your mouse over the link line between *Concept* (Task ID 1) and *Determine the layout of the site* (Task ID 14). You will be presented with a screen tip for the task dependency, which displays the type of task dependency, the names of the dependent tasks, and any lag time between the tasks.

Figure 21.

Screen tip for task dependency

17 From the *Task* tab, select Task 12, *Web Site Design*, and in the *Editing* group, click the *Scroll to Task* icon []. Selecting a task and clicking the *Scroll to Task* button shifts the start of the selected task's corresponding Gantt bar into view. Your screen will resemble the following:

Figure 22.

Scrolling to *Task* button

18 Move your mouse over the Gantt bar for the task *Evaluate current systems* (ID 2). The start date, finish date, and duration of the task will appear in a box.

19 Locate the task *Define specific functionality* (ID 8) and move your mouse pointer under the ID number until the icon changes to a double-ended arrow.

20 Hold your mouse button down and drag the bottom line downwards, and a dotted line will appear to help you determine where you want to set the row height:

Figure 23.

Drag line

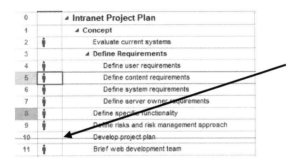

21 Release your mouse button when the dotted drag line is midway through the *Develop project plan* (ID 10) row to make the row for Task 8 double height.

22 Move your mouse pointer to the bar between the *Task* column heading and the *Duration* column heading until the icon changes to a double-ended arrow.

23 Hold the mouse button down and drag the line either left or right to adjust the column width as required, just as you did to adjust row height in the previous section.

24 To modify a task name, click to select the cell, and then click the same cell again to enter Edit mode. Locate the task *Define risks and risk management approach* (ID 9). Add the words "for corporate management" and press *Enter*. Notice that the long task name for Task 9 automatically wraps in the cell. Your screen will resemble the following:

Figure 24.

Auto-wrapped text for Task 9

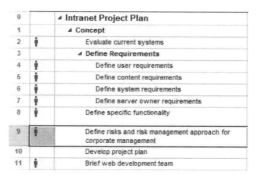

25 You can add a separate data entry bar to display and edit text. To do so, go to *File:Options* to see the **Project Options** dialog box.

Figure 25.

Project Options dialog box

26 In the **Project Options** dialog box select *Display* and then check *Entry bar* in the *Show these elements* section. Click *OK*. The contents of the active cell will display in an entry bar below the ribbon.

Figure 26.

Contents of
Task ID 9
displayed in the
entry bar

27 Alternatively, you can wrap text by selecting *Format:Columns* and then using the *Column Settings* dropdown list to select *Wrap Text*.

Microsoft Project 2016 allows you to modify the background of text cells, as well as the text itself.

28 Locate the task *Brief web development team* (ID 11) and select the *Task Name* cell. The *Task* tab contains several buttons that allow you to make formatting changes to the selected text cells.

Click the small boxed arrow at the bottom right of the *Font* group to open the **Font** dialog box. Change the *Color* from *Automatic* to *White* and the *Background Color* from *Automatic* to *Black*. Select a Background Pattern that seems appropriate (solid, in the following example).

Figure 27.

Modified font
background
instructions

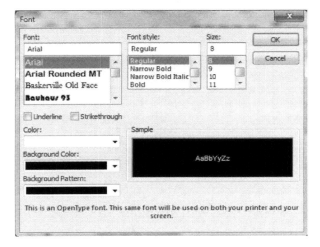

29 Click *OK* and the cell format is changed.

30 From the *File* menu click *Close*, and close **Navigation.mpp** without saving your changes.

3.4 Help Options in Microsoft Project 2016

Microsoft Project 2016 offers a variety of sources for help and additional information.

1 Start Microsoft Project 2016 without connecting to Project Server and click the *Help* button [**?**] in the upper-right corner of your screen. This icon will appear in the same place within every screen.

Figure 28.

New screen with *Help* button circled

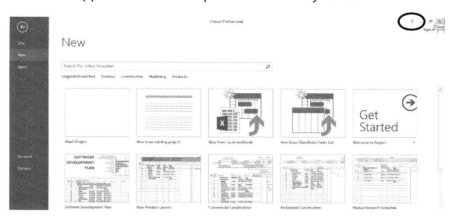

2 Microsoft Project will present a web page for **Project Help** dialog box similar to the following:

Figure 29.

Project Help page

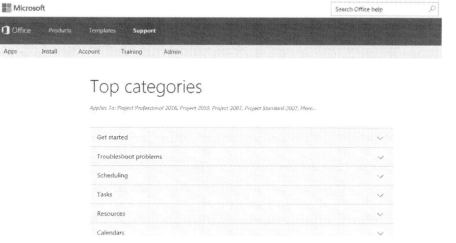

3 Use this interface to find a link to the information you need, or enter a search term to perform a more thorough search online.

4 Close the **Project Help** window by clicking the *X* in the upper right hand corner of the dialog box.

3.5 Finding the Right Information

The trick to using Microsoft Project effectively is first to know what type of information you are looking for, and then to know which view you can use to display this information. A view is a set of formatting instructions that tells Microsoft Project what data to present and how to organize it into a useful format so that each view displays a unique combination of project information. Once you are in the correct view, you can modify the display to view the exact information you require, as described later.

Views in Microsoft Project 2016 can be categorized into sheet views, chart and graph views, and form views. Each of the available views will provide different presentations of project information. Unfortunately, with 27 different views to choose from, simply deciding which one to use can be a challenge.

For example, the default Gantt Chart view includes a calendar bar chart on the right side of the screen and a table of data on the left side. A table is a set of formatting instructions that specifies which fields from the data storage area should appear on the screen. The default Entry Table, for example, contains ID (the task numbers), Name (titled Task Name), Duration, Start, Finish, Predecessors, and Resource Names (who is assigned to the task).

The decision tree in the next section is intended to help guide you to the six most useful views in Microsoft Project. Microsoft Project 2016 does help by automatically opening certain views for you (for example, custom tracking views when you set up the tracking method to be used for the project), but remembering these six views will save you valuable time.

For task information, the Gantt Chart (with and without a split window) is generally most useful. For resource information, the Resource Sheet (with and without a split window) is best. For assignment information, the Task Usage and Resource Usage views are the best starting points.

Selecting a View

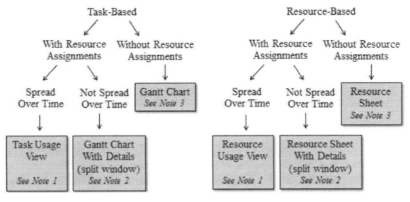

When selecting the best Microsoft Project view, you must first decide if you are looking for task-based or resource-based information.

❑ If you require task-based information, next decide if you are interested in information with or without resource assignments.

 o If the information you require is task-based, without resource assignments, the Gantt Chart should meet your needs (see Note 1 for additional detail).

 o If the information you require is task-based, with resource assignments spread over time, the Task Usage View should meet your needs (see Note 2 for additional detail).

 o If the information you require is task-based, with resource assignments not spread over time, the Gantt Chart with details in the lower pane (split window) should meet your needs (see Note 3 for additional detail).

❑ If you require resource-based information, next decide if you are interested in information with or without task assignments.

 o If the information you require is resource-based, without task assignments, the Resource Sheet should meet your needs (see Note 1 for additional detail).

 o If the information you require is resource-based, with task assignments spread over time, the Resource Usage View should meet your needs (see Note 2 for additional detail).

 o If the information you require is resource-based, with task assignments not spread over time, the Resource Sheet with details in the lower pane (split window) should meet your needs (see Note 3 for additional detail).

Note 1: Are you seeing the information you want to see in the Gantt Chart or Resource Sheet views?

❑ If you are not seeing the information you want on the left side of the divider of the Gantt Chart View:

 o Apply a table that contains the columns (or fields) you wish to view

 o Add columns to the existing table

 o Add columns to the existing table and then apply the table

 o Create a new table that contains the columns (or fields) you wish to view

Note 2: Are you seeing the information you want to see in the (Task or Resource) Usage view?

❑ If you are not seeing the columns you want on the left side of the divider on the (Task or Resource) Usage View, you can do one or more of the following:

 o Apply a table that contains the columns (or fields) you wish to view

 o Add columns to the existing table

- o Add columns to the existing table and then apply the table
- o Create a new table that contains the columns (or fields) you wish to view

❑ The grid on the right side of the (Task or Resource) Usage view contains time-phased information—work details broken down on a day-by-day basis (this time phasing can be modified). If you are not seeing the columns you want to see on the right side of the divider on the Usage View:

- o To change the timescale, in the *View:Zoom* section of the ribbon, use the *Zoom* dropdown arrow to *Zoom in/Zoom out*.
- o To see a short list of display options for this grid, right-click anywhere in the grid area. When you do so, you will see the following list:

Figure 30.

Time-phased
details list

❑ If the data in the timescale (for the task, resource or assignment you wish to view) is not appearing on the screen:

- o From *Task:Editing* click the *Scroll to Task* icon
- o Zoom in/Zoom Out
- o In the *Format:Zoom* section of the ribbon, adjust the timescale

❑ In the lower pane, if you are not seeing the fields you want to see:

- o Right-click in the lower pane and select *Predecessors & Successors, Resources & Predecessors, Resources & Successors, Schedule, Work, Cost, Notes,* and/or *Objects*, as appropriate
- o From *View: (Task or Resource) Views*, use the *Other Views* dropdown list to select *More Views* and then choose the appropriate "form" view.
- o From *View:Split View* use the *Details* dropdown list to select the appropriate view.

Note 3: Are you seeing the information you want to see in the Gantt Chart with Details or Resource Sheet with Details views?

❑ If you are not seeing the columns you want on the upper pane of the Gantt Chart View:

- o Apply a table that contains the columns (or fields) you wish to view
- o Add columns to the existing table

- Add columns to the existing table and then apply the table
- Create a new table that contains the columns (or fields) you wish to view

❑ If you are not seeing the fields you want to see on the lower pane:

- Right-click in the lower pane and select *Schedule*, *Work*, *Cost*, *Notes*, and/or *Objects*, as appropriate

- From *View: (Task or Resource) Views*, use the *Other Views* dropdown list to select *More Views* and then choose the appropriate "form" view.

- From *View:Split View*, use the *Details* dropdown list to select the appropriate view.

Evaluating the Most Useful Views

🗁 This exercise uses the file **Navigation.mpp**. Ensure this file is open.

1 When you open a Microsoft Project file, you will see the Gantt Chart view by default.

Figure 31.

Navigation.mpp – Gantt Chart view

2 Double-click a task name to see the **Task Information** dialog box, containing summary information about the selected task. The following figure shows a summary of the task information for *Define content requirements*:

Figure 32.

Define content requirements task Information

3 To view task-based information with resource assignments summarized over the project lifetime, the Gantt Chart (with window split) is the most useful view. As covered earlier, Microsoft Project defaults to the *Task* tab and Gantt Chart view upon opening.

4 In the ribbon, the *View* group (top-left of your screen) includes a Gantt
 Chart view icon []. Clicking on the arrow next to *Gantt Chart*
 displays a dropdown list of additional views.

Figure 33.

Gantt Chart
dropdown

5 To display the assignment information for these Gantt Chart tasks,
 from the *Task:Properties* group in the ribbon, click the *Details* button
 []. The Task Details Form view is the default view in the lower
 frame.

Figure 34.

Gantt Chart over
Task Details
Form

The *View* tab provides many different viewing options. For example, this
tab contains the Gantt Chart icon at the left in the *Task Views* group. In
the *Split Views* group, selecting details includes the Task Form as the
default, as well as several additional choices.

Notice that the information in the Task Form window(s) refers to an
individual task in the Gantt Chart above. This information is summarized
over the life of the task.

6 Several different types of summarized information can be shown in
 the Task Form. To see the options, right-click in the gray area on the
 right side of the Task Form. A box similar to the following will appear:

Figure 35.

Task Form
options

7 To view resource-based information without assignment details, go to
 Task:View and select the *Resource Sheet* view. Your screen will
 resemble the following:

Figure 36.

Resource Sheet
view

8 Double-click a Resource Name to see the **Resource Information**
 dialog box with details about that resource.

Figure 37.

Resource
information for
Jeffery Vineburg

9 As covered earlier, to view resource-based information with resource
 assignments summarized over the project lifetime, the Resource
 Sheet (with window split) is the most effective view. To get to this
 view from the Resource Sheet view, from the *View* tab select *Details*
 in the *Split View* group.

The Resource Form view should be the default view in the lower frame, as shown in the following figure. Alternatively, you can select the Resource Sheet (with window split) view from the *Task* and *Resource* tabs.

Figure 38.

Resource Sheet
(with details
selected, split
screen)

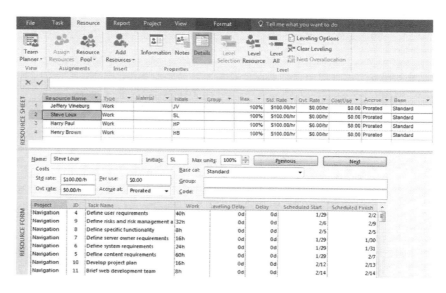

The preceding view provides the "big picture" about resources in the upper window (Resource Sheet), with details about their assigned tasks in the lower window (Resource Form).

10 As with the Task Form, various types of information can be presented in the Resource Form. To see the options, right-click in the gray area on the right side of the Resource Form view to see the following list of options:

Figure 39.

Resource Form
options

11 To view assignment details by task, from *Task:View* select *Task Usage.* Alternatively, you can go to *Task Views:Views:Task Usage.* Your screen will resemble the following:

Figure 40.

Task Usage view

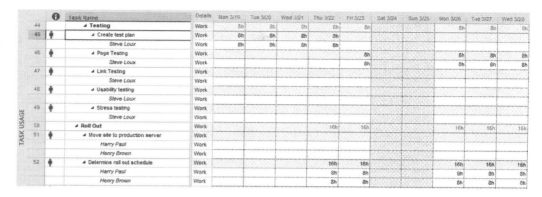

12 The italicized names below each task represent each person's assignment to that task. If you double-click a name under a task, you will see an **Assignment Information** dialog box with details about that person's assignment to the task.

Figure 41.

Assignment information for Jeffrey Vineburg for the task *Evaluate current systems*

13 The grid on the right side of the view contains time-phased information—task assignment details broken down on a day-by-day basis (this time phasing can be modified). To see a short list of display options for this grid, right-click anywhere in the grid area. When you do so, you will see the following dialog:

Figure 42.

Time-phased
details list

14 To see a complete list of fields you can modify, click *Detail Styles...*
 in the box displayed above. The **Detail Styles** dialog box will appear.

Figure 43.

Detail Styles
dialog box

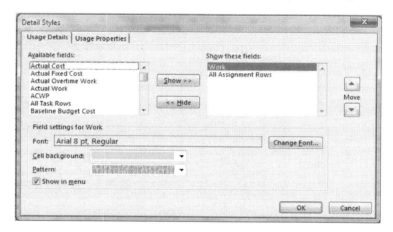

15 You can also view assignment information sorted by resource, rather
 than by task. For this option, from *View:Resource Views* select
 Resource Usage. You can also access the Resource Usage view via
 the *Task* and *Resource* tabs. Your screen will resemble the following:

Figure 44.

Resource Usage
view

16 As with the Task Usage view, you can double-click an italicized task
 name (an assignment) to view the **Assignment Information** dialog box.

Display the Information You Want

Once you have selected the appropriate view for your purposes, you can adjust
the view in various ways to show any specific information you need.

To see additional information (such as Cost, Summary or Tracking data) on the
left side of the Task Usage or Resource Usage views, on the left side of the
Gantt view, or on the Resource Sheet, you have two choices:

1 From *View:Data* click *Tables*. From the dropdown, select the appropriate table. You can also select *More Tables* to review other tables to apply to the view or to create new tables, as we'll describe shortly.

2 You can also insert a new data field into a table by clicking the *Add New Column* heading (the last column) and selecting a field from the list. A column may also be inserted by navigating to *Format:Columns* and clicking *Insert Column* per the following figure.

Select the column and drag to position it as desired.

Figure 45.

Inserting an additional column

NOTE

When you are working in an enterprise environment using Microsoft Project Professional, changes made to tables and views will apply to the modified project only. For modified or new tables to be available to all enterprise projects, or to be used in the published version of any project, they must be created as part of the enterprise global by a Project Server administrator.

Using the View Bar

A convenient shortcut for moving between views is the View Bar. To activate it, right-click at the far left in the vertical strip where the name of the current view shows, and click *View Bar*.

Figure 46.

Select View Bar

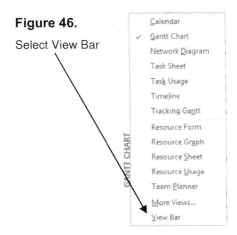

You will see icons for commonly used views. Click any of these icons to quickly apply the view. Your screen will resemble the following:

Figure 47.

View bar

Timeline View

Microsoft Project 2016 includes a timeline view that by default is displayed above other views, showing a concise overview of the entire schedule. You can add tasks to the timeline and even print it for a clear summary report of the entire project. You can also easily paste the timeline into an e-mail or other document for an instant report.

📂 This exercise uses the file **Timeline.mpp**. Be sure this project is open before beginning.

1 To enable the Timeline view, from *View:Split View*, select the *Timeline* checkbox. A timeline bar representing the entire project will display below the ribbon, as in the following figure:

Figure 48.

View of timeline with Gantt Chart

2 The Zoom commands found in *View:Zoom* (for the Gantt Chart) work in conjunction with the timeline as well. To display additional tasks on the timeline, select *Evaluate current systems* and then from *Task:Properties* click the *Add to Timeline* icon [🖾]. Alternatively, you can right-click on the task and from the resulting list select *Add to Timeline*.

3 You can also display milestones on the timeline. Select *User interface designed* and from *Task:Properties* click *Add to Timeline*. Your timeline will resemble the following:

Figure 49.

Sample timeline

4 By default tasks are displayed as a bar on the timeline, but they may also be displayed as a callout text box. Add the task *Evaluate current systems* to the timeline, and then right-click on this task in the timeline and select *Display as Callout* (or from *Format:Current Selection* click *Display as Callout*). Your timeline will resemble the following:

Figure 50.

Sample timeline with callout

5 Right-click the timeline bar and select *Detailed Timeline*. This will collapse the bar's height and shrink the display, while leaving the tasks visible on the timeline.

6 Close your project without saving the changes.

Calendar View

📂 This exercise uses the file **Navigation.mpp**. Be sure this project is open before beginning.

1 The Calendar view displays tasks in the form of a wall calendar. To access the Calendar view, from *View:Task Views* select *Calendar*. Your screen will resemble the following:

Figure 51.

Calendar view

2 By default, the current month appears in the view. Click the *Week* button at the upper left of the Calendar view to see the current week only.

3 Click *Custom* and you will see the **Zoom** dialog box. Change the number of *Weeks* to "*2*" and click *OK*. Your screen will resemble the following figure. You can use the **Zoom** dialog box to control the number of weeks the Calendar view includes or to specify a date range.

Figure 52.

Calendar **Zoom** dialog box

How Microsoft Project 2016 Uses Data

Entering data in Microsoft Project 2016 is often just the first step. Behind the scenes, Microsoft Project works to use the data to provide meaningful information for the project manager. This exercise explores how this process works for one specific example.

📂 This exercise uses the file **Navigation.mpp**. If this file is not already open, launch Microsoft Project 2016 without connecting to Project Server and open this project from the Exercise Directory before beginning.

1 By default you should be in the Gantt Chart view with the *Task* tab selected. Apply the Gantt Chart view if another view is displayed. From the *Properties* group click *Details* to see the Gantt Chart/Task Details Form combination described earlier.

2 Right-click anywhere in the Task Details Form and select *Cost* from the menu that appears. In the upper half of the screen, select *Define user requirements* (Task ID 4) to view details about that task in the Task Form. Your screen will resemble the following.

Figure 53.

Resource Cost details

Note that the cost of each assignment is now displayed in the lower details pane.

3 Click on the upper half of the screen anywhere to activate the Gantt Chart portion. Notice that the view name on the left side of the screen changes from gray to green to indicate the active view. Click the details box in the Split view group to remove the bottom pane.

4 From the *View* group select *Resource Sheet* to change the screen to display the Resource Sheet view to verify the hourly cost rate for each resource. Your screen will resemble the following:

Figure 54.

Resource Sheet

	Resource Name	Type	Material	Initials	Group	Max.	Std. Rate	Ovt. Rate	Cost/Use	Accrue	Base
1	Jeffery Vineburg	Work		JV		100%	$100.00/hr	$0.00/hr	$0.00	Prorated	Standard
2	Steve Loux	Work		SL		100%	$100.00/hr	$0.00/hr	$0.00	Prorated	Standard
3	Harry Paul	Work		HP		100%	$100.00/hr	$0.00/hr	$0.00	Prorated	Standard
4	Henry Brown	Work		HB		100%	$100.00/hr	$0.00/hr	$0.00	Prorated	Standard

5 Click on the *Gantt Chart* icon to return to the original split Gantt view
 by clicking the *Details* option in the *Split view* menu group. Click on
 any task to see the resource cost for that task. Microsoft Project used
 the *Std. Rate* value times the number of hours (work) each resource is
 assigned to calculate these costs.

6 To see the total resource cost for the project, from *View:Data* click
 the *Tables* icon, and from the dropdown list select the *Cost Table*.
 Move the divider bar between the table and the calendar bar chart to
 the right until you see the *Total Cost* column heading. Your screen
 will resemble the following.

Figure 55.

Total resource
cost for the
project

Behind the scenes, Microsoft Project uses data you provide to calculate
additional values that a project manager might want. This is a very useful
feature, but it can be confusing to users who don't realize what is happening,
as we will see later.

End of Chapter Quiz Questions

1. Fill in the blanks: A project consists of activities that have a distinct beginning and end (known as _____) and the people, equipment, and supplies used to complete those activities (known as _____).

2. What is an assignment?

3. True or False: A connection between a resource and a task is known as a dependency.

4. Where can you go customize the ribbon and the Quick Access Toolbar?

5 -8. Match the keyboard shortcut listed in the left column of the table below, to the correct description from the right column by entering the letter that the shortcut corresponds to in the blank line.

5. Press Ctrl + End _____	A. Your view will return to the first row and column of the task list.
6. Press Ctrl + Home _____	B. Your view will shift to the start of the project's Gantt bars.
7. Press Alt + End _____	C. Your view will jump to the last column in the task list.
8. Press Alt + Home _____	D. Your view will jump to the end of the project's Gantt bars.

9. How do you open the **Project Options** dialog box? _____

10. True or False: In Microsoft Project 2016, you can access help without connecting to Project Server.

11. Fill in the blank: Views in Microsoft Project 2016 can be categorized into 3 view categories: _____ views, _____ and _____views, and _____ views.

12. Fill in the blank: The default _____ view includes a calendar bar chart on the right side of the screen and a table of data on the left side

13. What can you do if you are not seeing the columns you want on the left side of the divider on the (Task or Resource) Usage View?

```

```

14 -18. Match the view listed in the left column of the table below, to the correct usage from the right column by entering the letter that the shortcut corresponds to in the blank line.

14. Gantt Chart ___	A. If the information you require is task-based, with resource assignments spread over time
15. Task Usage View ___	B. If the information you require is resource-based, with task assignments not spread over time
16. Gantt Chart + details in the lower pane (split window) ___	C. If the information you require is task-based, without resource assignments
17. Resource Sheet ___	D. If the information you require is resource-based, without task assignments
18. Resource Sheet + details in lower pane (split window) ___	E. If the information you require is resource-based, with task assignments spread over time
19. Resource Usage ___	F. If the information you require is task-based, with resource assignments not spread over time

20. What can you do if you are not seeing the fields you want on the lower pane?

21. What can you do if you are not seeing the information you want on the left side of the divider of the Gantt Chart View?

22. Fill in the blank: To view resource-based information without assignment details, go to *Task:View* and select the _____ _____ view.

23. How can you view resource-based information with resource assignments summarized over the project lifetime?

24. How do you view assignment information sorted by resource, rather than by task?

25. How can you insert a new data field to a view?

```
┌─────────────────────────────────────────────────────────────┐
│                                                               │
│                                                               │
│                                                               │
└─────────────────────────────────────────────────────────────┘
```

26. True or False: When you are working in an enterprise environment using Microsoft Project Professional, changes made to tables and views will apply to the modified project only.

27. What are some advantages of the timeline view?

28. How can you see the total resource cost for a project?

part II

Project Definition

chapter 4

Understanding Project Definition

- Defining Your Project and Understanding the Definition Process

- Initiating a Project

- Planning the Scope of a Project

- Scope Definition

- Scope Verification

Learning Objectives for this Chapter

At the end of the chapter, the reader should be able to:

- Understand the basic principles of the project definition
- Describe the process for initiating a project
- Define the key components of the project scope document
- Recognize the concepts of scope definition and scope verification

4.1 Defining Your Project and Understanding the Definition Process

The typical questions addressed in project definition documents are: Why are we doing this project? How many people are required and what types of skill will they need? How much will it cost? What are the deliverables? When will it be done?, and How will you do it?

Defining a Project Definition Document

Different organizations use different names for their definition documents. Some of the more common names are:

- ❑ **Business Plan** – Often used to gain support and approval for internal company projects

- ❑ **Proposal** – Used between two separate firms, such as a manufacturer and a consulting company, to sell a project to a company

- ❑ **Statement of Work (SOW)** – The formal attachment or appendix to the standard terms and conditions of a contract that describes the detailed approach for performing the project; sometimes part of a proposal

- ❑ **Scope of Work** – Another term used for a Statement of Work

- ❑ **Project Charter** – Like a business plan, it is often used to gain support and approval for internal company projects

The Anatomy of a Definition Document

"The most important and difficult part of the project is its beginning.... If done carefully, the project has a chance of success. If done carelessly, or not at all, the project is doomed to failure."

--Wysocki, Beck and Crane
Effective Project Management

In order to ensure that the project is properly defined, the project manager must meet with the key sponsor and stakeholders to develop a mutually agreed-upon definition for the project. Ideally, this step is completed before the project is funded and scheduled, but it may be necessary to fine tune it once you are sure the project is approved. As mentioned at the beginning of this chapter, a thorough definition document will consider a number of key questions. To answer these questions, the document will usually consist of the following sections:

❑ **Executive Summary** – A brief summary of the entire document

❑ **Objectives** – Clear, measurable statements defining the purpose of the project

❑ **Assumptions** – Documented answers to open key unknowns

❑ **Approach** – A plan of action for building the deliverables

❑ **Deliverables guidelines** – Outline of the project deliverables list

❑ **Business investment** – Estimated project cost

❑ **Estimated schedule** – Summary of the project work plan

❑ **Completion criteria** – How you'll know when each major phase and the overall project are done

Defining What "Done" Means

One of the keys to avoiding scope creep is to know exactly when you're done. The definition process is the project manager's first and most critical opportunity to limit the project scope through clearly articulated exit or completion criteria for the major project deliverables and for the overall project.

The project definition document provides an opportunity for the project manager to define this completion criteria. A solid completion statement will tie the deliverables and their acceptance together in a logical way.

A sample completion statement might look like the following:

> The design task will be complete when the project manager provides the Design Report, as outlined in the deliverables guideline section, and it is accepted by the project sponsor according to the acceptance procedure in Appendix C.

Statements like this should not only be included in the completion criteria section of the definition document, but also in the approach section to help clear up any doubts as to exactly what "done" means.

The most difficult part of writing a definition document is setting limits—that is, defining up front what the project does include, as well as what it does not include.

For example, a project charter that says, "The goal of this project is to network all facilities in Maryland," leaves the project manager vulnerable to the dreaded, "While you're at it, why don't you include the facilities in Virginia?" On the other hand, a project charter that says, "The goal of this project is to network all facilities in Maryland. Facilities in Virginia will be networked in a separate project during the next fiscal year," provides some defense when people ask for out-of-scope modifications.

Backing into Project End Dates

All too often, the project manager is assigned to a project *after* the project finish date, budget, and resources have been defined. If the project manager (or someone with similar skills) has not been involved in the initial definition of these important parameters, a work plan and schedule may not yet exist. The only way to achieve any degree of certainty in these figures is to lay out a schedule that demonstrates whether or not there is enough money, the right number and kind of people, and enough time to produce the expected deliverables.

Project managers affectionately call the process of forcing a project plan to fit into a pre-determined project scope, schedule, and set of resources as *backing into the schedule*. Most project managers would prefer to build the plan before they commit to any kind of project completion date. The painfulness of this process highlights the importance of involving the project manager early in the definition of a project.

In the event that the schedule cannot support the key parameters, it is important that the project manager communicate this issue to the project sponsors as quickly as possible.

In the later modules on the subject of planning, we'll take a look at what the project manager can do to build a plan against a fixed end date, budget, and number of resources.

4.2 Initiating a Project

The PMBOK Guide identifies four processes involved in the overall project definition process: project initiation, scope planning, scope definition, and scope verification.

Initiation involves formally recognizing that a new project exists or that an existing project should continue into its next phase. In some organizations, a project is not formally initiated until after completion of a feasibility study, a preliminary plan, or some other form of analysis. Some types of projects—especially internal service projects and new product development projects—are initiated informally, and a limited amount of work may be done to get the approvals needed for formal initiation.

Inputs to Initiation

Each aspect of the initiation process has its key components, as outlined below.

Product description – The product description documents the characteristics of the product or service that the project was undertaken to create. The product description will generally have less detail in early phases and more detail in later ones as the product characteristics are progressively elaborated.

Strategic plan – Plan projects should be supportive of the performing organization's strategic goals. As such, the strategic plan of the performing organization should be considered as a factor in project selection decisions.

Project selection criteria – Project selection criteria are typically defined in terms of the product of the project and can cover the full range of possible management concerns (e.g. financial return, market share, public perceptions).

Historical information – Historical information about the results of previous project selection decisions, and previous project performance should be considered to the extent it is available. When initiation involves approval for the next phase of a project, information about the results of previous phases is often critical.

Tools and Techniques for Initiation

Project selection methods – Project selection methods generally fall into one of two broad categories:

❏ Benefit measurement methods – Comparative approaches, scoring models, benefit contribution, or economic models

❏ Constrained optimization methods – Mathematical models using linear, non-linear, dynamic, integer, and multi-objective programming algorithms

These methods are often referred to as *decision models*. Decision models include generalized techniques (decision trees, forced choice) as well as specialized ones (Analytic Hierarchy Process, Logical Framework Analysis).

Expert judgment – Expert judgment will often be required to assess the inputs to this process. Such expertise may be provided by any group or individual with specialized knowledge or training and is available from many sources.

Outputs from Initiation

Project charter – A project charter is a document that formally recognizes the existence of a project. It should include, either directly or by reference to other documents:

❏ The business need that the project was undertaken to address

❏ The product description

The project charter should be issued by a manager external to the project and at a level appropriate to the needs of the project. It provides the project manager with the authority to apply organizational resources to project activities.

Identification of project manager – In general, the project manager should be identified and assigned as early in the project as is feasible. The project manager should always be assigned prior to the start of project plan execution and preferably before much project planning has been done.

Constraints – Constraints are factors that will limit the project management team's options. For example, a predefined budget is a constraint that will limit the team's options regarding scope, staffing, and schedule.

Assumptions – Assumptions are factors that, for planning purposes, will be presumed to be true, real, or certain. For example, if the date that a key person will become available is uncertain, the team may assume a specific start date. Assumptions generally involve a degree of risk.

4.3 Planning the Scope of a Project

Scope planning is the process of developing a written scope statement to serve as the basis for future project decisions. In particular, the scope statement will influence whether or not the project or phase has been completed successfully. The scope statement forms the basis for an agreement between the project team and the project customer by identifying both the project objectives and the major project deliverables. Under some circumstances, particularly if the major deliverables and project objectives have been identified, this process may involve little more than creating the written document.

Inputs to Scope Planning

- ❑ Product description
- ❑ Project charter
- ❑ Constraints
- ❑ Assumptions

Tools and Techniques for Scope Planning

Product analysis – Product analysis involves developing a better understanding of the product of the project. It includes techniques such as systems engineering, value engineering, value analysis, function analysis, and quality function deployment.

Benefit/cost analysis – Benefit/cost analysis involves estimating tangible and intangible costs (outlays) and benefits (returns) of various project alternatives, and then using financial measures—such as return on investment or payback period—to assess the relative desirability of the identified alternatives.

Alternatives identification – This is a catchall term for any technique used to generate different approaches to the project. There are a variety of general management techniques used here, the most common of which are brainstorming and lateral thinking.

Expert judgment – Expert judgment was described in Section 4.2: *Initiating a Project.*

Outputs from Scope Planning

Scope statement – The scope statement provides a documented basis for making future project decisions and for confirming or developing a common understanding of project scope among the stakeholders. As the project progresses, the scope statement may need to be revised or refined to reflect changes to the scope of the project. The scope statement should include, either directly or by reference to other documents:

- ❑ *Project justification* – The business need that the project was undertaken to address
- ❑ *Project product* – A brief summary of the product description

❑ *Project deliverables* – A list of the summary-level sub-products whose full and satisfactory delivery marks completion of the project; for example, the major deliverables for a software development project might include the working computer code, a user manual, and an interactive tutorial. When known, exclusions should be identified, but anything not explicitly included is implicitly excluded.

❑ *Project objectives* – The quantifiable criteria that must be met for the project to be considered successful; must include at least cost, schedule, and quality measures. Project objectives should have an attribute (cost), a yardstick (U.S. dollars), and an absolute or relative value (less than 1.5 million). Un-quantified objectives (customer satisfaction) entail high risk.

Supporting detail – Supporting detail for the scope statement should be documented and organized for easy use and should always include all identified assumptions and constraints.

Scope management plan – This document describes how project scope will be managed and how scope changes will be integrated into the project. It should also include an assessment of the expected stability of the project scope—that is, how likely is it to change, how frequently, and by how much. The scope management plan should also include a clear description of how scope changes will be identified and classified. This is particularly difficult, and therefore absolutely essential, when the product characteristics are still being elaborated.

A scope management plan may be formal or informal, highly detailed or broadly framed, depending on the needs of the project. It is a part of the overall project plan.

4.4 Scope Definition

Scope definition involves subdividing the major project deliverables identified in the scope statement into smaller, more manageable components to:

❑ Improve the accuracy of cost, time, and resource estimates

❑ Define a baseline for performance measurement and control

❑ Facilitate clear responsibility assignments

Proper scope definition is critical to project success. Poor scope definition leads to higher costs because of the inevitable changes (scope creep), which disrupt project efficiency, increase project time, and lower the productivity and morale of the project team.

Inputs to Scope Definition

Scope statement

Constraints – When a project is done under contract, the constraints defined by contractual provisions are often important considerations during scope definition.

Assumptions

Other planning outputs – The outputs of the processes in other knowledge areas should be reviewed for possible impact on project scope definition.

Historical information – Historical information about previous projects should be considered during scope definition. Information about errors and omissions on previous projects should be especially useful.

Tools and Techniques for Scope Definition

Work breakdown structure templates – A work breakdown structure (WBS) from a previous project can often be used as a template for a new project. Although each project is unique, WBSs can often be reused since most projects will resemble previous projects within a given organization with similar project lifecycles and similar deliverables required from each phase.

Decomposition – Decomposition involves subdividing the major project deliverables into smaller, more manageable components until the deliverables are defined in sufficient detail to support future project activities (planning, executing, controlling, and closing). Decomposition involves the following major steps:

1 *Identify the major elements of the project* – In general, the major elements will be the project deliverables and project management. However, the major elements should always be defined in terms of how the project will actually be managed.

2 *Decide if adequate cost and duration estimates can be developed at this level of detail for each element* – The meaning of "adequate" may change over the course of the project; decomposition of a deliverable that will be produced far in the future may not be possible. For each element, proceed to Step 4 if there is adequate detail and to Step 3 if there is not, as different elements may have differing levels of decomposition.

3 *Identify constituent elements of the deliverable* – Constituent elements should be described in terms of tangible, verifiable results in order to facilitate performance measurements. As with the major elements, the constituent elements should be defined in terms of how the work of the project will actually be accomplished. Tangible, verifiable results can include services as well as products. For example, *status reporting* could be described as *weekly status report*s. Repeat Step 2 on each constituent element.

4 *Verify the correctness of the decomposition*:

 ❑ Are the lower-level items both necessary and sufficient for completion of the item decomposed? If not, the constituent elements must be modified—added to, deleted from, or redefined.

 ❑ Is each item clearly and completely defined? If not, the descriptions must be revised or expanded.

 ❑ Can each item be appropriately scheduled? Budgeted? Assigned to a specific team or person who will accept responsibility for satisfactory completion of the item? If not, revisions are needed to provide adequate management control.

Outputs from Scope Definition

Work breakdown structure – A work breakdown structure (WBS) is a deliverable-oriented grouping of project elements that organizes and defines the total scope of the project; work not in the WBS is outside the scope of the project. As with the scope statement, the WBS is often used to develop or confirm a common understanding of project scope. Each descending level represents an increasingly detailed description of the project elements.

A WBS is normally presented in chart form. However, the WBS should not be confused with the method of presentation; drawing an unstructured activity list in chart form does not make it a WBS.

Each item in the WBS is generally assigned a unique identifier. These identifiers are often known collectively as the *code of accounts*. The items at the lowest level of the WBS are often referred to as *work* packages. These work packages may be further broken down in the activity definition process.

4.5 Scope Verification

Scope verification is the process of formalizing acceptance of the project scope by the stakeholders (sponsor, client, customer, etc.). It requires reviewing work products and results to ensure that all were completed correctly and satisfactorily. If the project is terminated early, the scope verification process should establish and document the level and extent of completion.

Scope verification differs from quality control in that it is primarily concerned with acceptance of the work results, while quality control is primarily concerned with the correctness of the work results.

Inputs to Scope Verification

Work results – Assessments such as which deliverables have been fully or partially completed and what costs have been incurred or committed; work results are an output of project plan execution.

Product Documentation – Documents produced to describe the project's products must be available for review; the terms used to describe this documentation (plans, specifications, technical documentation, drawings, etc.) vary by application area.

Tools and Techniques for Scope Verification

Inspection – Inspection includes activities such as measuring, examining, and testing undertaken to determine whether results conform to requirements. Inspections are variously called reviews, product reviews, audits, and walk-throughs.

Outputs from Scope Verification

Formal Acceptance – Documentation that the client or sponsor has accepted the product of the project or phase must be prepared and distributed.

End of Chapter Quiz Questions

1 -5. Match the project definition document name listed in the left column of the table below, to the correct description from the right column by entering the letter that the name corresponds to in the blank line. NOTE: One answer applies to two of the questions.

1. Business Plan _____ 2. Proposal _____	A. Used between two separate firms, such as a manufacturer and a consulting company, to sell a project to a company
3. Statement of Work _____	B. Another term used for a Statement of Work
4. Scope of Work _____	C. Often used to gain support & approval for internal company projects
5. Project Charter _____	D. The formal attachment or appendix to the standard terms and conditions of a contract that describes the detailed approach for performing the project.

6. What sections does a project definition document usually contain?

7. Define the term "project objectives"

8. Which of the following are clear, measurable statements defining the purpose of the project?
 A. Executive Summary
 B. Objectives
 C. Assumptions
 D. None of the above

9. What are deliverables guidelines?

10. Fill is the blank: The summary of the project work plan is the _____ _____.

11. Which section of the project definition document can you tell when each major phase are done?

12. Fill in the blank: A solid completion statement will tie the _____ and their _____ together in a logical way.

13. A project charter says, "The goal of this project is to network all facilities in Delaware." What is a potential issue with this charter, and how can it be improved?

14. Describe what is meant by "backing into the schedule"?

15. What are the four processes involved in the overall project definition as identified by the PMBOK Guide?

16. True or false: Some types of projects are initiated informally, and a limited amount of work may be done to get the approvals needed for formal initiation.

17. – 28. Fill in the Inputs, Tools and Techniques, and Outputs for each of the phases below.

Initiation

Inputs: _____

Tools and Techniques:_____

Outputs: _____

Scope Planning

Inputs: _____

Tools and Techniques:_____

Outputs: _____

Scope Definition

Inputs: _____

Tools and Techniques:_____

Outputs: _____

Scope Verification

Inputs: _____

Tools and Techniques:_____

Outputs: _____

chapter 5

Defining Your Project Using Microsoft Project 2016

- Creating a New Project

- Providing Project Information

- Setting File Properties

- Setting Local Calendar Information

- Project Definition Review Exercise

Learning Objectives for this Chapter

At the end of the chapter, the reader should be able to perform the following Microsoft Project 2016 functions:

- Start a new project from scratch or from a template
- Create a new project from an Excel workbook
- Provide project information, such as project start and default scheduling constraint
- Identify and update file properties
- Set up a project calendar

*P*roject Definition is the process of documenting the key scope parameters of the project. Within Microsoft Project 2016, project definition involves defining details about the developing project plan, such as the start (or finish) date of the project and the available dates and times for project work.

5.1 Creating a New Project

There are several methods of creating a new project in Microsoft Project Professional:

- ❑ Creating a new blank project
- ❑ Creating a new project based on an existing project
- ❑ Creating a project based on an existing project template
- ❑ Creating a new project from an Excel workbook
- ❑ Creating a new project from a SharePoint tasks list

Blank Project

To create a new blank project:

1 Open Microsoft Project 2016 and, from the introductory screen, select *Blank Project*. Alternatively, if Microsoft Project is already open, from the *File* tab select *New* and then click *Blank Project*.

Figure 56.

Microsoft
Project
introductory
screen (blank
project circled in
black)

2 From the *File* tab, select *Options* to see the **Project Options** dialog
 box.

Figure 57.

**Project
Options** dialog
box

3 In the sidebar, click *Save*. Your screen will resemble the following:

Figure 58.

Save tab in
**Project
Options** dialog

4 By default, Microsoft Project 2016 saves local project files in the
 *.mpp format. If you prefer a different format, click the down arrow in
 the first dropdown box to see other available options.

5 Another item you can change is where files are stored. To do so, use the *Browse* button by the *Default File location* field and select where you would like project files to be stored by default. For the purposes of this course, browse to your exercise directory. Click *OK*.

6 From the *File* menu, click *Save* and save your project to your exercise directory as **SampleProject.mpp**.

New from Existing Project

📂 This exercise uses the file **Navigation.mpp**. You do not need to open this file prior to beginning this exercise.

At times you might want to build a project similar to a previous one, since it might be quicker to simply edit the existing project to meet your needs rather than creating a new project from scratch.

1 To do so, from the initial Microsoft Project 2016 page, click *New from existing project*. Alternatively, if Microsoft Project is already open, from the *File* tab select *New* and then click *New from existing project*. Either way, you will see the **New from Existing Project** dialog box:

Figure 59.

New From Existing Project dialog box

2 Select **Navigation.mpp** and click *Open*. **Navigation.mpp** will open in Microsoft Project.

Figure 60.

Navigation.mpp
before saving as a
new project

3 From the *File* menu click *Save* to see the **Save As** dialog box, and
 save your project as **Navigation2.mpp**. Notice the new project name
 at the top of your screen:

Figure 61.

After changing
to
**Navigation2.m
pp**

4 Close **Navigation2.mpp**.

Project Templates

You can also create projects based on an existing project template:

1 To do so, click *File:New* and select one of the existing templates:

Figure 62.

Select a
template or
search for online
templates

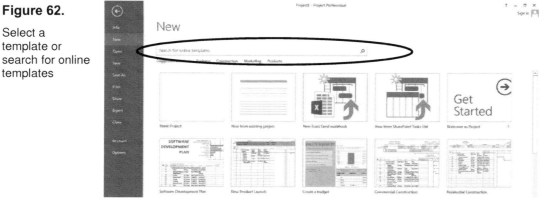

2 If you don't see a template that meets your needs, use the search bar
 toward the top of the screen (circled in black in the above figure) to
 find additional templates online.

Excel Workbooks

In much the same way as the previous examples, you can also create new
projects based on existing Excel task lists:

1 To do so, select *New from Excel workbook* from the Microsoft Project
 introductory page, or access this selection from the *File:New* menu.

Figure 63.

*New from Excel
workbook*

2 In the **Open** dialog box, navigate to the Excel file which your new
 project is to be based on. For this example, navigate to **TaskList.xlsx**
 and click *Open*. You will see the first screen of the **Import Wizard**:

Figure 64.

Excel **Import
Wizard**

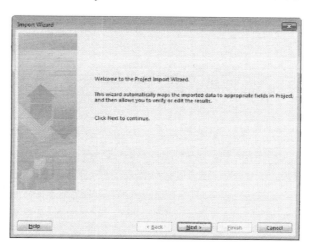

3 Click *Next*, ensure *New Map* is selected, and click *Next* again. Your
 screen will resemble the following:

Figure 65.

Excel **Import
Wizard –
Import Mode**

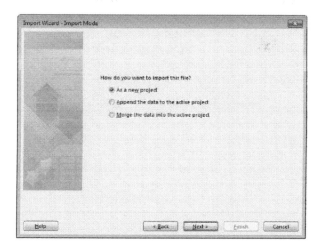

4 Select *As a new project* and click *Next* again to see the following
screen:

Figure 66.

Excel **Import
Wizard – Map
Options**

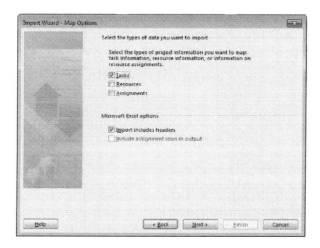

5 For this example we'll be importing only tasks, so select *Tasks* in the
first section and deselect *Import includes headers* in the second
section. Click *Next* to see the **Task Mapping** dialog:

Figure 67.

Excel **Import Wizard – Task Mapping**

6 In the **Task Mapping** dialog, in the *Source worksheet name* section, select *Sheet1*.

7 Because you are importing a simple list of tasks, in the *Verify or edit how you want to map the data* section, under *To: Microsoft Project Field*, use the dropdown arrow to select *Name*.

8 Click *Finish*. Your screen will resemble the following:

Figure 68.

Imported project

9 Your Excel task list has now become a project. Close your new project without saving it.

SharePoint Tasks List

In much the same way as the previous examples, you can also create new projects based on existing SharePoint tasks lists. Note: A SharePoint tasks list consists of a collection of tasks. Often SharePoint is used to create a preliminary tasks list that eventually becomes the core structure of a project.

1 To do so, select *New from SharePoint Tasks List* from the Microsoft Project introductory page, or access this selection from the *File:New* menu. You will see the **Import from SharePoint Site** dialog box:

Figure 69.

Import from SharePoint Site dialog box

2 Enter the SharePoint site's URL, click *Check Address* to confirm the URL is entered accurately, and in the *Tasks List* section select the name of the SharePoint tasks list you'd like to base your project upon.

3 Click *OK*. Your SharePoint tasks list has now become a project:

Figure 70.

Tasks list imported to Project

4 Close your new project without saving it.

5.2 Providing Project Information

The **Project Information** dialog box is where Microsoft Project 2016 allows you to set the scheduling and calendar methods to be used on your project. This information is necessary to allow the scheduling engine of Microsoft Project 2016 to do its job. When you create a new project from scratch, the **Project Information** dialog box can be automatically activated.

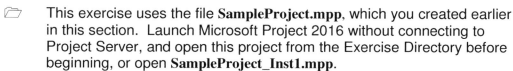 This exercise uses the file **SampleProject.mpp**, which you created earlier in this section. Launch Microsoft Project 2016 without connecting to Project Server, and open this project from the Exercise Directory before beginning, or open **SampleProject_Inst1.mpp**.

1 From *Project:Properties*, click the *Project Information* icon [] to access the **Project Information** dialog box for **SampleProject.mpp**.

Figure 71.

Project Information dialog box

NOTE

You can automate the launch of this dialog box when creating a new project by navigating to *File:Options*, **selecting** *Advanced* **in the sidebar, and selecting the** *Prompt for project info for new projects* **checkbox from the** *General* **section.**

2 Change the value entered in the *Start date:* field to today's date. The default is the date that the project is created. New tasks will use the start date specified here if no predecessors or constraints exist.

The *Schedule from* field indicates the scheduling method that Microsoft Project 2016 will apply to your project plan. Two options are available:

1 *Project Start Date* (default) – This option indicates that the project is scheduled from the start date. When it is selected, the **Finish Date** field is automatically deactivated; you cannot enter a finish date and must instead allow Microsoft Project to calculate it.

2 *Project Finish Date* – This option indicates that the project is scheduled from the finish date. When this option is selected, the **Start Date** field is automatically deactivated; you must allow Microsoft Project to calculate the start date. Though building a schedule back-to-front is a reasonable behavior, many people find it difficult, so the best practice may be to begin by scheduling from a start date and change to finish date scheduling later in the process.

NOTE

The recommended approach we will follow in this course is to schedule projects from a selected start date. Microsoft Project 2016 does not permit you to set both a start and finish date at the project level, but you can set a targeted finish date at the task level when you set task constraints, which is covered in a later lesson.

If you choose to use the *backwards scheduling* **technique, select** *Project Finish Date* **from the** *Schedule from* **dropdown list. Then, instead of selecting a project start date, select a project finish date from the dropdown calendar.**

The *Status Date* field enables you to specify the date that Microsoft Project 2016 should use to perform earned value calculations, identify the complete-through date in the **Update Project** dialog box, and place progress lines on the Gantt Chart. If you leave the status date as "NA" (default), Microsoft Project uses the current date as the status date.

The Calendar field indicates the calendar you want to use as the base calendar for your project. The base calendar specifies when project work is possible.

There are three pre-defined calendars available in Microsoft Project 2016 when using the Computer Profile:

Calendar	Description
Standard	The Standard calendar is the base calendar that is used as the default for project, resource, and task calendars. It reflects a traditional work schedule: Monday through Friday, 8:00 A.M. to 5:00 P.M., with an hour off for break.
24-Hours	The 24-Hours calendar does not allow for any nonworking time in the project schedule. The 24-Hours calendar is ideal for when tasks and resources are scheduled for different shifts around the clock, or when certain material resources (e.g. computer equipment, machinery) can work on tasks continuously.
Night Shift	The Night Shift calendar reflects the "graveyard shift" schedule of Monday night through Saturday morning, 11:00 P.M. to 8:00 A.M., with an hour of nonworking time for break.

When connected to Project Server, base calendars must be defined at the enterprise level (that is, in Project Server) by the Project Server administrator to maintain consistency across all enterprise projects. The Project Server administrator can define as many base calendars as needed for enterprise projects.

There is an option to allow individual projects to use their own local base calendars, rather than a consistent set of enterprise calendars, but it must be activated by the Project Server administrator.

The *Priority* field indicates the order in which tasks will be delayed when you level the resources across multiple projects. Microsoft Project 2016 enables you to assign a priority number between 0 and 1000 to a project. By entering "1000" in this field, you are designating the current project as having the highest priority of all of your projects. In practical terms, that means its schedule will be unaffected if you level resources across projects.

5.3 Setting File Properties

The calendar and scheduling method are properties of the project that are necessary for the scheduling engine of Microsoft Project 2016 to do its job. But you also can provide information about the project file, such as a title that can be different from the file name. This information is then available to include in the project plan itself or in headers and footers of printed information.

The **File Properties** dialog box contains several tabs of information:

- ❏ **General Tab** – Provides information on the file that stores the project plan
- ❏ **Summary Tab** – Provides fields to further describe the project
- ❏ **Statistics Tab** – Provides statistics about your work on the project file
- ❏ **Contents Tab** – Provides current project schedule statistics
- ❏ **Custom Tab** – Provides additional properties you can add to the file

The **File Properties** dialog box cannot be automated like the **Project Information** dialog box. Users have to remember to open it to provide or modify information about the file.

 📂 This exercise continues to use the file **SampleProject.mpp** (or **SampleProject_Inst1.mpp**).

1 Now that you have chosen start date scheduling and set the start date for your project, select *Advanced Properties*, which is found under *File:Info:Project Information*. You will be presented with the following screen (note the *Summary* tab is selected by default).

Figure 72.

Advanced properties + Properties dialog box

2 In the *Title* field, overwrite *SampleProject.mpp* with *Office Relocation Project*. This will appear as the Project Summary Task (Task ID 0).

3 In the *Author* and *Manager* fields, key in your name.

4 In the *Company* field, key in the name of your company.

5 In the *Comments* field, key in "This is the preliminary plan for moving the local office."

The information in the upper portion of the tab—(project) title, subject, author, (project) manager, and company name—can then be included in reports as header or footer text. The *Subject*, *Category*, and *Keywords* fields are most often used to enhance search capability. The free-form text box for additional comments will appear as a task note associated with the project summary task (title). The hyperlink base can be used to enter the file path to the directory where your project files are located, but it need not be filled in.

The *Save preview picture* option allows a thumbnail view of the project Gantt Chart to appear in the lower left-hand corner of selected directory views. It is generally not needed.

Your screen will resemble the following:

Figure 73.

Updated project
properties

6 Click *OK*.

Although we provided a user-friendly title for the project, making it appear in
the Gantt Chart can be confusing since Microsoft Project itself does not use
the term "title." To view the title of your project in the Gantt Chart:

7 From *File:Options* select *Advanced* in the sidebar. Scroll down to
 Display options for this project and check *Show project summary
 task*, as shown in the following figure:

Figure 74.

Showing the
Project Summary
task
(Task 0)

8 Click the *OK* button. The title you entered in the **File Properties** dialog
 box will be shown as Task 0 in the *Task Name* field. If no title is
 entered, the file name is used by default. You can enter your own text
 in the project summary task name as well, and it will change the title.
 Your screen will resemble the following:

Figure 75.

Gantt Chart
showing project
title (Task 0)

9 Along with the title, the row 0 of Task Name contains a Note icon [🗒
] in the Indicator [ℹ] column. Place your mouse pointer over the
 Note icon to read it. Your screen will resemble the following:

Figure 76.

Task note
attached to the
project summary
task [title]

These notes are intended as internal reminders for the project manager and
are not visible by default except through Microsoft Project. They can also be
read by navigating to *Task:Properties* and selecting the *Information* [▣]
icon.

10 Save your project.

5.4 Setting Local Calendar Information

Calendar Options

In addition to the project calendar, Microsoft Project 2016 also has calendar
options—such as default start time and hours per day—that are used to assign
dates to tasks when no date or time is specified. For example, if the first task is
scheduled using the project start time, the task will be scheduled to start at the
default start time of 8:00 AM unless otherwise specified. If changes are made to
the default calendar options, the base calendar should be updated with those
changes. If the calendar options and the base calendar do not display the same
basic information, tasks and resource assignments may conflict.

📁 This exercise uses the file **SampleProject.mpp**. Be sure this project is
open before beginning, or open **SampleProject_Inst2.mpp**.

1 From *File:Options* select *Schedule* from the **Project Options** dialog
box. Your screen will resemble the following:

Figure 77.

Schedule under
Project Options

The *Hours per day*, *Hours per week*, and *Days per month* values are essentially conversion factors which allow Microsoft Project to accept durations in values other than days and still create an accurate schedule.

 2 Click *Cancel.*

Adding a Holiday to the Project Base Calendar

Before you begin adding tasks and resources to your project, it is important to make sure the project base calendar includes information such as company holidays and other non-working times.

When you turn your project into an enterprise project by publishing it to Project Server, you will have to use an enterprise base calendar created by the Project Server administrator. The administrator will then presumably add any company holidays to the enterprise standard calendar.

Let's say that the second Monday in your project has been declared a national holiday, Project Management Day, and everyone will be off work. To inform Microsoft Project about this non-working day, we will have to modify the standard calendar we applied to **SampleProject.mpp.**

 3 From *Project:Properties* click the *Change Working Time* icon []. You will be presented with the following dialog box:

Figure 78.

**Change
Working Time**
dialog box

4 Click the appropriate date for the second Monday of your project. On the *Exceptions* tab, enter "Project Management Day" in the first row and press *Tab*. The following example uses March 25 as the exception.

Figure 79.

New holiday added

If Project Management Day were to be an annual holiday, the *Details...* button would allow you to set a recurrence pattern for this exception to the standard calendar. Clicking on *Details...* leads to the following dialog box:

Figure 80.

Exception *Details*

5 Click *Cancel* to close the **Details** dialog box. Then, click *OK* in the **Change Working Time** dialog box. Save and close your project.

5.5 Project Definition Review Exercise

This review exercise will reinforce the project definition process covered in this chapter.

1 Open Microsoft Project 2016 without connecting to Project Server.

2 From *File:New* select *Blank Project.*

3 Ensure that you are scheduling from the project start date and make the project start date "June 3."

4 Enter a project title of "Implement Microsoft Project 2016."

5 Identify yourself as the author and project manager.

6 Mark the following days as holidays in the standard calendar: Independence Day (July 4 of the current year), Labor Day (September 2 of the current year), Thanksgiving (November 28 and 29 of the current year), and Christmas (December 25 of the current year).

7 Save your project as **DefinitionReview.mpp**.

End of Chapter Quiz Questions

1. How can you change the default location where files are saved?

2. Fill in the blank: You can create new projects based on existing Excel _____ lists.

3. Fill in the blank: The _____ _____ dialog box is where Microsoft Project 2016 allows you to set the scheduling and calendar methods to be used on your project.

4. Fill in the blank: The _____ _____ field indicates the scheduling method that Microsoft Project 2016 will apply to your project plan.

5. Which of the following is NOT an option in the Schedule form field?
 a. Project Start Date
 b. Project Finish Date
 c. Current Date
 d. None of the above

6. What does the *Status Date* field enable?

 []

7. What are the three pre-defined calendars available in Microsoft Project 2016 when using the Computer Profile?

 _____ _____ _____

8. How many base calendars can the Project Server administrator define?
 a. 1
 b. 2
 c. 3
 d. As many as needed for enterprise projects.

9. Fill in the blank: The _____ field indicates the order in which tasks will be delayed when you level the resources across multiple projects.

10. Before you begin adding tasks and resources to your project, it is important to make sure the project base calendar includes what information?

11. Fill in the blank: In order to set the project working time and non-working time you use _____ _____ _____ feature.

12. What is the *Exceptions* tab used for in the **Change Working Time** dialog box?

part

III

Project Task Planning

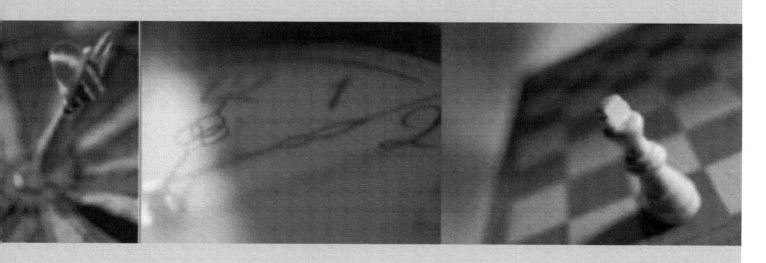

chapter 6

Developing a Work Breakdown Structure

- Creating a Project Work Plan

- Determining the Logical Relationship of Tasks in Your WBS

- Resource Planning and Acquisition

- Team Development

- Cost Estimating and Budgeting

Learning Objectives for this Chapter

At the end of the chapter, the reader should be able to:

- Describe the best practices for building a project schedule
- Understand the concept of using an organizing principle for developing the Work Breakdown Structure
- Describe the types of task dependencies
- Define the critical path and understand why it is important to project planning
- Understand effort versus duration
- Be familiar with the various types of resources that are typically assigned to projects, including non-human and material resources
- Define an optimized project plan
- Describe why baselines are important to project tracking
- Understand the basic principles for cost estimating and budgeting
- Become familiar with the PMBOK concepts of resource planning, staff acquisition, and team development

\mathcal{R}eal project planning begins with a work breakdown structure (WBS), which is the formal project management term for a set of tasks that are configured into an outline structure, with phases at the highest level and detailed tasks at the lowest level. From there, the WBS can be expanded into a project schedule and used to guide resource assignments.

This chapter will discuss the process of building a complete project work plan, beginning with a list of tasks.

6.1 Creating a Project Work Plan

Project Planning Summary

Before beginning a detailed discussion of developing a project work plan, consider the following questions that form a logical summary of the process:

❑ What is the primary goal? What is the main product or outcome of this project?

❑ What are the sub-goals? What are the intermediate steps and deliverables needed to achieve the primary goal?

- How are we going to organize the project? Do we expect that there will be multiple remote teams with distinct deliverables that will be handed off between teams? Or will there be close knit groups collaborating on a sequence of joint deliverables?

- What are the detailed activities? What more detailed tasks are needed to achieve the sub-goals?

- In what order do the detailed activities have to be done? What is the necessary sequence of the tasks?

- What kind of tasks are they? What determines how much time or effort they take?

- What skills are needed to do the tasks? What attributes do the resources need to have? Who are the named resources who actually will perform the work?

- How big are the tasks? What are our estimates of how much time or effort each one takes?

- When will the work be done? What does the schedule look like?

- Who will actually do the work, and when?

Referencing the Project Definition Document to Start Your Work Plan

Much of the information from the project definition document can be used as reference to start the work plan.

- Identify all project deliverables and determine how they will be documented.

- Refer to your methodology.

- Make sure the template suits your situation.

- Decide if the detail for the summary schedule is appropriate.

- Determine how the project budget was developed; validate it.

In order to build a plan, the project manager needs to know what deliverables have been designated for the project. This information can be found in the definition document created in the concept phase.

Methodologies and Planning

Many methodologies are accompanied by suggested work plans that have been built based upon successful projects that used the work plan. These work plan templates are a valuable source of information that can be used by the project manager in building the work plan.

A word of caution: Work plan templates sometimes contain hundreds, or even thousands, of pre-defined tasks. It is important that you validate these work plan templates even though it is tempting to think that a plan with that much detail already loaded must be right.

Determining How the SOW Summary Schedule was Built

If the SOW contains a summary schedule, you might assume that a detailed work plan must have been built to support the summary schedule. If one has been built, then you already have a good starting point and may only need to validate what was already created.

The same holds true for the budget. As you may recall from the definition process, the project budget should be built from the detailed work plan, which states the total resource labor hours. Again, you should already have a good starting point for the plan.

Starting a Plan with a New Task Outline

If there is no methodology and no previous work plan that has been converted to a template, you may have to start with the proverbial "blank sheet of paper." In the following sections, we will consider what processes and tools have been suggested to support this process.

Defining Activities

Activity definition involves identifying and documenting the specific activities that must be performed to produce the deliverables and sub-deliverables identified in the definition document. Ideally, the project manager will have the support of the project team throughout this process, but in many organizations the project team is not identified until activity definition is complete.

To start activity definition, the project manager should consider four major items:

Definition document – The project justification and the project objectives contained in the scope statement of the definition document are necessary inputs to the process.

Historical information – The activities required on previous similar projects can provide insight into the activities needed in this project.

Constraints – The factors that will limit the project team's options, such as a predetermined finish date or a firm budget limit, must be considered.

High-level work breakdown structure – A work breakdown structure at the phase level may be available to guide activity definition.

Creating a Work Breakdown Structure (WBS) for Deliverables

The process of building the WBS starts by clustering tasks around logical groupings, such as related activities (e.g. design, programming, testing), related geographies (e.g. East coast, Midwest, West coast sites), or functions (e.g. accounting, human resources, shipping).

In the absence of a methodology that provides a template to guide activity definition, this can be as much art as science. The templates installed with Microsoft Project 2016 can be a useful source of insight into the options available.

A graphical representation of the WBS might look a lot like a family tree:

Figure 81.

A WBS "family tree"

Once you've clustered the tasks into logical groupings, you need to decide if the WBS contains the appropriate level of detail. A plan with three phases that contain 1,000 hours each is not enough detail. However, if you loaded every step in a procedure into your work plan, this would probably be too much detail (for example a plan that contains 3,000 tasks, each documenting one hour of effort).

So what's the difference between a methodology procedure step and a task? Tasks are estimated, are scheduled, and have resources assigned. You wouldn't want to go through all that effort for a procedure step. It's not worth it. What we need are some rules of thumb for determining the right amount of detail.

Completing the WBS

The *Rule of 80* is one way to test whether the WBS contains enough detail. Donald Plummer writes in <u>Productivity Management</u>, "The 80-hour rule stipulates that you break a project into tasks of 80 hours or less, each of which must result in a tangible product or deliverable."

This rule is just a guideline. You have to decide what the right level of detail is for your project. A small network upgrade project that occurs over a weekend might contain 50 tasks that each requires 30-60 minutes of effort. Early software developers used the guideline that tasks should be greater than 4 hours of effort and less than 40 hours of effort.

Another useful approach is to ask if you have enough detail to be able to manage effectively. The longer the task, the more you will have to rely on the progress reports of the resource assigned to it and the harder it will be to ask probing questions about their progress. When you think you have enough detail, you should refer to the list of deliverables to be certain that tasks exist to build each of the deliverables. This is a good preliminary test of completeness, but it is still possible to overlook some important activities.

Working with Tasks that Are Not Deliverables Related

If you look only at the list of deliverables to build the WBS, there are some tasks you may miss. These are called *scaffolding tasks*, a term from the construction management industry. The scaffolding is used to put up the building, but when the building is delivered the scaffolding is gone.

Scaffolding tasks fall into three general categories:

1 **Support tasks** – Such as writing the program used for a one-time database conversion; the database gets converted, but the program to convert it does not get delivered; other examples include: configuring a test environment or converting database records to a new format.

2 **Project management tasks** – Such as the processes of tracking, analysis, and scope management; such tasks *do not* produce project deliverables, but still need to be included in the plan.

3 **Administrative tasks** – Such as filing and copying; the deliverables guidelines in the SOW may not be any help in reminding you to include administrative tasks in the plan, but they are important enough to include; other examples include: printing, non-project meetings, and other non-project activities that impact the schedule.

Scaffolding tasks can take a significant amount of effort, so it is important they be uncovered through some means other than the deliverables list.

Using the Gantt Chart with the WBS

The Gantt Chart is a visible representation of the project schedule. Each task represents a row on the chart accompanied by a bar, which is drawn to represent the start and finish date of the task. The Gantt Chart provides an excellent graphical representation of the WBS.

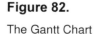

Figure 82.

The Gantt Chart

6.2 Determining Logical Relationships of Tasks in Your WBS

Task Dependencies

Once the WBS is built, you are ready to decide the order tasks will be performed. Some tasks depend on one or more tasks before they can start. For example, you can't put up the walls until you pour the foundation. Some tasks need to start or finish at the same time, while other tasks can't start until another one is already underway.

The predecessor and successor relationship you define provides the foundation for the critical path of your project. There are four different kinds of task dependencies:

Finish-to-Start Dependencies (FS)

This relationship means that the first task, the *predecessor,* must be finished before the next task, the *successor*, can start. It is the most common type of task dependency. On the Gantt Chart it is usually represented as follows:

Start-to-Start Dependencies (SS)

This relationship means that the successor task cannot start until the predecessor task starts. On the Gantt Chart it is usually represented as follows:

Finish-to-Finish Dependencies (FF)

This relationship means that the successor task cannot finish until the predecessor task finishes. On the Gantt Chart it is usually represented as follows:

Start-to-Finish Dependencies (SF)

This relationship means that the successor cannot finish until the predecessor starts. It is the least common type of task dependency. On the Gantt Chart it is usually represented as follows:

Variations of Task Dependency Types

Of course tasks sometimes overlap, which is called lead (or lead time). Tasks can also be delayed (for example, to wait while concrete dries), which is called lag (or lag time).

Activity Sequencing

The PMBOK Guide calls the process of establishing dependencies *activity sequencing*. This is the process of identifying and documenting dependencies between activities to be able to develop a realistic and achievable schedule.

Sequencing can be done manually as well as with project management software. Manual methods are often used on smaller projects. Project management software is more effective when the project is longer than six weeks, requires managing multiple resources, and requires frequent repetitive reports.

There are some specific items the project manager should consider in determining these logical relationships:

Product characteristics—such as the physical layout of a plant to be constructed or subsystems on a software project—often affect activity sequencing.

Mandatory dependencies are those that are inherent in the nature of the work being performed. These dependencies often involve physical limitations (e.g. software must be written before it can be tested), but they can also be based on the logic of the tasks.

Discretionary dependencies are not required, but instead are determined by the project manager or team. Discretionary dependencies are usually based on knowledge of:

- ❑ Best practices within a particular application area

- ❑ Some aspect of the project that makes a specific sequence desirable, even though there are other approaches available. One justification might be the availability of necessary resources.

External dependencies is a relationship between project activities and non-project activities. For example, an activity in a project may depend on delivery of hardware from an external source, or environmental hearings may be required before site preparation on a construction project.

Once the logical relationships are determined, the project manager can create visual representations of the activities, including project network diagrams and Gantt Charts. Gantt Charts are most commonly used, but network diagrams are often helpful in complex projects involving relationships among sub-projects.

These visual representations are helpful in determining and using the *critical path method* (CPM).

The Critical Path

The *critical path* is the longest path through the network, based on task duration, which dictate the shortest amount of time the project can be completed.

Though the critical path had originally been used by DuPont to sequence activities in chemical plant construction, the critical path was popularized when Lockheed was building the Polaris submarine in the 1950s. Project managers noticed that some seemingly important tasks could be late without impacting the end date of the project, while other less important tasks that were late were delaying the overall project. This problem led them to rediscover DuPont's concept of the critical path.

Calculating the critical path

The critical path can be calculated using a project activity network, such as the one in the following figure:

Figure 83.

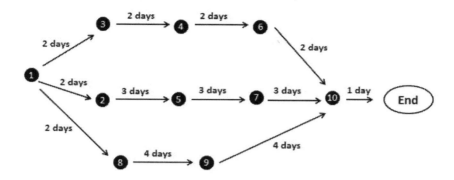

The longest path through the activity (task) network is the critical path.

Path	Length of Path	Longest?
1-3-4-6-10	9 days	No
1-2-5-7-10*	12 days	Yes*
1-8-9-10	11 days	No

These calculations can also provide you with the slack. *Slack* is the amount of time that a task can be delayed without impacting the project end date. Tasks not on the critical path have slack, while tasks on the critical path have zero slack.

Tasks 3, 4, or 6 can be up to 3 days late without changing the critical path. These tasks each have three days of slack.

On the other hand, tasks on the 1-2-5-7-10 path are on the critical path and have zero days of slack.

- ❑ What would happen if Task 2 consumed 5 days instead of 3 days?
- ❑ What would the length of the 1-2-5-7-10 path become?
- ❑ In this case would the 1-2-5-7-10 path still be critical?

Another process for calculating the critical path and slack is the Program Evaluation and Review Technique (PERT). This process evaluates probable outcome based on three scenarios: a best-case, expected-case, and worst-case scenario. The outcome in question may be the duration of a task, its start date, or its finish date.

The Critical Path As an Estimate

The critical path is an estimate because its analysis requires several assumptions, including:

❑ **All tasks are known**. If you forget to add some tasks and add them later, the original critical path may change. Most project plans are missing tasks when they are initially built.

❑ **All links are accurate**. A complicated plan with hundreds of tasks is likely to have some incorrect task dependencies defined.

❑ **All estimates are accurate**. Inaccurate estimates can cause the original critical path to change.

❑ **Other non-critical paths may have small amounts of slack**. A complicated activity path can have multiple non-critical paths. A change in any one of these paths can cause the original critical path to change.

Given the amount of assumptions we rely on in our analysis, the only time you know the actual critical path is after the project is finished.

Despite these potential problems, the critical path method gives the project manager a good indication of where to focus attention. The most important application of CPM is to realize a late task on the critical path will cause the project end date to change.

Estimating the Duration of Activities

The PMBOK Guide covers a process called *activity duration estimating*. This is a process of determining the number of work periods needed to complete each activity.

This estimation will often require consideration of elapsed time as well. For example, if *concrete curing* will require four days, that means it will require four work days if it begins on Monday, but only two work days if it begins on Friday.

There are several items the project manager and project team should consider in developing task estimates:

Resource availability – The duration of most activities will be influenced by the resource assignments. Two people may be able to complete an activity in half the time it would take either of them alone, while a person working half-time will generally take at least twice as much time to complete an activity as the same person working full-time.

Resource capabilities – The duration of most activities will be significantly influenced by the capabilities of the resources assigned. An experienced employee will generally complete an activity in less time than an inexperienced employee.

Historical information – Historical information can be very helpful in this estimating process. Common sources of such information include:

❑ *Project files* – Previous project results may be detailed enough to provide insights into the duration of activities.

❑ *Commercial duration estimating databases* – Historical information is often available commercially, which is especially useful when the activity duration is not driven by the work involved (e.g.: How long does it take concrete to cure? How long does a government agency usually take to respond to certain types of requests?).

❑ *Project team knowledge* – Members of the project team may be aware of previous results or estimates.

Other tools defined by the PMBOK Guide include:

Analogous estimating – Analogous estimating, also called *top-down estimating*, means using the actual duration of a previous, similar activity as the basis for estimating the duration of a future activity. It is frequently used to estimate project duration when there is a limited amount of detailed information about the project, for example, when the project's in the early phases.

Analogous estimating is a form of expert judgment. This form of estimating is most reliable when (1) the previous activities are similar in fact and not just in appearance, and (2) the individuals preparing the estimates have the needed expertise.

Simulation – Simulation involves calculating multiple durations with different sets of assumptions. The most common is *Monte Carlo Analysis* in which a distribution of probable results is defined for each activity and used to calculate a distribution of probable results for the total project.

Schedule Development

Once the durations of the activities in the project have been determined, the project manager and project team can move to *schedule development*. Schedule development, as defined by the PMBOK Guide, means determining start and finish dates for project activities. If the start and finish dates of individual activities are not realistic, the project is unlikely to be finished on schedule.

As with estimating duration, there are several items the project manager and project team should consider in this process:

Resource requirements

Resource pool description – Knowing what resources will be available at what times and in what patterns is necessary for schedule development. Shared resources can be especially difficult to schedule unless their availability can be negotiated in advance.

Calendars – Project and resource calendars identify periods when work is allowed. Project calendars affect all resources; some projects will work only during normal business hours while others will work a full three shifts. Resource calendars affect a specific resource or category of resources; for example, a project team member may be on vacation or in a training program or a labor contract may limit certain workers to certain days of the week.

Constraints – There are two major categories of constraints that must be considered during schedule development:

❑ *Imposed dates* – Completion of certain deliverables by a specified date may be <u>required</u> by the project sponsor, the project customer, or other external agency.

 ❑ *Key events or major milestones* – Completion of certain deliverables by a specified date may be <u>requested</u> by the project sponsor, the project customer, or other stakeholders, and may be connected with contract payments. Once scheduled, these dates become expected and often extremely difficult to move.

Leads and lags – Any of the dependencies may require a lead or a lag to accurately define the relationship (there might be a two-week delay between ordering a piece of equipment and installing or using it).

The Importance of the Estimate

The entire project plan and schedule revolves around the estimated effort for each task. For this reason, the estimates play a key role in building a reliable schedule for the project.

The amount of effort is usually stated in hours, but minutes, days, weeks, months, or even years may be appropriate depending on the type of project. A voicemail system upgrade may be measured in minutes, due to the fact that the project team has only a small amount of time to accomplish the project objectives. A large program with a high amount of uncertainty that will span multiple years may be estimated in units of weeks or months. In all cases, the schedule will only be as reliable as the underlying estimates.

Effort versus Duration

Duration is the amount of time estimated to complete the estimated effort. The effort for a task may be estimated at 40 hours, but its duration is uncertain until you have more information. You'll need to know how many people will work on the task and the percentage of time each will devote to the task. For example, a person working 100% of an 8-hour day will require 5 days to complete the 40-hour task, while a person devoting 25% of an 8-hour day will need 20 days to complete the task.

Assign 5 people to the task working 100% of an 8-hour day and the task will be done in one day, or will it? Adding resources to a task may reduce its duration, but new considerations must be taken into account. Will the resources need to spend more time on communication and coordination than a single person working on the task does? Can the task really be split amongst multiple resources? These factors will affect both effort and duration.

Estimating Work

Work is the total amount of effort scheduled to be performed on a task by all assigned resources. Work can also be estimated in a variety of ways:

 ❑ **Historical** – Data based on past, identical projects that sets a precedent for task duration estimates

- **Participative** – Data based on past, similar projects that sets a precedent for task duration estimates

- **Intuitive** – Data based on past, dissimilar projects that sets a precedent for task duration estimates

- **Unknown** – Foresight without any precedent or relevant information

Determining Resource Requirements

The first challenge in resourcing a project is to decide what skills will be needed to complete it. A look at the tasks in the WBS will provide some meaningful insight into this inquiry. Once the skill types are determined, the next step is to estimate how many people with these skill types will be needed. Consider the following example:

The project is scheduled for 12 months and the estimated number of programmer hours is 4,500. Assuming each programmer can productively work 30 hours per week, how many programmers will you need?

If you divide the total effort of 4,500 hours by 30 hours, you will need 150 weeks of programmer time. If you divide the total weeks by 50 productive weeks over the 12-month project span, you'll need three programmers assuming they can all start on day one and finish on the last day of the project.

The programmers can't start until the end of the 3rd month, and must be done by the end of the 9th month.

Given this new factor, the work must be done in 25 weeks of duration instead of 50. Now you'll need 6 programmers.

Another variable is the actual skill level of the resources that will perform the work. Since you may not know the names of the people who will be assigned to the project, you may need to make assumptions. You might assume that all programmers will have at least five years of real programming experience with the technology that will be used in the project. Be sure to clearly document such assumptions.

Non-human and Material Resources

Not all resources are people. The project manager should keep in mind other resources that may be needed—concrete, steel, pipe, wood, glass, computers, test time, equipment, etc. Such resources can be critical factors in the project manager's ability to complete the project successfully. They should also be scheduled to the tasks that require them.

Avoiding Over-allocation with Load Leveling

Load leveling is the process of assigning resources to the plan without giving them too much work to do in any given time period. You can do 40 hours of work next week, but you can't do 40 hours of work on Monday.

A note of caution: When using automated tools, care should be taken to ensure that resources are not being given too much work in any given time period while you are assigning resources to tasks. If you wait until you are done assigning all of your resources to level your plan, you may be faced with a hopeless mess.

It is tempting to assume that your full-time resources will be able to devote 40 hours per week to the project. Unfortunately, this is usually not realistic. It's better to take a more conservative approach and assume that full-time people will not be able to devote more than 30 hours per week to the plan.

Another thing to keep in mind is the problem of under-allocation. Full-time resources that are only scheduled for 10 hours per week can be a problem too.

Task versus Resource Leveling

Load leveling can be done two different ways: by task or by resource. Leveling by task is what you do when you assign resources to a task and then make sure the resources are available to work on the task.

Leveling by resource means that after you create resource assignments, you look at each resource and all of the tasks assigned to each resource to see if tasks need to be rescheduled to provide for a realistic workload for each resource. However, this approach may present problems—as you reschedule tasks to more realistically allocate one resource, you may over-allocate another.

Leveling against a Fixed Project End Date

Unrealistic project plans are often built to a fixed end date coupled with insufficient resources. The best way to avoid this situation is a sound approach to resource leveling.

Optimizing the Plan

The planning steps reviewed up to this point should produce a reasonable first draft of the work plan. Planning is like writing—several drafts may be required.

Several of the steps may be repeated as the plan is optimized: resources may be added to meet the target end date; estimates may be adjusted as resource skills or roles are converted to real names; new tasks may be discovered as details are filled in; links may change to accommodate other schedule constraints; assignments may shift to load level the plan. Tools like Microsoft Project provide an automatic load-leveling capability.

All of these changes often force the project manager to iterate the steps of planning until a realistic plan is built. The work plan and schedule is not optimized until the scope, schedule, and resources have been configured to meet the project objectives!

The Baseline and Project Manager Accountability

Why Baseline the Plan?

The baseline is recorded so that the project manager has a stake in the ground against which to measure progress as the project begins. The baseline is the foundation for reporting the "plan vs. actual" that is so fundamental to gauging whether a project is or is not on course.

It is one of the final steps before the project starts.

The Case for Baselining Only the Earlier Phases

For a long, multi-phase project, there may be so much uncertainty in the later phase of the project that the baseline is only valid for the earlier parts of the schedule. For this type of project, the project manager should set the expectation that the baseline is only reliable for the parts of the plan for which there can be any reasonable level of certainty.

This is often a formal part of the organization's project methodology, usually referred to as *rolling wave planning*. In this approach, a time period, or *planning horizon*, for detailed planning is defined. For example, the organization might decide that six months is a realistic length of time for detailed planning—beyond six months, only a high-level plan would be required.

A Caution on Automated Project Management Tools

Today's powerful computers and complex software can produce some awesome outputs, especially graphics. But don't be satisfied with a plan that looks good just because it was produced by a tool. As the saying goes, "A fool with a tool is a faster fool!" If it used to take you three hours to build a plan that won't work, you can now do it in 15 minutes and print it on a color printer. Project plans produced using color Gantt Charts are still failing at an unacceptable pace.

Project management software will not make you a better planner; you still have to know how to plan to build a solid project plan.

6.3 Resource Planning and Acquisition

Since resources have such a profound effect on the project plan and schedule, the project manager must be aware of methods and processes relevant to resource management that are available for use.

Resource Planning

The PMBOK Guide defines a process called *resource planning*, which involves determining what resources (i.e. people, equipment, and materials) should be used to perform project activities, and what amount of each resource is required by each activity. This is closely connected to cost estimating.

This process will be affected by another process defined by the PMBOK Guide called *organizational planning*. Organizational planning involves identifying, documenting, and assigning project roles, responsibilities, and reporting relationships.

Organizational planning is often tightly linked with communications planning, since the project's organizational structure will have a major effect on the project's communications requirements. Clearly, the project manager cannot perform resource planning without an awareness of the organizational structure and style that will be imposed on the project and its structure.

The combination of the needs of the project manager and the organizational considerations should produce:

Role and responsibility assignments – Project roles (who does what) and responsibilities (who decides what) must be assigned to the appropriate project stakeholders. Most roles and responsibilities will be assigned to stakeholders who are actively involved in the work of the project, such as the project manager, other members of the project management team, and the individual contributors.

Staffing management plan – The staffing management plan describes when and how human resources will be brought onto and taken off the project team. The staffing plan may be formal or informal, highly detailed or broadly framed, depending on the needs of the project. It is part of the overall project plan.

Organization chart – An organization chart is a graphic display of project reporting relationships, which may be formal or informal, highly detailed or broadly framed, depending on the needs of the project.

Staff Acquisition

Another planning process defined by the PMBOK Guide is *staff acquisition*. This is the process of assigning the required human resources to the project and getting them to work on it. The project management team has to make sure that the available resources will meet project requirements. To do this, the project manager and project team, if possible, will have to consider:

Staffing management plan – This includes the project's staffing requirements.

Staffing pool description – When the project management team is able to influence or direct resource assignments, it must consider the characteristics of the potentially available staff. Considerations include, but are not limited to:

❑ *Previous experience* – Have the individuals or groups done similar or related work before? Have they done it well?

❑ *Personal interests* – Are the individuals or groups interested in working on this project?

❑ *Personal characteristics* – Are the individuals or groups likely to work well together as a team?

❑ *Availability* – WII the most desirable individuals or groups be available in the necessary time frames?

Recruitment practices – Recruitment practices of the organizations involved in the project also constrain the staff acquisition process.

The project manager (and project team, if possible) will usually have to negotiate for human resources, either with functional managers (especially in a matrix organization) or with other project management teams in the organization that share scarce or specialized resources.

In a projectized organization, the project manager may have the responsibility of procuring resources specifically for the project. Procurement is required when the organization lacks the in-house staff needed to complete the project.

6.4 Team Development

Once the resources for the team have been identified and assigned, the next process defined by the PMBOK Guide is team development. Team development includes improving the ability of individuals to contribute to the project as well as enhancing the ability of the team to function as a unit. Individual development is a necessary requirement of any job for growth and morale, while development as a team determines the project's ability to meet its objectives.

Team development on a project is often complicated when individual team members are accountable to both a functional manager and the project manager. Effective management of this matrix relationship is a critical success factor for the project and the project manager. Team development continues throughout the project.

There are a variety of tools used for team development:

Team-building activities include management and individual actions taken to improve team performance. Activities such as establishing ground rules for dealing with conflict may improve team performance. Specific team-building activities can vary from a five-minute agenda item in a regular review meeting to a multi-day off-site meeting focused on improved interpersonal relationships among key team members.

Reward and recognition systems are formal management actions that promote or reinforce desired behavior. To be effective, such systems must make the link between performance and reward clear, explicit, and achievable.

Projects often have their own reward and recognition systems. For example, willingness to work overtime in order to meet an aggressive schedule objective should be rewarded or recognized; needing to work overtime as the result of poor planning should not be.

Reward and recognition systems must also consider cultural differences. For example, developing an appropriate team reward mechanism in a culture that prizes individualism may be very difficult.

Collocation refers to placing the project team members in the same physical location—such as a "war room"—where the team congregates or leaves work items.

Training includes all activities designed to improve the skills, knowledge, and capabilities of the project team. Training may be formal (e.g. classroom training, computer-based training) or informal (e.g. feedback from other team members).

6.5 Cost Estimating and Budgeting

Cost Estimating

The PMBOK Guide identifies two additional processes which are used in the planning process: *cost estimating* and *cost budgeting*. Cost estimating involves developing an estimate of the costs of the resources needed to complete project activities.

Cost estimating involves an assessment of how much it will cost to provide the product or service desired. Pricing, on the other hand, is a business decision—how much the organization charge will for the product or service—that uses the cost estimate as well as other considerations.

In order to calculate project costs, the project manager will need to reference two artifacts for each resource: the work breakdown structure helps to organize the cost estimates and to ensure that all identified work has been estimated; and the unit rates should be referenced for information such as staff cost per hour and bulk material cost per cubic yard. If actual rates are not known, the rates themselves may have to be estimated.

A chart of accounts—which describes the coding structure used by the organization to report financial information in its general ledger—is often used to ensure project cost estimates are assigned to the correct accounting category.

There are two approaches commonly used for this process:

❑ ***Top-down estimating*** is similar to the "analogous estimating" approach to estimating duration. As covered in Section 6.2: *Determining Logical Relationships of Tasks in Your WBS*, top-down estimating uses the actual cost of a previous, similar project as the basis for estimating the cost of the current project. It is frequently used when there is a limited amount of detailed information about the project (e.g. in the early phases) or when the projects are essentially repetitive (e.g. building homes).

❑ ***Bottom-up estimating*** involves estimating the cost of individual work items, then summarizing or rolling-up the individual estimates to get a project total. Bottom-up estimating is commonly used when there is little historical data or the project involves a great deal of uncertainty (e.g. research).

Cost Budgeting

Cost budgeting involves associating the overall cost estimates with individual work items to establish a cost baseline for measuring project performance. The cost estimates developed above, the WBS, and the project schedule will be used to carry out cost budgeting.

This process will result in a *cost baseline,* a time-phased forecast that will be used to measure and monitor cost performance on the project.

The cost baseline is developed by summing estimated costs by period and is usually displayed in the form of an S-curve, as illustrated in the following figure.

Figure 84.

Cost baseline display

End of Chapter Quiz Questions

1. What is a WBS?

2. What are some of the questions that you should consider before beginning a detailed discussion of developing a project planning summary?

3. True or False: You can validate work plan templates by seeing that it has lots of detail.

4. To start activity definition, the project manager should consider what four major items?

 1. _____

 2. _____

 3. _____

 4. _____

5. Which of the following are examples of WBS that contain the appropriate level of detail.
 a. A plan with three phases that contain 1,000 hours each.
 b. A plan that contains 3,000 tasks, each documenting one hour of effort.
 c. None of the above.
 d. Both A and B.

6. What is the "Rule of 80"?

7. True or False: If you look only at the list of deliverables to build the WBS, there are some tasks you may miss.

8. Which of the following is NOT a type of scaffolding task category:
 a. Deliverable
 b. Support
 c. Project management
 d. Administrative

9. What are the four basic types of task dependencies?

 1. _____
 2. _____
 3. _____
 4. _____

10. Fill in the blank: When tasks overlap, they are said to have _____ time.

11. Fill in the blank: When there's a delay between dependent tasks, they have _____ time.

12. What is activity sequencing?

13. What are external dependencies? Provide an example to make your point.

14. What is the critical path?

For questions 16– 19, use the project activity network below:

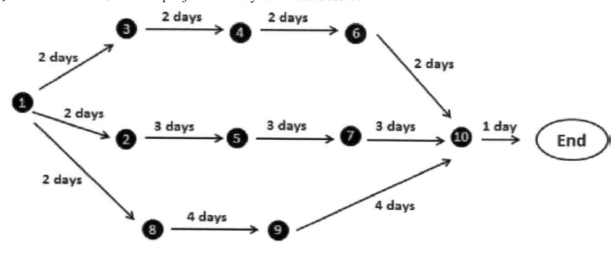

15. Fill in the blanks in the table below:

PATH	LENGTH
1-3-4-6-10	_____ days
1-2-5-7-10	_____ days
1-8-9-10	_____ days

16. Which of the above of paths are on the critical path? _____

17. What is the slack for tasks 3, 4 or 6? _____

18. The slack for tasks 1, 2, 5, 7 or 10 is:
 a. 1 day each
 b. 2 days each
 c. 3 days each
 d. None of the above

19. Fill in the blank: _____ is a process in which a probable
 outcome is evaluated based on a best-case, expected-case, and worst-case scenario.

20. True or false: Critical path is an estimate because its analysis requires several assumptions.

21. Fill in the blank: The most important application of CPM is to realize a late task on the critical path will cause the project _____ _____ to change.

22. What are some of the items the project manager and project team should consider in developing task estimates (list at least 3)?

 1. _____
 2. _____
 3. _____
 4. _____
 5. _____

23. What are some of the items the project manager and project team should consider in the schedule development process (list at least 3)?

 1. _____
 2. _____
 3. _____
 4. _____
 5. _____

24. Fill in the blank: The entire project plan and schedule revolves around the estimated _____ for each task.

25. Explain the difference between effort and duration.

26. What are some of the different ways of estimating work (list at least 3)?

 1. _____
 2. _____
 3. _____
 4. _____

27. Fill in the blank: The first challenge in resourcing a project is to decide what _____ will be needed to complete it.

28. What is resource leveling?

29. What is resource leveling by task?

30. What is leveling by resource? What problem can it present?

31. What is resource planning?

```
┌─────────────────────────────────────────────────────────────┐
│                                                               │
│                                                               │
│                                                               │
│                                                               │
│                                                               │
│                                                               │
└─────────────────────────────────────────────────────────────┘
```

32. What three (3) things does the project manager and project team, have to consider in order to make sure that the available resources will meet project requirements?

_____, _____, & _____.

33. When is procurement required?

34. What are some ways to foster team development?

35. What are the two approaches commonly used for cost estimating?

chapter 7

Building a Work Breakdown Structure with Microsoft Project 2016

- Building the WBS

- Modifying and Editing the WBS

- Creating Task Dependencies

- Task Types and Scheduling

- Estimating Task Size

- Manual Task Scheduling

- Task Planning Review Exercise

 Learning Objectives for this Chapter

At the end of the chapter, the reader should be able to use Microsoft Project to:

- Build a basic task list into a WBS using the indent and outdent functions
- Modify and edit the WBS
- Creating task dependencies (link tasks) using finish-to-start [FS], start-to-start [SS], finish-to-finish [FF], and start-to-finish [SF] link types
- Use the task inspector to identify how the scheduling engine sets task dates
- View task outline numbers
- Insert and delete tasks
- Understand scheduling
- Import tasks from Microsoft Excel and Microsoft Outlook
- Use the "split screen" (task details option)
- Use the task information dialog box
- Enter basic task estimates using the Work and Duration fields
- Use the task types: fixed unit, fixed duration, and fixed units
- Use Manual Task Scheduling

*N*ow that we have described the theoretical background for developing a work breakdown structure and project plan, this chapter will describe how Microsoft Project 2016 can easily be used to create a project plan. This lesson will describe the best practices that experienced project managers generally use to accomplish the desired results.

7.1 Building the Work Breakdown Structure

Determining the Primary Goal and Creating the Project Shell

The project charter is a logical starting point when developing a WBS. The charter details the project's objective(s), major constraints (such as cost or scope boundaries), the expected timescale, and the name of the person responsible for achieving each of the project's goals.

For this exercise we will use the following project charter:

"Following the recent merger of Pan-Trans and Maryland Blue Airlines, our Board of Directors has decided to hold an east coast company conference in May of next year. Robin Q. Project is charged with leading the team to arrange the venue, timing, logistics, and communications required to make this event a success."

1 Start Microsoft Project 2016, ensuring you are not connected to Project Server. If you do not see a blank project, click **Blank Project** or select **File:New:Blank project** to create one. Your screen will resemble the following:

Figure 85.

New blank project

3 Select **File:Save As** to save this new project as: **PanTransConference.mpp**. We will be using this project over the course of this chapter.

3 Navigate to **Format:Show/Hide** and ensure the **Project Summary Task** is selected. Your screen will resemble the following:

Figure 86.

PanTrans Conference.mpp with summary task visible

4 At the bottom-left corner of the screen, you will notice that new tasks are currently set to be scheduled manually. While there are some cases where you do not want the Microsoft Project scheduling engine to perform normal calculations, you generally want the software to schedule the dates of new tasks for you. Select **Auto Scheduled - Task dates are calculated by Microsoft Project.**

Determining the Project's Sub-Goals

Developing the sub-goals of the project is also known as developing the project's initial scope. Typically this job is performed by a group that might include the project sponsor and others with expertise in the field. These people work together to outline the project's general and more detailed requirements. They will also include additional information about limitations or assumptions.

For project **PanTrans Conference**, project requirements include the following:

❑ General planning: Board approval of plan and budget

- o Venue
- o Agenda and schedule
- o Budget

- o Communication plan
- o Personnel commitments

❑ Detailed planning

- o Venue arrangements
- o Attendance
- o Travel arrangements
- o Agenda planning and timetable

- o Meeting facilities
- o Contingency planning
- o Cost planning
- o Catering

Organizing the Project

The project processes, discussed in Chapter 2: *Understanding Project Management*, affects how the project is structured and therefore what the WBS will look like. The goal, of course, is for the structure to be sensible and useful to the people who are managing the project or working with the WBS.

One common approach to organizing the WBS is to have a major section for each phase of the project, with the phases appearing sequentially. This is particularly valuable when there is a stage gate approval process or a portfolio management strategy with a metric for the number of projects in different phases.

Another common organizational strategy is often used for product-development projects, when components of the final product are produced simultaneously by different groups working in parallel.

On larger projects, the structure is often phase- and product-based.

For our training project, the WBS will be organized by two sequential phases:

❑ **General planning**, which is complete when the Board approves the general plan

❑ **Detailed Planning**, which is complete when the final arrangements are distributed and organization is handed over to the hospitality team

5 Begin creating the WBS by entering the two project phases—*General Planning* and *Detailed Planning*—in the Task Name column of your project, as in the following figure.

Figure 87.

PanTrans Conference.mpp project phases

Entering Project Tasks

Once the overall structure of the project is determined, the next step is to perform *progressive elaboration* of the WBS. This is the process of detailing the activities needed to deliver the required results. Depending on the scale of the project, this effort often requires several iterations with input from many subject matter experts and stakeholders. All but the smallest projects require more than two WBS levels.

In step 5 above you entered the top level tasks, or phases. Now it's time to drill down to a second (and maybe third or fourth) more detailed level of task requirements. Following are several best practices to use when determining the level of detail required for each task in your project:

❏ Every detailed task should belong naturally within the hierarchy. Tasks should not be isolated outside the main branches of the WBS.

❏ The lowest level tasks should be written in a way that the task's current status is easy to determine. Resources and supervisors should be able to clearly determine how far the task has progressed and when it is likely to be completed. On the other hand, it should not be so detailed that you are spending more time planning and tracking the activity than is warranted. These boundaries are often represented as the *8-80 rule*—that is, tasks should take not less than 8 hours of effort, nor more than 80 hours. This is a spinoff of the Rule of 80 covered under the *Entering Project Tasks* heading of Section 7.1.

❏ Required deliverables should be shown as resulting from specific, detailed tasks.

❏ When writing the task names for detailed tasks, always include a verb and an object—e.g. "Develop Phase 1 draft report" or "Approve budget for design work". This is not always applicable to summary tasks.

6 Under *General Planning*, in the Task Name field key in the following tasks:
 o Venue arrangements
 o Attendance
 o Travel arrangements
 o Agenda planning and timetable
 o Meeting facilities
 o Contingency planning
 o Cost planning
 o Catering
 o Publish final detailed plan

Your screen will resemble the following:

Figure 88.

Sample of
creating a new
WBS

Right now each task in the project, including the top level-project phases, appears on the same level. To identify specific tasks as sub-tasks:

7 Select the nine (9) tasks that follow *General Planning,* and from **Task:Schedule** click the **Indent Task** arrow [→].

Your screen will resemble the following:

Figure 89.

Creating a
WBS by
indenting tasks
to create a
summary task

At this point in the WBS development process, it is common to continue to enter detailed tasks and sub-tasks for the entire project. However, for large projects or ones where the scope of later phases depends on the outcome of earlier phases, you may adopt a rolling wave approach. As covered in Section 6.2: *Determining Logical Relationships in the WBS* in the subsection on baselining, rolling wave planning is the approach of developing the immediate next phases in detail and only covering the later ones generally.

For this exercise, we will now add a starting task for the project, as well as additional tasks under the first two *General Planning* sub-tasks.

9 Under *General Planning* add a new sub-task, *Hold project kick-off meeting.*

10 Under *Venue,* include the following sub-tasks, ensuring you indent the tasks properly:

 o Decide on venue criteria

 o Perform brief research on possible venues

 o Select top three potential venues

 o Perform detailed research on top three potential venues

- o Calculate cost and other criteria scores
- o Select winning venue

11 Under *Agenda and schedule*, include the following sub-tasks, ensuring you indent the tasks properly:

- o Develop list of key agenda items
- o Develop draft agenda around key items
- o Prepare list of secondary agenda item candidates
- o Estimate time required for agenda
- o Prepare list of presenters
- o Develop list of entertainment events
- o Develop draft agenda and schedule

Project management is essential for the successful execution of the project, and this activity needs to be accounted for in the WBS. Depending on the scale and organization of the project, project management may or may not have specific sub-tasks. Because project management generally occurs across all phases of a project, it is often identified as a set of top-level tasks or phases with the associated detailed project management activities.

12 At the beginning of your project, add a new top-level task called *Project Management*, and include the following two sub-tasks: *Project tracking* and *Issue management*.

Your screen will resemble the following:

Figure 90.

Sample WBS results

Figure 91.

Highlighted Project Management tasks

Additional examples of tasks/phases without specific product-related deliverables—but that are important for successful project execution—include safety inspections and personnel management tasks.

Note: You may notice that for all the tasks you have entered, the duration appears as *1 day?* If you enter a task without a specific duration, and your project is set to Auto Schedule new tasks, Microsoft Project 2016 assigns an estimated one-day duration to each task. The question mark, which remains in the Duration field until you adjust these values, indicates that the value is not a careful estimate and has a great deal of uncertainty. In other words, it is a guess. To show that a duration is uncertain, type the question mark when you enter the duration value.

13 Select Task 30, *Contingency Planning*, and from *Task:Insert* click the *Task* icon. A new task line is inserted with the task name *<New Task>*. You can also use the *Insert* key on your keyboard and a blank line will be inserted above *Contingency Planning*. In the newly inserted task line, type *Arrange break-out rooms* and press *Enter*. By default, new tasks in Microsoft Project assume the same outline level as the task displayed immediately above.

Your screen will resemble the following:

Figure 92.

New task added

Notice that the new task *Arrange break-out rooms*, is treated like all other tasks for the moment.

14 To make *Arrange break-out rooms* a detailed task under *Meeting facilities*, select the new Task 30 and in *Task:Schedule* click the *Indent Task* icon. Task 30 has become a subordinate tasks of the new summary task *Meeting facilities* (Task ID 30). Your screen will resemble the following:

Figure 93.

Creating a summary task

The left-pointing arrow next to the *Indent Task* icon is the *Outdent Task* icon [≡←], which can be used to reverse the outlining process or to promote a task to a higher outline level.

15 Select the task *Arrange break-out rooms* (Task ID 30) and click the *Outdent Task* icon. Notice the task is now at the same outline level as the task above it. Delete the task **Arrange break-out rooms**.

16 Save and close your project.

7.2 Modifying and Editing the WBS

Microsoft Project 2016 provides several different methods to modify your work breakdown structure. You can insert, move, delete and multiply the occurrences of tasks as your project plan undergoes changes. This lesson will review some of the alternate approaches available for working with project tasks.

Alternate Methods for Adding New Tasks to Your WBS

📂 This exercise uses the file **WBSEditing.mpp**. Be sure this project is open before beginning.

1 Select the task *Locate new site* (Task ID 4).

2 Above *Locate new site*, insert *Develop preliminary design* and give it a duration of 5 days. Your screen will resemble the following:

Figure 94.

Inserted task

Several cells turned blue as a result of inserting this task, and they will remain blue until the project is saved or another change is made that affects the project schedule. This feature is designed to make it easier for users to identify changes caused by modification to individual cells.

3 Insert the task *Select target moving date* (duration 1 day) above *Hire mover* (Task ID 13).

4 On further thought, you have decided this doesn't make sense; the possible moving date will be produced as part of the project and doesn't need to be a separate task. Click the down arrow next to the *Undo* button []—located by default at the top-left corner of your screen—several times until your project plan reverts to its condition before you inserted *Select target moving date*. At this point, the *Redo* button [] will become active, allowing you to change your mind back.

5 You're curious about the task *Negotiate new lease* (Task ID 10) and wonder why it's scheduled to start on April 29th. The *Task Inspector* is a good way to see the factors affecting a task's scheduling, as well as recommendations if there are conflicts with the task.

Select the task *Negotiate new lease* and from *Task:Tasks* click the *Inspect* icon []. The *Task Inspector* sidepane will appear, similar to the following:

Figure 95.

Task drivers
for Task 10

6 Click the *X* in the upper right-hand corner of the sidepane to close it and save your project.

Moving a Task in Your Task List and Cutting/Pasting a Summary Task

While you can use the cut, copy, and paste functions found in the *Task:Clipboard* area of the ribbon to rearrange the sequence of tasks, you may find it easier to use the drag-and-drop approach. This section continues the use of **WBSEditing.mpp**. Please ensure this file is open before beginning, or open **WBSEditing_Inst1.mpp**.

1 Click to select the entire task row of *Hire mover* (Task ID 13). When using drag-and-drop, it is important to select the entire row by clicking the task number, not just the task name.

2 Click again and drag the row up until you see a gray line appear above *Select subcontractors* (Task ID 12). Your screen will resemble the following:

Figure 96.

Using drag-and-drop to move a task

3 Release your mouse button. *Hire mover* will replace *Select subcontractors* as Task ID 12, and *Select subcontractors* will become Task ID 13.

4 Select the task row of summary task *Phase Two* (ID 6).

5 From *Task:Clipboard* click the *Cut* [✂] icon. The **Planning Wizard** dialog box will appear to remind you that because *Phase Two* is a summary task, deleting it will also delete all of its subtasks. (When you paste the summary task somewhere, all of its subordinate tasks will move with it). From the **Planning Wizard** dialog box select *Cancel. Don't delete any tasks.* and click *OK* to close the box.

6 What if you really wanted to delete a task? Select the task *Hire architect* (Task ID 3) and press the *Delete* key on your keyboard. Notice the "Smart Tag" (the large *X*) in the Indicator field of the following figure. This means Microsoft Project doesn't know whether you want the task name or the entire task deleted.

Figure 97.

Smart Tag options

7 Click the arrow by the *X* in the Indicator field to see your options. Select the default option: *Delete the task name.*

NOTE

> You will only see the Smart Tag if you select the *Task Name* cell. If you select the entire row by clicking on the task ID number and then hit the *Delete* key, Microsoft Project will assume you know what you're doing and delete the task without any questions. Thank goodness for *Undo*!

8 Use the *Undo* button to restore the original task name.

9 Save and close your project.

Viewing Outline Numbers

When you create your schedule, Microsoft Project 2016 automatically assigns an outline number to each task, based on the outline structure. Each number indicates the task's position within the outline hierarchy. The first task in the outline is assigned the number 1. The subtask immediately below is then assigned the number 1.1; the next subtask is assigned the number 1.2; etc. Outline numbers can be useful for reporting purposes.

The outline number format is comparable to a WBS code, but outline numbers are created automatically by Microsoft Project, while the WBS code can be customized by the user. The number of digits in the code indicates the outline level; Task 1.1.1.1 is the first task in the fourth outline level, under Task 1.

☞ This exercise uses the file **OutlineNumbers.mpp**. Be sure the project is open before continuing.

1 From *Format:Show/Hide* select the *Outline Number* checkbox. Outline numbers will appear in your project plan. Your screen will resemble the following:

Figure 98.

Outline numbers

2 If you prefer not to have outline numbers attached to the task names, you can insert the WBS field in the table to show the outline numbers in a separate column. To do this, right-click *Task Name* and select *Insert Column...* from the menu that appears. Then, select *WBS* as the title of your column. Finally, from *Format:Show/Hide* uncheck the *Outline Number* checkbox. Your screen will resemble the following:

Figure 99.

Separate WBS
column showing
task outline
numbers

3 Click *Undo* several times to remove the WBS column. Save and close your
 project.

Bringing in a Task List from Excel

You can import information from Microsoft Excel into any defined Microsoft Project
field. Although you can enter values in some calculated fields, Microsoft Project
may recalculate these values, either automatically or when you specify.

To transfer information between Microsoft Project 2016 and other programs, use
the Import/Export Wizards to help you create an import map to ensure that the
information is placed into the proper fields in Microsoft Project.

1 Before beginning this exercise, confirm that you are able to import tasks
 from Excel spreadsheets that were created in an earlier version (pre-2013)
 of Microsoft Excel. To do so, open Microsoft Project and from *File:Options*
 select *Trust Center*. Click the *Trust Center Settings...* button and then click
 Legacy Formats in the sidebar.

2 Check the *Allow loading files with legacy or non-default file formats.*
 option. Your screen will resemble the following:

Figure 100.

Trust Center
(security)
options

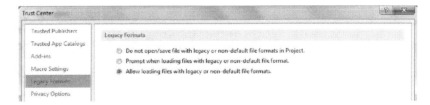

3 Click *OK* twice to accept the new setting and close the dialog boxes.

4 Now, from *File:New* click *New from Excel workbook.*

5 You will be presented with the **Open** dialog box. Navigate to the *Exercises
 Directory* folder on your computer (if necessary), select **Task List.xlsx**, and
 click *Open*. You will be presented with the first **Import Wizard** screen:

Figure 101.

Import Wizard
welcome screen

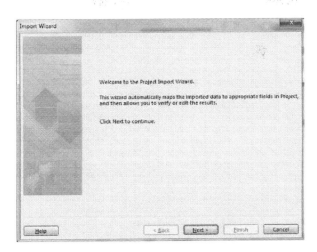

6 Click *Next*. The Wizard prompts you to select whether you want to use a *New map* or *Use existing map*.

Figure 102.

New or existing
map prompt

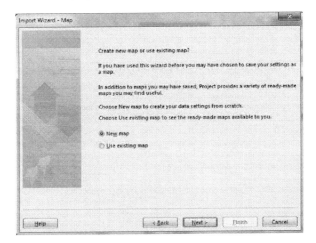

7 Accept the default *New map* option and click *Next* to see the **Import Mode** screen:

Figure 103.

Import Mode choices

NOTE

> **Microsoft Project 2016 enables you to append or merge Excel data to an existing project file, as well as create a new project file.**

8 Ensure the default *As a new project* option is selected and click *Next* to see the *Map Options* screen.

Figure 104.

Import Map options

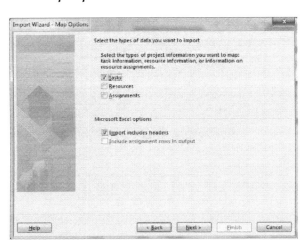

Each type of data (tasks, resources, assignments) imported will require a separate mapping screen to define where each Excel field corresponds to which Microsoft Project field.

9 Select *Tasks* in the top section and *Import includes headers* in the bottom section, and click *Next* to see the **Task Mapping** dialog box. From the *Source worksheet name* dropdown list, select *Sheet 1* as follows:

Figure 105.

Task Mapping dialog

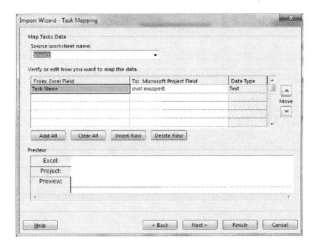

10 In the *To: Microsoft Project Field* dropdown list, select *Name.* To see a preview of the mapping, press *Enter* or click in the cell below the field.

Figure 106.

Selecting the project field

11 Click *Next* to see the **End of Map Definition** screen.

Figure 107.

**End of Map
Definition**
screen

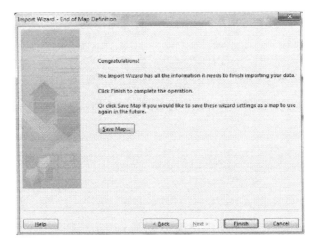

Notice this screen gives you the option to save and re-use your map.

12 Click *Finish*. The task list from Excel will import to your new project plan. Your screen will resemble the following (only the first fifteen tasks are shown in this figure):

Figure 108.

New Project file
from Excel

13 Save your new project plan with the default name **TaskList.mpp**.

14 Close your project.

Importing Outlook Tasks Dialog

To access this feature, first open a blank project. From *Task:Insert* use the dropdown on the *Task* icon to select *Import Outlook Tasks....* The **Import Outlook Tasks** dialog box will appear.

Figure 109.

Import Outlook Tasks dialog box

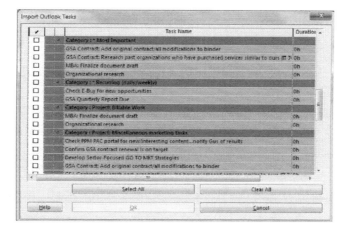

This box displays all your task folders from Outlook, but not tasks from public folders. The tasks are grouped by folder name and then category name.

Select tasks to import by clicking the checkbox to the left of the task name. Multiple tasks can be selected by holding down the *Control* or *Shift* key while selecting the tasks or by choosing a group of tasks (click the checkbox next to the category name). There is a *Select All* button as well as a *Clear All* button for more efficiency.

Once you've made your selections for import, click the *OK* button. The Outlook tasks will be appended into the currently open project.

7.3 Creating Task Dependencies

Setting Task Dependencies

📁 This exercise uses the file **TaskDependencies.mpp**. Be sure this project is open before beginning.

1 Click the *Task Name* column header to select all tasks in the project and then from *Task:Schedule* click the *Link Tasks* icon [∞]. Your screen will resemble the following:

Figure 110.

All tasks linked

Notice that by linking all the tasks in this way, the project's duration jumped from 36 days to 54 days. Ideally, the new project finish date would be acceptable to the client, but it's far more common for project managers to have to look for ways to speed up the schedule.

The way the tasks are linked above, all tasks in Phase One must be completed before any task in Phase Two can begin. You might decide that you could speed up the project by doing Phase One and Phase Two at the same time.

2 To do so, double-click the black line linking the bars for Phase One and Phase Two. The **Task Dependency** dialog box will appear.

Figure 111.

Phase link

3 Click *Delete* to remove the link. Your screen will now resemble the following:

Figure 112.

Unlinked phases (summary tasks)

Another way to remove the link is to click *Phase One* and *Ctrl+Click* on *Phase Two* to select the noncontiguous tasks. Then, from *Task:Schedule* click the *Unlink Tasks* icon [⊱].

4 Although you have saved some time (the project duration is now 36 days instead of 54 days), you realize this work schedule is impossible. According to this logic we can review the proposal (Task ID 7) before we're done writing it (Task ID 2). Click *Write proposal* and *Ctrl+Click* on *Review proposal* to select only those tasks, and then click the **Link Tasks** button to link them.

Your screen will resemble the following:

Figure 113.

Corrected link logic

The process of shortening a project by doing tasks at the same time (in parallel) is called *fast-tracking*. Fast tracking is the most common method used for shortening a project because it appears to be less expensive than the only alternative: *crashing*. Crashing requires applying additional resources to critical path tasks to shorten individual tasks. We will present a more detailed discussion of this concept in Section 14.2: *Plan Revision and Scope Management*. Unfortunately, risk increases when tasks are done at the same time.

5 Click the **Undo** button in the upper-left corner of your screen, and save and close your project.

Note: Microsoft Project 2016's default when linking tasks is to create a finish-to-start task dependency since it is the most common type of task dependency. You can begin by selecting the preferred dependency or start with the default link and change the dependency type later. In the long run, it may be less work to link groups of tasks finish-to-start and modify the exceptions rather than establish all task dependencies individually.

Alternate Ways to Link Tasks

In this lesson we'll examine additional ways to create and modify logical task links.

📁 This exercise uses the file **TaskDependencies.mpp**. Be sure this project is open before beginning.

Dragging the Link Line from One Task to Another

1 Place your mouse pointer over the Gantt bar for *Write proposal* (Task ID 2) so that the cursor turns into a four-way arrow.

2 Click and drag the link line to the Gantt bar of *Review proposal* (Task ID 7). Your screen will resemble the following:

Figure 114.

Link path
(linking by
mouse)

3 Release your left mouse button. You have successfully linked Task 2 with
 Task 7 in a finish-to-start fashion.

NOTE

> Task dependencies rely on the order you selected. For example, if
> you had selected *Review proposal* (Task ID 7) first in the previous
> exercise and dragged its link line to *Write proposal* (Task ID 2),
> *Review proposal* would be shown as the predecessor of *Write
> proposal.*

Linking Tasks in a Split Screen

4 From *Task:Properties* select *Details* to see the Split Gantt Chart view.

5 Right-click in the Task Details Form (bottom pane). Click *Predecessors &*
 Successors from the resulting menu. Your screen will resemble the
 following:

Figure 115.

Split screen
view for linking
tasks

6 Click in the *Predecessor Name* field and then click the dropdown arrow to
 see the list of tasks in the project.

7 Select *Hire architect* (Task ID 3) in the Gantt Chart (top pane). Notice that
 its predecessor and successor are listed in the Task Details Form (lower
 pane). From this pane you can delete predecessor or successor tasks or
 add new ones.

NOTE

When working in this split view, changes made in the Task Details Form (lower pane) are not implemented until you click OK or hit **Enter** twice in succession (with no changes between hits).

8 Double-click the window divider to remove the split, or click the *Details* icon again.

Linking Tasks in the Entry Table

9 Move the vertical divider bar to the right until you can see the entire *Entry Table*. You can assign predecessors (only) by typing the task ID number in the *Predecessors* field for a task.

Using the Task Information Dialog Box

10 Double-click any task name to see the associated **Task Information** dialog box, or select a task and click the *Information* icon found in *Task:Properties*.

11 Select the *Predecessors* tab to assign a predecessor or modify the type of dependency. Click OK to close the dialog box.

Figure 116.

Task Information dialog

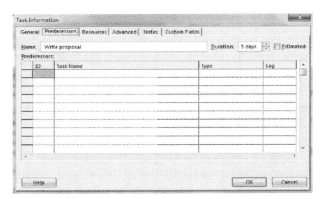

Establishing Other Types of Dependencies

If a finish-to-start task dependency does not accurately reflect the relationship between two tasks, you can use the **Task Dependency** dialog box to select a different type. To access the **Task Dependency** dialog box, simply double-click the dependency link line between the tasks in the Gantt Chart.

In the following example, we have decided that in the interest of time the beginning of the task *Negotiate new lease* would allow the task *Finalize drawings* to begin, so we want to change the present finish-to-start dependency to a start-to-start relationship.

12 Double-click the link line between *Negotiate new lease* and *Finalize drawings.* In the resulting dialog box, click the down arrow in the *Type:* window. Your screen will resemble the following:

Figure 117.

Task Dependency
dialog box

13 From the *Type:* dropdown list, select *Start-to-Start (SS)* and click *OK*. The two tasks are now shown to start at the same time. Your screen will resemble the following:

Figure 118.

Start-to-start task
dependency

NOTE

> **Dependencies can also be changed in the Task Details Form (in the split window) by clicking in the Type column for a dependency. They can also be changed in the Task Information dialog box; be sure to work with the successor task, since only the predecessor task(s) are shown in this dialog. Double-click the successor task name to open the Task Information dialog easily.**

Adding Lag or Lead Time to Modify Task DependenciesIn addition to establishing task dependencies, you can specify any necessary delay between tasks by inserting lag. As covered in Section 6.2: *Determining Logical Relationships of Tasks in Your WBS*, lag is a required waiting period, generally used to allow something to happen—concrete to set, paint to dry, etc. Lag time lengthens the project duration, but it is logically necessary.

We have decided we really can't start the *Finalize drawings* task until some of the *Negotiate new lease* task is complete. The negotiators feel that they will need at least three days' discussion before the second task can begin.

14 Double-click the link line between *Negotiate new lease* and *Finalize drawings*, then in the **Task Dependency** dialog box enter "*3d*" in the *Lag* field.

15 Click *OK*. Task 11 now starts three days after Task 10 starts. Your screen will resemble the following:

Figure 119.

SS
dependency
with lag

Even when tasks are linked finish-to-start, it is not always necessary for the first task to completely finish before the second task can begin. To show that two tasks can overlap, you can specify lead time after establishing a task dependency such as finish-to-start. Ultimately, lead time shortens the duration of a project.

Lead time is expressed as a negative number in the lag field.

16 Save and close your project.

Determining the Proper Order of Tasks in a Project

The order in which tasks are performed is an important piece of the logic for a project.

This exercise uses the file **PanTransConference.mpp** which you created earlier in this chapter. Be sure this project is open before beginning, or open **PanTransConference_Inst1.mpp**.

As you can see from our previous work with this project, the starting assumption is that all the detailed tasks we have listed can be done on the same day. However, when we look at the detailed task descriptions it is clear that is not the case; some tasks depend on the outcome of another one. We can visualize a chain of activities each depending on the successful completion of the one before. The sequence is defined using dependencies which link one task as a predecessor with another that is a successor.

1 We will first identify tasks where the outcome of one task is used directly by another task. For instance, *Decide on venue criteria* and *Develop list of key agenda items* should immediately follow *Hold project kick-off meeting*. Using the methods discussed earlier in this chapter, link these tasks by establishing two finish-to-start dependencies.

Figure 120.

Linking tasks
using finish-to-
start
dependencies

2 It is also possible to link several tasks at one time. Select all the *Venue* sub-
 tasks (Task ID 7 through Task ID 12), and from *Task:Schedule* click the *Link*
 icon. Your screen will resemble the following:

Figure 121.

Linking a series
of tasks

3 In the same manner, link all the *Agenda and schedule* sub-tasks (Task IDs
 14 to 20)

Note: *Hold project kick-off meeting* (Task ID 5) now has two successors (Task IDs 7
and 14). Tasks may also have multiple predecessors.

4 The WBS structure often becomes even more complicated. *Develop list of
 entertainment events* (Task ID 19) is dependent on the venues being
 considered, and so must be a successor to *Perform detailed research on
 top three potential venues* (Task ID 10). Update the project accordingly.

5 Because it is necessary for the first five *General Planning* sub-tasks (Task
 IDs 7, 14, 21, 22, and 23) to be completed prior to completing the final sub-
 task, link each of these tasks as a predecessor to *Present general plan*
 (Task ID 24). Your screen will resemble the following:

Figure 122.

Linking
multiple
predecessor
tasks to key
successor
tasks

6 Sometimes, it can be difficult to discern the many predecessors to a key
 successor by looking at the links in the Gantt Chart. When that happens,
 choose *View:Split view* and click on *Details*. Next, right-click in the lower
 pane of the split window to select the *Predecessors & Successors* details.
 Click on Task 24, *Present general plan*, to see a list of the task's
 predecessors.

Figure 123.

Detailed list of
predecessors
& successors
in the lower
pane

7 Save your project.

7.4 Task Types and Scheduling

When you assign a resource to a task in Microsoft Project 2016, there is a well-defined
mathematical relationship between three fields: Work, Duration, and Units. Microsoft
Project uses the following formula to calculate the values of these fields:

$$Work = Duration \times Units$$

As covered in the *Schedule Development* sub-section of Chapter 6.2, *work* is the effort that will be expended by a resource to complete the task. *Units* refers to the percentage of the resource's working time (as defined in their calendar) that will be allotted to the task. *Duration* is the number of days it will take to complete the task.

For example, if a resource is assigned 40 hours of work at 100% units, the duration of the task will be 40 hours, or 5 days. If the resource is working only 50% of their time on this task, then the duration is 80 hours, or 10 days.

As there are three variables in this equation, the simplest rendering you can produce is a solid three-dimensional curve showing the relationship of the variables—not terribly useful for practical answers. By eliminating a variable, the equation becomes simple algebra and can easily be solved for concrete values, which is much more useful to a project manager.

You can decide which value should be a constant by determining which of the three you could estimate most accurately during planning. Microsoft Project will then calculate the other two values as assignments are made. (Using the approach in this course, until an assignment is made, the only value Microsoft Project has for each task is its duration). Once an assignment is made, all three values for this formula are known, and Microsoft Project will continue to calculate the values when changes are made.

You control which value is treated as a constant and which can be re-calculated by Microsoft Project by the use of task types. To do so, a clear understanding of how this process works is necessary; otherwise, it will appear that Microsoft Project is misbehaving when it is actually working perfectly.

Microsoft Project 2016 defines three different task types:

- ❑ **Fixed Units** – The default, unless you change Microsoft Project's options; assumes you know each resource's % availability for project work)

- ❑ **Fixed Work** – The most common in a consulting environment

- ❑ **Fixed Duration** – Determined by the nature of the task

The general rule is:

If one of the three values (work, duration, or units) is fixed, and you change a second value, the third will be re-calculated and changed by Microsoft Project.

This rule works predictably and is fundamental to understanding how Microsoft Project manipulates resource assignments.

For example, for a fixed units task, if you modify an assignment's work, the task duration will be recalculated. Or, if you modify the task duration on a fixed work task, the resource assignment's units will change.

The Smart Tags feature of Microsoft Project 2016 makes this process easier because Microsoft Project asks you what you have in mind when you make a change in a resource assignment, as you'll see shortly.

Determining Task Types

As we continue to develop the WBS for our project, it is important to understand the kind of things that influence the effort required to perform a task. With this information we are better able to determine the task type: fixed work, fixed duration or fixed units.

Fixed work tasks are the most common. The size of a fixed work task is driven by how much effort is needed to complete it. Remember the school mathematics exercises: "If it takes 3 men 7 days to dig a ditch 50 feet long, how long will it take 4 men to dig a ditch 70 feet long?" This type of problem refers to a fixed work task. The assumption is that the task only progresses while resources are actively working on it.

Fixed duration tasks are performed over a specific period of time, regardless of how hard the resources are working. Natural processes, such as growing a culture in a Petri dish, tend to be fixed duration tasks. There is likely to be involvement of resources for supervision or maintaining the environment for the culture to grow, but typically adding extra resources does not affect the speed at which the task progresses.

Fixed units refers to support tasks for which the duration is the same as the activity being supported. Fixed units tasks generally do not drive the schedule. It is typical for these tasks to have no successors. By default, Microsoft Project identifies new tasks as fixed units. You can change this by navigating to *File:Options:Schedule* and using the *Default Task Type* dropdown arrow to set the desired default task type.

Figure 1.

Changing the task type

📁 This exercise continues to use file **PanTransConference.mpp** created earlier in this chapter. Be sure this project is open before beginning, or open **PanTransConference_Inst2.mpp**.

1 Double-click *Hold project kick-off meeting* to view the **Task Information** dialog box for this task.

Figure 2.

Task Information dialog box

2 In the **Task Information** dialog box, select the *Advanced* tab and use the dropdown arrow in the *Task type* field to select *Fixed Duration*. Click *OK* to close the dialog box.

Figure 3.

Selecting *Fixed Duration* in the **Task Information** dialog

3 Select *Project tracking* and *Issue management,* and from *Task:Properties* click the *Information* button to view the **Multiple Task Information** dialog box.

4 Select the *Advanced* tab and use the dropdown arrow in the *Task type* field to select *Fixed Units*. Click *OK* to close the dialog box.

Figure 4.

Multiple Task Information dialog

Another method for identifying a task's type is to insert a new column (Type) in your Gantt Chart view.

5 Right click in the Duration column header and select *Insert Column*. In the new column, select *Type*. Your screen will resemble the following:

Figure 5.

Display the task
Type column

	❶	Task Mode ▾	Task Name ▾	Type ▾	Duration ▾	Start
0		⚡	⊿ PanTransConference_Inst2	Fixed Duration	9 days?	3/18
1		⚡	⊿ Project Management	Fixed Duration	1 day?	3/18
2		⚡	Project tracking	Fixed Units	1 day?	3/18
3		⚡	Issue management	Fixed Units	1 day?	3/18
4		⚡	⊿ General Planning	Fixed Duration	9 days?	3/18
5		⚡	Hold project kick-off meeting	Fixed Units	1 day?	3/18
6		⚡	⊿ Venue	Fixed Duration	6 days?	3/19
7		⚡	Decide on venue criteria	Fixed Units	1 day?	3/19
8		⚡	Perform brief research on possible venues	Fixed Units	1 day?	3/20
9		⚡	Select top three potential venues	Fixed Units	1 day?	3/21
10		⚡	Perform detailed research on top three potential venues	Fixed Units	1 day?	3/22
11		⚡	Calculate cost and other criteria scores	Fixed Units	1 day?	3/25
12		⚡	Select winning venue	Fixed Units	1 day?	3/26
13		⚡	⊿ Agenda and schedule	Fixed Duration	7 days?	3/19

6 For the purpose of this exercise, use the dropdown arrows in the Type
 column to change the task type to *Fixed Work* for all remaining detailed
 tasks. Try changing a few task types to get a feel for how this feature works.
 Note: We can change the task types any time, as we progress through the
 planning process.

Figure 6.

Using the drop
down to set
task type.

7 Save your project.

7.5 Estimating Task Size

Once you identify tasks, the next step in developing a WBS is to estimate the size, or
duration, of each task. You must gather estimates for all fixed work tasks (how much
resource effort is required during task performance?) and fixed duration tasks (how
much time will elapse during task performance?).

📁 This exercise continues the use of file **PanTransConference.mpp.** Be sure this
 project is open before beginning, or open **PanTransConference_Inst3.mpp.**

1 Right-click in the Start column header and select *Insert Column*. In the
 new column, select *Work*. Your screen will resemble the following:

Figure 7.

Inserting the
Work column
to the Gantt
Chart view

2 For *Hold project kick-off meeting* (currently our only fixed duration task), enter a task duration of "0.5 days" in the Duration column.

Note: Microsoft Project 2016 will accept duration estimates in minutes (type an "m"), days (d), weeks (w), and months (mo). The default value is days, so typing "3" or "3d" will both result in a duration of 3 days. It's best to use the same setting to avoid confusion from task to task, particularly if working with multiple projects or if others are reviewing your project.

4 For each of the fixed work tasks, enter the work required in the Work column according to the following table:

Task Name	Work
Decide on venue criteria	4 hours
Perform brief research on possible venues	16 hours
Select top three potential venues	4 hours
Perform detailed research on top three potential venues	24 hours
Calculate cost and other criteria scores	8 hours
Select winning venue	4 hours
Develop list of key agenda items	4 hours
Develop draft agenda around key items	4 hours
Prepare list of secondary agenda item candidates	16 hours
Estimate time required for agenda	4 hours
Prepare list of presenters	8 hours
Develop list of entertainment events	4 hours
Develop draft agenda and schedule	8 hours
Budget	8 hours
Communication plan	8 hours
Personnel commitments	8 hours

Task Name	Work
Present general plan	8 hours
Venue arrangements	8 hours
Attendance	8 hours
Agenda planning and timetable	8 hours
Meeting facilities	8 hours
Contingency planning	8 hours
Cost planning	8 hours
Catering	8 hours
Publish final detailed plan	8 hours

Your screen should match the following:

Figure 8.

Entering work at
the task level

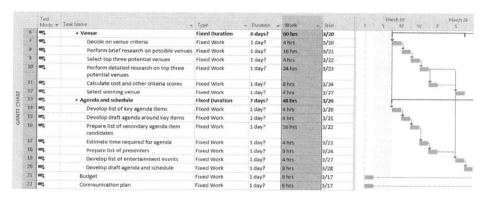

Note that because resources are not yet assigned to the tasks in this project, the Units value does not yet apply and Duration have not yet been calculated (*1 day?*) for fixed work tasks.

We have yet to assign a resource to a fixed units task. In this project, we have two fixed units tasks: *Project tracking* and *Issue management* (Task IDs 2 and 3). Remember, fixed units tasks are support tasks that only affect the project schedule when there is a shortage of resources to perform these tasks. In the case of these project management tasks, they will be performed over the length of the project, and it's important that the estimated task duration is shorter than the tasks they are supporting so they are not mistaken for critical path tasks.

4 Currently the *General Planning* phase of the project has a scheduled duration of 8.5 days, so set the duration of the fixed units tasks to 8 days each.

5 Save and close your project.

7.6 Manual Task Scheduling

Microsoft Project 2010 introduced a major shift in how projects are scheduled. Since then, project managers have been able to choose to manually schedule individual (or all) tasks in a project.

When a task is manually scheduled, changes due to factors such as task dependencies (covered in Section 6.2: Determining Logical Relationship of Tasks in Your WBS) and the project calendar (covered in the *Schedule Development* sub-section of 6.2) no longer automatically adjust task dates. You can also place a manually scheduled task anywhere in your schedule, and Microsoft Project won't move it.

Project managers who prefer automatic scheduling can turn off the new manual scheduling feature for specific tasks or for the entire project. Some projects, especially complicated ones, may still require Microsoft Project's powerful scheduling engine.

Note: Except for in the following exercise, it is still recommended that you use auto-scheduling for new tasks.

Manually Scheduling New Tasks

📁 This exercise uses the file **TaskScheduling.mpp**. Ensure this file is open before beginning.

1 To change the default manual setting for scheduling of new tasks, at the bottom-left of your screen click *New Tasks* and select *Auto Scheduled – Task dates are calculated by Microsoft Project*. Alternatively, from *Task:Tasks* use the *Mode* dropdown to select *Auto Schedule*. For this exercise we will continue to use manual scheduling, so ensure this setting is restored.

2 Insert a new task before *Review project plan with team* (Task ID 5) and call it *Edit project plan*. As you can see at the bottom left of your screen, the default scheduling setting for new tasks is *Manually Scheduled.*

Figure 9. ✦ NEW TASKS : MANUALLY SCHEDULED

3 In *Manually Scheduled* mode, tasks can be used as placeholders when schedule details are not yet be known; in this case, text can be added to the scheduling fields. For your new task, *Edit project plan*, enter "tbd" in the Duration field. Enter "After July" in the Start field. Enter "December" in the Finish field. The task will retain the text entries and Microsoft Project will not automatically schedule the task.

Figure 10.

Inserting and
entering
information for a
manually
scheduled task

	Task Mode ▾	Task Name ▾	Duration ▾	Start ▾	Finish ▾
0	⬛	⊿ Software System Implementation	102 days	6/6	10/25
1	⬛	⊿ Build Project Plan	23 days	6/6	7/6
2	⬛	Create Statement of Work	10 days	6/6	6/19
3	⬛	Obtain approval of Statement of Work	1 day	6/20	6/20
4	⬛	Create project plan	10 days	6/21	7/4
5	⭐?	Edit project plan	TDB	after July	December
6	⬛	Review project plan with team	1 day	7/5	7/5

4 Select *Edit project plan again* and from *Task:Tasks* click the *Auto Schedule* icon. Notice the task now has scheduled dates. Click *Undo* in the upper-left corner of your screen to return to the manually scheduled task.

5 To change the default task mode for all projects, from *File:Options* click *Schedule* and then by the *Scheduling options for this project* section, use the dropdown arrow to select *All New Projects*, as in the following figure:

Figure 11.

*File:Options:
Schedule:
Scheduling
options for
this project:
All New
Projects*

6 Click *Cancel* (we do not want to save this option).

Top-Down Summary Tasks

At the beginning of the planning phase, project managers may only have some high-level information on key deliverables and major milestones of their projects. The project manager can use Microsoft Project 2016 to divide projects into high-level phases based on the overall timeline and budget. This means that dates for individual work items do not necessarily need to line up exactly with dates for the high-level phases.

7 Select *Edit project plan* and change the new task scheduling mode to *Auto Schedule*. To make this task a top-down summary task, enter a new task immediately following it called *Review project plan edits*.

8 Select the new task and from *Task:Schedule*, click the *Indent Task* icon. *Edit project plan* becomes a summary task with rolled-up schedule information. This allows detailed tasks to be planned and executed within a summary task, while the summary task can represent higher-level schedule goals.

Figure 12.

Converting a
new task to a
summary task

	Task Mode	Task Name	Duration	Start	Finish
0	▪	◢ **Software System Implementation**	**102 days**	**6/6**	**10/25**
1	▪	◢ **Build Project Plan**	**23 days**	**6/6**	**7/6**
2	▪	Create Statement of Work	10 days	6/6	6/19
3	▪	Obtain approval of Statement of Work	1 day	6/20	6/20
4	▪	Create project plan	10 days	6/21	7/4
5	▪	◢ **Edit project plan**	**1 day**	**7/5**	**7/5**
6	▪	Review project plan with team	1 day	7/5	7/5
7	▪	Obtain approval of project plan	1 day	7/6	7/6

9 Save your project.

Respect Links

When you are using manual scheduling, Microsoft Project 2016 does not automatically reschedule tasks when you edit predecessor information. If you want Microsoft Project 2016 to do this, you must change the task mode to auto-scheduled or, as an alternative, from *Task:Schedule* click the *Respect Links* icon [🖫]. This reschedules the task but keeps it manually scheduled.

Inactive Tasks

The inactive tasks functionality allows you to remove tasks from your project while maintaining a record of the tasks you've removed.

Inactivating tasks helps you to manage scope. When a project runs over budget or over schedule, you can remove tasks but give yourself an option to re-add them later as funding and time allow. You can also use the inactive tasks functionality to perform "What-If Analysis" by experimenting with different combinations of adds or cuts to your project. To inactivate a task or group of tasks:

1 Continuing our work with **TaskScheduling.mpp** (or open **TaskScheduling_Inst1.mpp**), select *Review project plan edits* (Task ID 6). Go to *Task:Schedule* and click the *Inactivate* icon [▭]. Your screen will resemble the following:

Figure 13.

Setting an
Inactive task

	❶	Task Mode	Task Name	Duration	Start	Finish
0		▪	◢ **Software System Implementation**	**102 days?**	**5/6**	**9/26**
1		▪	◢ **Build Project Plan**	**23 days?**	**5/6**	**6/7**
2		▪	Create Statement of Work	10 days	5/8	5/19
3		▪	Obtain approval of Statement of Work	1 day	5/22	5/22
4		▪	Create project plan	10 days	5/23	6/5
5		▪	◢ **Edit project plan**	**0 days?**	**5/6**	**5/6**
6		▪	~~Review project plan edits~~	~~1 day?~~	~~5/8~~	~~5/8~~
7		▪	Review project plan with team	1 day	6/6	6/6

Notice that the inactive task no longer affects the schedule, and is not able to be updated. This change also triggered a re-calculation of the summary task above (Task 5 *Edit Plan*) and its duration was set to 0 days

2 To reactivate this task, right-click the task and from the dropdown list click *Inactivate Task* to uncheck it.

Figure 14.

Inactivate Task in the task right-click menu

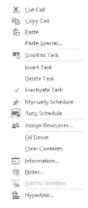

3 Save and close your project.

7.7 Task Planning Review Exercise

1 Start a new project to begin one week from today and save the file as **MeetingTasks.mpp** in the exercise directory.

2 Enter "Shareholders Meeting" as the project title, "2012 Annual Report" as the subject, and your name as author and manager. Show the project title as Task 0 in the Gantt Chart view.

3 Enter the following tasks and durations in the task list:

Task	Duration
Schedule conference date	1 day
Print letter	2 days
Book keynote speaker	2 days
Develop letter	1 day
Get corporate approval	1 week (estimated)
Plan food with caterer	3 days
Print catering menu	1 day
Meeting occurs	milestone

4 Insert a new task, *Reserve conference center*, with a duration of 2 days before Task 2 (*Print letter*).

5 Move Task 3 (*Print letter*) after Task 6 (*Get corporate approval*) using drag-and-drop.

6 Insert a new Task 1, *Meeting Details*, and make all following tasks part of this phase (i.e. indent them).

7 Link all tasks in the *Meeting Details* phase finish-to-start, and then change the link for *Print letter* and *Plan food with caterer* to start-to-start.

8 Show a delay of 2 days between *Reserve conference center* and *Book keynote speaker*. Overlap *Plan food with caterer* and *Print catering menu* by 1 day. Your screen should resemble the following:

Figure 15.

Tasks with lag

9 Save and close your project.

End of Chapter Quiz Questions

1. What 4 things does the Project Charter include?

 1. _____
 2. _____
 3. _____
 4. _____

2. How can you display the project summary task?

3. When could organizing the WBS to major sections for each phase of the project, with the phases appearing sequentially be valuable?

4. What is the next the step after the overall structure of the project is determined?

5. Describe the "8-80 rule."

6. What are some of the best practices to use when determining the level of detail required for each task in your project?

```

```

7. Why does the duration appear as "1 day?" by default when you start entering tasks in your project plan?

```

```

8. What is the Task Inspector?

9. You accidently delete a task that was not supposed to be deleted. What can you do?

10. What is the difference between the outline number and the WBS code?

11. How can you get outline numbers to appear in your project plan, attached to the task names? How can you get them to appear NOT attached to the task names?

12. True or False: You can import information from Microsoft Excel into any defined Microsoft Project field.

13. When mapping fields, each type of data imported will require a separate _____ _____ to define where each Excel field should correspond to which Microsoft Project field.

14. What is fast tracking? _____

15. What is crashing? Why is it generally a secondary option to fast-tracking?

16. What kind of dependency is the default when linking tasks in Microsoft Project 2016?

17. If you had selected *Review proposal* (Task ID 7) first in a project plan and dragged its link line to *Write proposal* (Task ID 2), which task would be shown as the predecessor?

18. How can you display the Split Gantt Chart view?

19. When working in Split Gantt Chart view, what do you have to do, in order to ensure that the changes made in the Task Details Form are implemented?

20. What are some of the ways that task dependencies can be changed (list at least 2 different ways)?

21. Task A has to start 3 days after task B starts. How can you make this happen?

22. Fill in the blank: Lead time is expressed as a _____ number in the lag field.

23. What is the duration, if a resource is assigned 40 hours of work at 100% units? What happens to the duration if the resource is working only 50% of their time on this task?

24. What are the three different task types as defined by Microsoft Project 2016?

```
┌──────────────────────────────────────────────────────────────┐
│                                                                │
│                                                                │
│                                                                │
│                                                                │
└──────────────────────────────────────────────────────────────┘
```

25. Fill in the blank: If one of the three values is fixed, and you change a second value, the third will be _____ by Microsoft Project.

26. In which of the following units, will Microsoft Project 2016 NOT accept duration estimates?
 a. Minutes (m)
 b. Days (d)
 c. Weeks (w)
 d. Months (mo)
 e. None of the above (It will accept all of these)

27. True or False: You can place a manually scheduled task anywhere in your schedule, and Microsoft Project won't move it.

28. What are two ways to change the default setting for scheduling new tasks?

```
┌──────────────────────────────────────────────────────────────┐
│                                                                │
│                                                                │
│                                                                │
│                                                                │
└──────────────────────────────────────────────────────────────┘
```

29. What is the benefit of using the inactive tasks feature?

```
┌──────────────────────────────────────────────────────────────┐
│                                                                │
│                                                                │
│                                                                │
│                                                                │
└──────────────────────────────────────────────────────────────┘
```

30. How do you inactivate tasks?

```
┌──────────────────────────────────────────────────────────────┐
│                                                                │
│                                                                │
│                                                                │
│                                                                │
└──────────────────────────────────────────────────────────────┘
```

chapter 8

Managing Project Resources and Assignments

- Defining Project Resource Types with Microsoft Project 2016

- Assigning Resources to Tasks

- Cost Planning

- Task Constraints and Scheduling

- Resource Assignment Review Exercise

Learning Objectives for this Chapter

At the end of the chapter, the reader should be able to:

- Define project resource types: work, cost, and material
- Assign resources to tasks
- Use cost features to develop a project budget
- Set and modify task constraints
- Split work on a task
- Use the team planner
- Effectively define task types using fixed work, fixed units, or fixed duration
- Explain the effect of effort-driven scheduling on task assignments
- Appropriately apply the task usage or resource usage view to display assignment information
- Assign costs to tasks and apply cost rate tables
- Determine which views are most appropriate to show relevant cost information by task, resource, or assignment
- Understand and apply task constraints to develop a realistic schedule

*M*icrosoft Project 2016 users will most often be working in an enterprise environment connected to Project Server. In this situation, the Project Server administrator creates a resource pool and modifies it as necessary while project managers staff their projects from the resource pool. This allows the organization to track assignments for team members across all projects.

The enterprise resource pool and enterprise resource management will be addressed in a later chapter (Section 10.3: *Enterprise Resource Management*). In this chapter, we will focus on the various ways Microsoft Project 2016 enables you to assign resources to tasks, which will help you determine how long a task will take and how much the task will cost. As noted earlier, a resource can be a specific person, a generic group of people (e.g. programmer or carpenter), a piece of equipment (e.g. crane or computer), a material consumed in the course of completing the task (e.g. lumber, printer paper), or a cost associated with an individual task (or the entire project, if designated as a budget resource).

8.1 Defining Project Resource Types with Microsoft Project 2016

Up until this point we've addressed the logic of project activities: What deliverables are required? In what order must they be completed? What affects the amount of work needed to complete them? Now we must consider the type and availability of resources required to accomplish the work and how this will affect the project schedule.

Note: Creating an internal resource list is useful when resources are to be used exclusively by your project. In the case of an enterprise resource pool, resources created within an individual project are flagged as local resources.

The first step in this process is to examine the tasks identified in your WBS and determine the skills and other resources needed to accomplish each task. You want to be certain the resources on your project team have the right skills. Keep in mind that some tasks must be performed by qualified professionals and/or specialists while others can be performed by generalists with broader capabilities.

Viewing Resources in the Resource Sheet

📁 This exercise uses the file **ResourceAssignment.mpp**. Be sure this project is open before beginning.

1 From the *Resource:View* tab in the ribbon, use the dropdown list to select the *Resource Sheet* view.

2 The first Resource Name field contains *Patrick Rierdon*.

3 Tab over to the *Type* dropdown list and notice the resource type options now available.

Figure 16.

Resource types

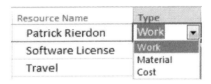

Work resources are not consumed by the project, *material resources* are used up, and *cost resources* only have costs associated with them and can be used for high-level project budgeting. Cost resources can be assigned to individual tasks (or to the project summary task, if they are flagged as budget resources).

4 Tab through the default Resource Sheet fields for each of the three resource types and notice the differences.

5 Add the following generic resources to your project by keying them into the Resource Name column in the lines following *Travel*:

Resource name	Type	Initials
Analyst	Work	Anlst
Designer	Work	Dsgnr
Project Manager	Work	PM

Note: Generic resources are almost always replaced with named resources as the project progresses. It is reasonable to assign a generic resource at more than 100% if you expect to be assigning multiple named resources to that task later.

6 Right-click in the Resource Name column header and select *Insert Column*. Choose *Generic* from the dropdown list. You will see a new column titled "Generic." Use the dropdown list in each row to identify the three new resources as generic resources (*Yes* in the Generic column). Your screen will resemble the following:

Figure 17.

Adding generic resources

	ⓘ	Generic	Resource Name	Type	Material Label	Initials	
1		No	Patrick Rierdon	Work		PR	
2		No	Software License	Material	License	SW	
3		No	Travel	Cost		Travel	
4	👥	Yes	Analyst	Work		Anlst	
5	👥	Yes	Designer	Work		Dsgnr	
6	👥	Yes	Project Manager	Work		PM	

Adding a Local Resource to Your Project

Named resources are added to the project in the same way as generic resources.

7 Click the first available Resource Name field and type "Susan Smith."

8 Press *Tab* and notice the default values assigned to a new resource.

Adding a Resource through the Resource Information Dialog Box

9 Double-click on a blank row in the Resource Sheet view. The **Resource Information** dialog box appears, showing the *General* tab by default:

Figure 18.

**Resource
Information**
dialog box

Notice you can provide the same kind of information entered in the Resource Sheet view. There are also tabs for *Costs*, *Notes*, and *Custom Fields* associated with the resource. The *General* tab also contains a *Budget* checkbox to allow you to flag a resource for high-level budgeting purposes.

Using the Resource Notes Button

In addition to the **Resource Information** dialog box, there is a shortcut to provide notes on resources.

10 Click *Cancel* to close the **Resource Information** dialog box and return to the Resource Sheet view, and select *Patrick Rierdon*.

11 In *Resource:Properties* click the *Notes* icon []. You will be presented with the following dialog box:

Figure 19.

**Resource
Information**
dialog

12 In the *Notes* field enter the text, "Patrick's contract calls for payment at the end of each task he is assigned to, with a minimum payment period of two weeks."

13 Click *OK*. A resource note icon will appear in the Indicators field for *Patrick Rierdon*. Move your pointer over the icon to read the associated note.

14 Save your project.

Figure 20.

Note for *Patrick Rierdon*

	ⓘ	Generic	Resource Name
1	📝	No	**Patrick Rierdon**
2		📝 Notes: 'Patrick's contract calls for	
3		payment at the end of each task he is assigned to, with a minimum	
4	🖉	payment period of two weeks.'	

> If you create a resource note that is too lengthy to view in its entirety as a ScreenTip, you can double-click on the resource notes icon in the Indicator field to read the entire note.
>
> **NOTE** You can also include this note in a printed report or view.

8.2 Assigning Resources to Tasks

Microsoft Project 2016 enables you to assign resources to tasks in a variety of ways. Resource assignments clarify responsibility for doing tasks and also help you to determine how long a task will take and how much it will cost.

Microsoft Project 2016 uses two different fields to express the allocation of a work resource: maximum units and assignment units. The maximum units field represents the amount of a resource's time that is available to accomplish any project tasks during any time period. The default value is 100%, which can be thought of as one full-time equivalent of the resource for the number of project hours in a day (by default, 8).

The assignment units value indicates the allocation of a resource to a particular task assignment. A specific resource can work full-time (100%) on one task or half-time (50%) on two tasks, and so on, before Microsoft Project flags that resource as over-allocated. You can also specify assignment units for material resources to indicate the quantity of material being used for the assignment, even though there is no maximum units value available for material resources.

The following exercise demonstrates how you can assign resources in various ways and avoid some over-allocations by using tools available through the **Assign Resources** dialog box. These techniques apply whether you are working with local resources or those from the enterprise resource pool.

Assigning a Resource to a Task

📁 This exercise continues the use of **ResourceAssignment.mpp** from the previous section. If you did not work on that exercise, you can also open **ResourceAssignment_Inst1.mpp** from your exercise directory.

1 From *Task:View* apply the Gantt Chart view, and in *Task:Properties* click *Details*. Select Task ID 2, *Create Statement of Work*.

2 Click the first Resource Name cell in the Task Details Form (bottom pane). Type "Frank Goren". Your screen will resemble the following:

Figure 21.

Using a split screen view to add assignments

3 Click *OK* in the Task Details Form to assign Frank Goren to the task and add him to your resource sheet. Note that the Microsoft Project scheduling engine automatically calculates the assignment effort (work), based on the task duration.

You can also add a name directly to the Resource Name field in the Gantt Chart Entry Table or in the **Assign Resources** dialog box. In these cases, just like in the preceding split screen example, the default values will be applied in the Resource Sheet until changed. Since these methods are only necessary for local resources, the Resource Sheet view is the most efficient approach to use.

Note: The above method of adding resources is dangerous as you could spell a name incorrectly and end up with two or more of the same resources on your project. It is a good practice to choose from resources, as in the following methods.

A Project Server administrator can create entries for the enterprise resource pool manually using the techniques already described, but s/he will generally use an existing resource database to populate the resource pool.

4 If necessary, from *Task:Properties* click the *Details* icon to split the window. Right-click in the gray area of the Task Details Form (lower pane) and click *Cost* from the dropdown list to view cost information.

5 Select Task ID 3, *Obtain approval of Statement of Work*, in the upper pane.

6 In the upper section of the pane, click the *Assign Resources* icon [👥] under *Resource:Assignments*. You will see the **Assign Resources** dialog box.

Figure 22.

Gantt Chart or Task Form with **Assign Resources** dialog box

7 Select *Patrick Rierdon* in the **Assign Resources** dialog box, and then click *Assign*. Your screen will resemble the following:

Figure 23.

New task assignment

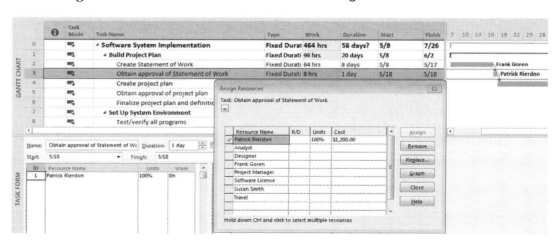

Notice in the bottom pane that Microsoft Project has automatically calculated the work at 8 hours based on the task duration of 1 day.

8 Click *Create Project Plan* (Task ID 4) and *Ctrl-click* on *Obtain approval of project plan* (Task ID 5) to highlight both tasks. Then, click *Patrick Rierdon* in the **Assign Resources** dialog box and click *Assign*. Patrick Rierdon is now assigned to both tasks. Your screen will resemble the following:

Figure 24.

Multiple task
assignment

Just as you can assign one resource to multiple tasks, you can assign
multiple resources to one task or several tasks at the same time:

9 Select the task *Create project plan* (Task ID 4). Notice that Microsoft
 Project has calculated work of 24 hours based on the task duration of
 3 days. Note: If you use this method of assigning resources, you will
 only see this result if you have inserted the Work column in the Gantt
 Chart or show the details of assignment information in the lower pane.

10 Assuming that Patrick needs a software license for the task, click
 Software License in the **Assign Resources** dialog box, and then click
 Assign. Your screen will resemble the following:

Figure 25.

Material
resource
assigned

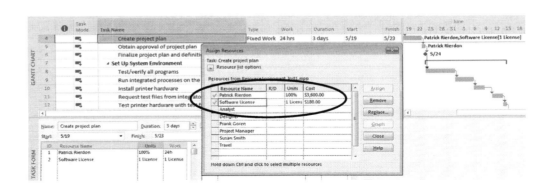

Notice that Microsoft Project has assigned 1 software license to the task (by
default) and calculated the cost as $180. Patrick's cost was also calculated
based on his work and resource standard rate (as seen in the Resource
Sheet). Cost calculations will be covered in greater detail later in this section.

11 Because you think Patrick will need 2 licenses, change the value in
 the lower pane appropriately and click *OK*.

12 There will also be travel costs associated with this task. Click the
 Cost cell for *Travel* in the **Assign Resources** dialog box. Enter "$3,000"
 and click *Assign*. Your screen will resemble the following:

Figure 26.

Cost resource
assigned

Notice the recalculated cost for 2 software licenses ($260) and the travel cost next to the Gantt bar for this task.

NOTE

> **When assigning material resources to a task, assign the resource first, accepting the default units value, and then modify the Units field in the Task Form (lower pane). For cost resources, type the predicted value in the Cost cell for the resource and press *Enter*. Using the *Assign* button with a cost resource can lead to unexpected and undesirable results if other resources are already assigned.**

13 Save your project.

Replacing Resources on Task Assignments

This exercise continues the use of **ResourceAssignment.mpp** from the previous section (or you can open **ResourceAssignment_Inst2.mpp** from your exercise directory).

On further consideration, you have decided that one of the assignments should be changed: Susan Smith has more time available to create the statement of work and has done several of them, so she might be a better choice for that task than Frank Goren.

1 Select *Create Statement of Work* (Task ID 2). In the **Assign Resources** dialog box, select *Frank Goren* and click *Replace*.

2 In the **Replace Resource** dialog box, click *Susan Smith*. Your screen will resemble the following:

Figure 27.

Replace Resource dialog box

3 In the **Replace Resource** dialog box, click *OK* to complete the replacement process.

4 Choose *View:Split view* to verify *Susan Smith* is assigned to Task 2.

Figure 28.

Verify resource assignment replacement

5 If you wish to verify the cost of this replaced assignment, right mouse click in the lower pane and choose *Cost* from the drop down.

Figure 29.

Verifying the cost of a replaced assignment

6 Save your project.

Note: Generic resources are replaced by named resources in the exact same manner as named resources replace each other. So once you determine, for example, that John Smith is the analyst that will be assigned to this project, you would use the method just described to replace the generic resource "Analyst" with the named resource "John Smith".

Also, Microsoft Project considers the specific resources calendar of all assigned resources when scheduling a task. Because of this, you will have to look into each resource's calendar details to figure out why an assignment date might have change when replacing an assigned resource with another resource who may have a different calendar setup. That might not be a problem (e.g. in the previous example, you might remember that Susan has vacation plans that may affect the scheduling of her new assignment), but over a long project, many of these details can get lost. When you're in the middle of a stakeholder review with top management and someone asks, "Why does your Gantt Chart say 10 days duration but show 15 days?" it's easy for your mind to go blank. You'd like to be able to show that the task takes 10 days of work, but there is a break in the middle.

We will see some ways to investigate these kinds of situations when we review the Task Usage and Resource Usage views. These views can show you how resource assignment work is spread over time.

Interrupting Work on a Task

📂 This exercise continues the use of **ResourceAssignment.mpp** from the previous section (or you can open **ResourceAssignment_Inst3.mpp** from your exercise directory).

Microsoft Project 2016 allows you to split a task to show that work has been interrupted and then resumed at a later point in a project. A task can be split more than once, and each of its splits is graphically depicted in the Gantt Chart, where the length of the interruption is shown by the width of the gap in the Gantt bar.

1 Verify you can see the entire Gantt bar for Task 4. If so, scroll to the right side of the Gantt Chart (the timescale) to ensure that you can see all of *Create project plan* (Task ID 4).

4 From *Task:Schedule* click the *Split Task* icon [✳]. Position your mouse over the Gantt bar for task *Create project plan* (ID 4), until the *Start Date* on the ScreenTip reads "5/25" (the date you want the split to begin) and release your mouse button to initiate the task split function. The ScreenTip will resemble the following:

Figure 30.

Split task
ScreenTip

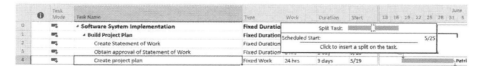

5 Now, place your mouse over the right side of the split task. Continue to hold down the left mouse button and drag your pointer to the right. The dates in the ScreenTip will change to show the start and finish dates for the delayed segment of the task.

Figure 31.

ScreenTip while dragging split task

6 When the start and finish dates on the ScreenTip read 5/28 to 6/4, release the mouse. The task will be split into two segments. Your screen will resemble the following:

Figure 32.

Successful split task (delays remainder of task segment that was split)

Notice that the task duration field in the Entry Table remains unchanged because no work is done during the gap in the task. This can be verified by displaying the Task Usage view.

Removing a Task Split

7 Move your mouse pointer over the right-hand portion of the split Gantt bar for the task *Create project plan* (task ID 4) until the cursor changes into a four-way arrow.

8 Left-click the right-hand segment of the Gantt bar and drag it back towards the left half of the bar. Your screen will resemble the following:

Figure 33.

Removing task split

9 Release the left mouse button when the two halves of the bar touch. The segments of the Gantt bar are reunited, and work on the task is no longer split.

10 Save and close your project.

Team Planner

The Team Planner view allows you to easily see what tasks are assigned to resources. Using the Team Planner view, a simple dragging motion also allows you to change existing assignments to over-allocated resources or assign currently unassigned tasks to available resources.

📂 This exercise uses the file **TeamPlanner.mpp**. Be sure this project is open before beginning.

1 From *Resource:View* click *Team Planner*. You will see a timeline with tasks displayed. Resources and the tasks to which they are assigned are displayed on the top portion of the screen, and unassigned tasks are displayed in the bottom portion.

Figure 34.

Primary Team
Planner view

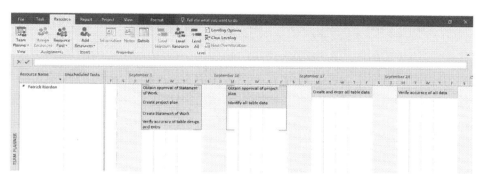

2 Hovering over a task bar displays information about the task. The task can be rescheduled simply by dragging the task on the timeline. The task can also be assigned to a different resource by dragging to the desired resource's "swim lane."

3 To see the effects of rescheduling and reassigning tasks, click the *Gantt Chart* icon in *Task:View*.

4 The Team Planner function has several limitations. There are more effective ways to identify and resolve resource over-allocations that will be covered later in this section

5 Save and close your project.

Modifying Assignments When Work Is the Basis for Your Schedule

📂 This exercise uses the file **TaskTypes.mpp**. Be sure this project is open before beginning.

If your resource demand and project budget are based on labor (work) estimates, then fixed work is the recommended task type. Organizations that focus on forecasting the work to be done (and on using statements of work to define charges for that work) usually use fixed work as the default task type. By entering work estimates for each task, they can evaluate resource allocation for the project. When work is fixed, Microsoft Project won't change the work estimate, but you can modify the specific work value for a task.

1 Split the window in the Gantt Chart view and select the task *Locate new site* (ID 4). Be sure the **Resources** and **Predecessors** option is showing in the Task Form view (lower pane). Your screen will resemble the following:

Figure 35.

Fixed work task with split screen

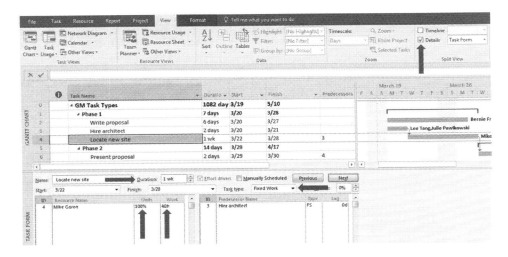

3 Note the fields that have arrow pointers to follow how the information changes in this exercise.

What is the duration of the task?

What is Mike's work assignment?

Mike has other obligations during this time, and he can only devote six hours each day to the task (75% of his time). Change the units for Mike Goren's assignment to "75%" and click *OK* in the Task Form window. What is the revised duration for this task?

Did the work change?

3 Return Mike's assignment units value to "100%" and click *OK*. Now increase the task duration to "2w" and click *OK*.

Did Mike's units change?

Did the work change?

If not, why not? (HINT: Should a fixed work task change its work?)

4 Click in the Resource Name column directly under *Mike Goren* and use the pull-down menu to add *Bernie Frazer* to the task. What are you actually changing when you add a resource?

5 Click *OK*. What happens to the task?

Since work is fixed, when you change units, Microsoft Project recalculates duration. This is why the *Effort driven* option (above *Task Type*) is grayed out—fixed work tasks must become shorter when resources are added.

Microsoft Project will not change the work value on a fixed work task, but you can. What happens if you do? Mike and Bernie have now estimated that they will need 40 hours each to complete the task.

6 Change the Work value to "80h" for both Mike and Bernie. Microsoft Project could keep the equation in balance either by assuming each would work 16 hours per day (200% units) or by allowing the task to take twice as long. What actually happens to the task assignment when you click *OK*? Change the Work value for Mike and Bernie back to "40h".

As a general rule, the Units value is preserved when possible, so the task became twice as long (back to one week duration).

NOTE

> **When working in the Task Form or Task Details Form half of a split view, changes are not effective until you click *OK* or press *Enter* twice. Users occasionally get frustrated because they press *Enter* and nothing happens!**

Modifying Assignments When Task Duration Is the Basis for Your Schedule

In some situations the length of the task is known or, more commonly, the estimated work must be completed within a specific time period. For example, if you are renting a piece of equipment for a few days, then the resources using that equipment must complete the work during that time. If the work estimates increase, then the percentage of their time a resource is assigned to the task would increase. In this situation, a task type of fixed duration would fit the expected behavior of the schedule.

7 Select the task *Move into new location* (ID 16). Your screen will resemble the following:

Figure 36.

Fixed duration task with split view

8 The actual office relocation must occur over two days. On further consideration, you have decided the work estimates need to be increased.

What is the units value for the resources?

Increase the work effort for each resource from "8" hours to "12" hours and click *OK*.

What is the revised units value for the resources?

Did the duration change?

If not, why not? (HINT: Should a fixed duration task change its duration?)

9 A few resources have volunteered to be fully available both days. Increase the units to "100%" for Bernie Frazer, Lee Tang and Julie Pawlkowski.

What is the revised work effort for these resources?

Did the duration change?

10 Return all the *Work* estimates to "8 hours" and all *Units* to "50%" and click *OK* to go back where we started.

Fixed duration means Microsoft Project won't change the duration value for the task—but it doesn't mean you can't change it. Assume you were able to get the moving equipment rental extended for a third day. How would that affect the assignments?

11 Increase the duration of Task 16 to "3 days." What changes in the lower pane?

12 Reset the duration to "2 days" to return to the original values.

13 Save your project.

The Effect of Effort-Driven Scheduling

In addition to defining the task type, Microsoft Project 2016 allows you to define the scheduling type appropriate for each task—effort-driven or not effort-driven.

An effort-driven task goes faster with more resources. For example, if Steve is assigned full time to a task with 40 hours of work and you assign Mary to the same task, Mary will pick up 20 of Steve's hours if the task is effort-driven, leaving the total work for the task at 40 hours. The duration of the task, however, will decrease by half since two people doing 20 hours of work at the same time can finish the task in half the time.

There are situations, of course, where assigning another person will not shorten the duration of the task. If the people involved have different skill sets, for example, the work is more likely to double than to be split between them.

The scheduling type becomes important mainly when adding or removing resources on a task. The first task assignment simply defines the starting point (work, units and duration) for Microsoft Project and usually behaves simply. Later changes can cause frustration because the scheduling engine in Microsoft Project operates five different ways, depending on whether the task is fixed work, fixed duration effort-driven, fixed duration not effort-driven, fixed units effort-driven, or fixed units not effort-driven. All fixed work tasks behave as effort-driven tasks.

🗁 This exercise continues the use of the file **TaskTypes.mpp**. Be sure this project is open before beginning, or open **TaskTypes_Inst1.mpp**.

1 For the fixed duration task *Move into new location* (ID 16), clear the check box next to *Effort driven*. (Navigate to *View:Split view:Details* to see the *Task Type* option in the lower Task Form pane).

2 Click to create a name cell directly under *George Brody* and type in "April Faraday." Since duration is fixed and you are adding units, you might think that Microsoft Project will recalculate the work. Is that what happens when you click *OK*? (See the next figure for help to this quesiton)

3 Click on *April Faraday* in the lower Task Form and use the *Delete* key to remove her from the task. Click *OK* to get back to where we started with this task.

4 Switch *Effort driven* on by checking the box next to it, and add April Faraday back to the task again. This time her name will be on the pick-list of names. Consider what's happening—duration is fixed, and you are adding units, but effort-driven means more people get the work done faster. Click *OK* to see how Microsoft Project deals with this apparent contradiction. Your screen will resemble the following:

Figure 37.

Fixed
duration
task, with 2
different effort-
driven scenarios

5 Save your project.

This is one of the few occasions when Microsoft Project recalculates two of
the three values (work, units, and duration) rather than just one.

Modifying Assignments When Assignment Units Is Set

Another way to think about the three task types is to associate fixed work with a
situation where you know (or must forecast) the amount of work to be done. This
is typically done when the client is paying for hours of work done on the task, not
the duration (length) of the task. Fixed duration tends to be a characteristic of
the task itself—certain things take a specific amount of time, no more and no
less. Fixed units applies to situations where the project manager knows how
much of each resource he or she "owns" for the project, regardless of work or
duration for any specific task. Microsoft selected fixed units as the default task
type because that is the most common situation in project management.

The assignment units field, simply labeled *Units* in the Task Form, determines
what percentage of a resource's available working time will be dedicated to the
specific task. As demonstrated in the preceding exercises, if you change the
duration on a fixed work task or change the work on a fixed duration task, Project
recalculates the assignment units.

Unless the (Assignment) Units value is changed when making an assignment, Microsoft Project uses the Max. Units value, which we saw in the Resource Sheet view (by default, 100%).

If using fixed work or fixed duration as the default task type, you would change to fixed units for those tasks in which a change to the duration or work should not modify the assignment units. One example would be a situation when a task spans the duration of the project and the resource will be working an established percentage of its time on that task.

📂 This exercise continues the use of the file **TaskTypes.mpp**. Be sure this project is open before beginning, or open **TaskTypes_Inst2.mpp**.

1 Select the task *Write proposal* (ID 2). Choose *View:Split View* then *Details*. Your screen will resemble the following:

Figure 38.

Fixed units
task with details

2 Note that the task duration spans the entire project duration and that 100% of Bernie Frazer time is allocated to the task.

3 What is Bernie Frazer's work effort?

Assume that a scope change request increases the project length by 5 days and increases the task duration to "10 days."

What is Bernie's revised work effort? (Did it increase?)

Why didn't the assignment units change? (HINT: Should a fixed units task change its units?)

4 Decrease the task duration to "2 days" and look at the assignment units and assignment work values. You should see the work increase and the units stay constant

Microsoft Project selected effort-driven as the default scheduling type, since project managers most often assign additional resources to a task to get it done sooner. Let's examine the effect of effort-driven scheduling on a fixed units task.

5 For *Resolve project issues* (Task 2), deselect *Effort driven* in the lower pane (Task Form).

6 Assign April Faraday to work on the task with Bernie Fraser. What happens to the work, units, and duration values for the task?

7 Remove April Faraday from the task, select *Effort driven* in the lower pane (Task Form), and reassign April Faraday to the task. Click *OK*. What happens to the work, units, and duration values for the task this time?

Using Smart Tags to Simplify Making Changes

Smart Tags alert you to possible options when you make changes in a file.

8 Remove the window split (deselect *Details*) and select *Write Proposal* (Task ID 2). Increase its duration to "20 days" and press *Enter*. A Smart Tag indicator with a yellow caution icon will appear in the corner of the Duration field for *Write proposal*. Your screen will resemble the following:

Figure 39.

Smart Tag alert

9 When you hover your cursor over the Smart Tag, you will see the following Smart Tag alert message: *Click to set the reason for the duration change so that the task can be properly scheduled.*

10 Click on the Smart Tag alert to see the following scheduling choices:

Figure 40.

Scheduling options for Smart Alerts

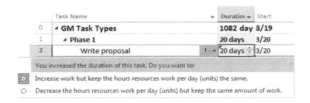

It is not uncommon to increase the duration of a task and prefer the second option to keep work constant even though it is a fixed unit task.

If you're not sure which option to select, split the screen (i.e. *Details*) as we did earlier and review the new calculations that resulted from your duration input of "20 days."

11 Save and close your project.

Viewing Your Resource Assignments

Microsoft Project 2016 gives the project manager several different options to look at resource assignments in a project. The two most useful assignment views are the Task Usage view (which lists tasks and the resources assigned to each one), and the reverse: the Resource Usage view (which lists resources and their assigned tasks).

The Task Usage View

📁 This exercise uses the file **AssignmentUsage.mpp**. Be sure this file is open before beginning.

1 If the Task Usage is not already displayed, from *View:Task Views* click the *Task Usage* icon to apply the Task Usage view to the project.

2 Adjust the Task Name column to accommodate the task name text (if necessary) by dragging the right border of the column to the right. Alternatively, you can double-click the right border of the column title box.

3 Select the resource *Bernie Frazer* under the task *Write Proposal* (ID 2), and in *Task:Editing* click the *Scroll to Task* icon [🔲].

4 Bernie's planned work for the task is shown, as in the following figure. Notice these values are calculated from the work, duration, and units relationship previously discussed. The Task Usage view shows resource assignments listed by task in the same order as in the Gantt Chart view.

Figure 41.

Task Usage view

5 Double-click Bernie's name to see the **Assignment Information** dialog box. This dialog shows Bernie's specific assignment data for the *Write Proposal* task. Notice that Bernie's Units value is 75%, which explains the 6 hours per day calculated in the Task Usage view.

Figure 42.

Assignment Information dialog box

The Resource Usage View

6 From *Task:View* select *Resource Usage*.

7 Locate resource number 1, *Bernie Frazer*, and select the task *Write proposal*.

8 From *Task:Editing* click the *Scroll to Task* icon to view the work assigned to Bernie on this task on the week of March. Your screen will resemble the following:

Figure 43.

Resource
Usage view

9 In the preceding figure, Bernie is shown as having 14 hours of work to do on the Wednesday of the week of March 26, so he is marked as over-allocated on that date (boldface red). We will delve deeper into the value of using the Resource Usage view to identify and resolve resource over-allocations later in this section.

10 Save and close your project.

8.3 Cost Planning with Microsoft Project

Microsoft Project calculates basic cost at the assignment level. These calculations are then rolled up to the task level:

❑ Assignment Work X Resource Cost Rate* = Assignment Cost

❑ Task Cost = Assignment Cost** (summary of all assignments) + Fixed Cost***

* See step two of the following exercise to learn how to view this information

** Summary of all assignments

*** Task-level field

Determining Costs in Microsoft Project

📁 This exercise uses the file **ResourceCost.mpp**. Be sure this file is open before beginning.

1 Apply the Resource Sheet view to your project.

2 From *View:Data* click *Tables* and select *Cost* to apply the cost table to the Resource Sheet view. Note you can now see the total cost for each resource.

Figure 44.

Resource Sheet
view with Cost
Table applied

	Resource Name	Cost	Baseline	Variance	Actual Cost	Remaining
1	John Tierney	$12,000.00	$0.00	$12,000.00	$0.00	$12,000.00
2	Rebecca Burns	$10,320.00	$0.00	$10,320.00	$0.00	$10,320.00
3	Bernie Frazer	$16,800.00	$0.00	$16,800.00	$0.00	$16,800.00
4	George Brody	$26,880.00	$0.00	$26,880.00	$0.00	$26,880.00
5	David Crawford	$13,900.00	$0.00	$13,900.00	$0.00	$13,900.00
6	Joan Higgins	$15,240.00	$0.00	$15,240.00	$0.00	$15,240.00
7	Mike Goren	$6,020.00	$0.00	$6,020.00	$0.00	$6,020.00
8	Julie Pawlkowski	$7,520.00	$0.00	$7,520.00	$0.00	$7,520.00
9	Ted Haley	$1,200.00	$0.00	$1,200.00	$0.00	$1,200.00
10	Mary Remington	$8,400.00	$0.00	$8,400.00	$0.00	$8,400.00

3 From *Resource:Properties* click *Details*. You will see a split screen with the Resource Sheet view on the top and the Resource Form on the bottom.

4 Right-click in the lower pane and select *Cost* from the dropdown list.

5 In the upper pane, select *John Tierney*. Note that John Tierney's Cost in the upper pane ($12,000) equals the sum of the Cost of the individual assignments in the lower pane.

Figure 45.

John Tierney's
cost details

6 In the upper pane, right-click on *Bernie Frazer*, and from the dropdown list, select *Information*. You will see the **Resource Information** dialog box for Bernie Frazer.

7 In some cases, a resource may have different costs depending on the roles and tasks they are performing. Microsoft Project provides the capability to use different resource rates for different roles and assignments. In the **Resource Information** dialog box, select the *Costs* tab. You will see that in cost rate table A (which is where Microsoft Project puts resource assignments by default), Bernie's Standard Rate is $70/hour, as follows:

Figure 46.

Resource Information dialog box; *Costs* tab for Bernie Frazer

8 On the second line of the cost rate table, enter an Effective Date of "10/1," and a new Standard Rate of "$80". This rate will be used for any task assigned after the new rate effective as of 10/1. Your screen will resemble the following:

Figure 47.

Additional cost rate effective 10/1 for $80 per hour

9 Click *OK* to accept the change and close the **Resource Information** dialog box.

10 Ensuring Bernie Frazer is selected in the upper pane, double-click
 Task ID 2 (*Create Statement of Work*) in the lower pane to see the
 Task Information dialog for this task. Note Bernie's work on this task:
 10 days = 80 hours.

Figure 48.

**Task
Information**
dialog box for
*Create Statement
of Work*

11 Click *OK* to close the **Task Information** dialog box. As you can see in
 the following figure, the total cost of Bernie's work on this task is
 $5,600 (Bernie's rate of $70/hour X 80 hours).

Figure 49.

Bernie's cost at
the assignment
level, as shown
on the Resource
Form on the
lower pane.

12 In the lower pane, double-click Task 14 (*Send out prep packet*) to
 view the **Task Information** for this task. Note the task is scheduled to
 begin on 10/10, after the 10/1 hourly rate increase, and it's expected
 to take 2 days (16 hours).

Figure 50.

**Task
Information**
dialog box for
*Send out prep
packet*

13 Click *OK* to close the dialog box. Look in the lower pane and note
 Bernie's total cost for Task 14 is $1,280 (16 hours X $80 = $1,280).

Figure 51.

Bernie's total
assignment cost
for Task 14

14 Save your project.

Alternate Cost Rate Tables

Each resource can have up to five (5) separate resource rates, labeled A, B,
C, D, and E. As mentioned above, when you assign a resource to a task,
Microsoft Project will, by default, assign the resource rate using the value(s)
in cost rate table A. This information is typically entered on the Resource
Sheet in the column called "Standard Rate."

Additional rates can be assigned to a resource using cost rate tables B, C, or
D at the assignment level of detail. The following exercise will show you how
to use rates from tables other than cost table A.

☞ This exercise continues the use of **ResourceCost.mpp** from the preceding
 section. Alternatively, you can open **ResourceCost_Inst1.mpp** from your
 exercise file. Ensure you're looking at a split view with the Resource
 Sheet in the upper pane and the Resource Form in the lower pane with
 cost details (you can refer to Steps 1 – 4 in the preceding exercise for
 help with this).

1 In the upper pane, right-click on *Joan Higgins* and select *Information*
 to open the **Resource Information** dialog box.

2 Select the *Costs* tab and note that Joan's hourly cost is $60/hour in cost rate table A.

Figure 52.

Cost rate table

3 In Joan's **Resource Information** dialog box, select tab *B* (where cost rate table B is displayed) and enter a Standard Rate of "$90/hour." Click *OK* to save this change, and close the dialog box.

4 Change the upper pane view to Task Usage (right-click on *Resource Sheet* on the left side of the upper pane and select *Task Usage*).

5 From *View:Data* click the *Tables* icon, and from the dropdown list, select *Cost* to apply the Cost Table to this view.

6 In the upper pane, scroll to Task 8, *Determine current architecture*. Note that the Total Cost for Joan's work on this task is $3,000 (50 hours X $60/hour).

7 Right-click on *Joan Higgins* under Task 8 to display the **Assignment Information** dialog box. Your screen will resemble the following:

Figure 53.

Assignment Information dialog box for Joan Higgins' assignment to *Determine current architecture*

8 In the **Assignment Information** dialog box, change *Cost rate table* from "A" to "B." This directs Microsoft Project to calculate Joan Higgins' cost for this task based on the information in cost rate table B. Click *OK* to close the dialog box.

9 Note that switching the cost rate table changed Joan Higgins' Total
 Cost for that task from $3,000 (see Step 6) to $4,500 (50 hours X
 $90/hour).

Figure 54.

Changed cost for
Joan's work on
*Determine
current
architecture*

10 Save your project.

Adding Fixed Cost to a Task

As a reminder:

❑ Assignment Work X Resource Cost Rate = Assignment Cost

❑ Task Cost = Assignment Cost + Fixed Cost

📁 This exercise continues the use of the file **ResourceCost.mpp** from the
 preceding section. Alternatively, you can open **ResourceCost_Inst2.mpp**.

1 If your screen is still split, remove the split either by double-clicking
 the line between the panes or by deselecting the *Details* checkbox
 under *View:Split View.*

2 Apply the Gantt Chart view to the project. Then go to
 View:Data:Tables, and choose *Cost* from the dropdown list to apply
 the Cost Table to this view. Note the Total Cost for Task 18, *Send out
 draft and review with key sponsors*, is $9,120, per the following figure:

Figure 55.

Gantt Chart with
Cost Table
applied

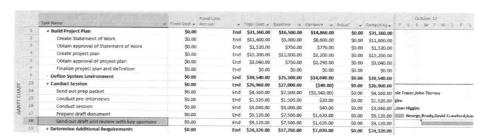

3 In the Fixed Cost column for Task 18, enter "$2,000." Note the Total
 Cost for this task is now $11,120.

Figure 56.

Fixed Cost
impact on total
Cost

Task Name	Fixed Cost	Cost Accrual	Total Cost	Baseline	Variance	Actual	Remaining
13 ▲ Conduct Session	$0.00	End	$28,960.00	$27,000.00	$1,960.00	$0.00	$28,960.00
14 Send out prep packet	$0.00	End	$4,160.00	$7,500.00	($3,340.00)	$0.00	$4,160.00
15 Conduct pre-interviews	$0.00	End	$1,520.00	$1,500.00	$20.00	$0.00	$1,520.00
16 Conduct session	$0.00	End	$3,040.00	$3,000.00	$40.00	$0.00	$3,040.00
17 Prepare draft document	$0.00	End	$9,120.00	$7,500.00	$1,620.00	$0.00	$9,120.00
18 Send out draft and review with key sponsors	$2,000.00	End	$11,120.00	$7,500.00	$3,620.00	$0.00	$11,120.00

4 Save your project.

Displaying Cost over Time, by Task (Or Phase)

📂 This exercise continues the use of **ResourceCost.mpp** from the preceding section. Alternatively, you can open **ResourceCost_Inst3.mpp**.

1 From *Task:View* click the arrow by the *Gantt Chart* icon, and from the dropdown list, select *Task Usage*.

2 Right-click on the right side of the vertical view divider (i.e. in the time scale data area). From the dropdown list, select *Cost* and deselect *Work* (*Work* is selected by default) to view cost details on this side of the view. Your screen will resemble the following:

Figure 57.

Task Usage view
with Cost Table
applied, showing
Cost details

Task Name	Fixed Cost	Fixed Cost Accru	Total Cost	Details	T	W	T	F	S	August 27 S	M	T
0 ▲ Software System Implementation	$0.00	Prorated	24,180.00	Cost	$1,520.00	$1,520.00	$1,760.00	$1,040.00			$1,040.00	$1,040.00
1 ▲ Build Project Plan	$0.00	End	$31,360.00	Cost	$1,520.00	$1,520.00	$1,280.00	$1,040.00			$1,040.00	$1,040.00
2 ▲ Create Statement of Work	$0.00	End	$11,600.00	Cost	$1,520.00	$1,520.00	$1,280.00	$1,040.00			$1,040.00	$1,040.00
John Tierney			$4,000.00	Cost	$400.00	$400.00	$400.00	$400.00			$400.00	$400.00
Rebecca Burns			$1,200.00	Cost	$480.00	$480.00	$240.00					
Bernie Frazer			$6,400.00	Cost	$640.00	$640.00	$640.00	$640.00			$640.00	$640.00
▲ Obtain approval of Statement of Work	$0.00	End	$1,520.00	Cost								
John Tierney			$400.00	Cost								
Rebecca Burns			$480.00	Cost								
Bernie Frazer			$640.00	Cost								
1 ▲ Create project plan	$0.00	End	$15,200.00	Cost								
John Tierney			$4,000.00	Cost								
Rebecca Burns			$4,800.00	Cost								
Bernie Frazer			$6,400.00	Cost								

3 By default you will see a daily view of your project's time-scaled data, by days. To change the timescale, choose *View:Zoom* and click on the dropdown under *Timescale* to change *Days* to *Weeks*, *Months*, etc.

Figure 58.

The Timescale
setting drop down

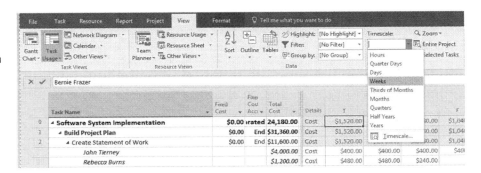

5 Select the *Months* setting. Your screen will resemble the following:

Figure 59.

Quarterly
timescale on the
top tier and
monthly on the
bottom tier of
timescale

7 Perhaps you would like to see a more high-level view of your project.
 Choose *Select All* above the ID column and left of the Task name
 header. All tasks should become highlighted. From *View:Data* click
 Outline, and from the dropdown list select *Level 1*. This will display
 the highest level phases of the WBS.

8 You are now presented a summary of total cost by phase of the left of
 the vertical divider and cost by phase by month on the right side of the
 vertical divider.

Figure 60.

Cost by phase by
month

9 Save your project.

Displaying Cost over Time, by Resource

This exercise continues the use of the file **ResourceCost.mpp** from the
preceding section. Alternatively, you can open **ResourceCost_Inst4.mpp**.

1 Apply the Resource Usage view to your project (from *Resource:View* click the dropdown arrow and select *Resource Usage*).

2 Use the method we covered in the preceding exercise (right-clicking in the *Timescale Data* area) to apply the *Cost Table* to the left side of this view, and show *Cost* details on the right; remove *Work* details.

3 Change the timescale to show a quarterly view, by months, as we covered in the preceding exercise (*View:Zoom:Timescale:Months*).

4 Select all resources by clicking on the little square that is above the ID column and left of the Resource Name header. This will highlight all tasks. From *View:Data* click the *Outline* icon and from the dropdown list select *Hide Subtasks*. Your screen will resemble the following:

Figure 61.

View of Resource Usage summarized by resource, by month

		Resource Name	Work	Add New Column	Details	May	Jun	Jul	Aug	Sep	Oct	Nov
		▷ Unassigned	1 hr		Cost							
1		▷ John Tierney	240 hrs		Cost				$3,200.00	$6,000.00	$1,200.00	$1,600.00
2		▷ Rebecca Burns	172 hrs		Cost				$1,200.00	$6,240.00	$480.00	$2,400.00
3	✦	▷ Bernie Frazer	240 hrs		Cost				$5,120.00	$12,800.00	$1,280.00	
4	✦	▷ George Brody	336 hrs		Cost					$7,680.00	$15,360.00	$3,200.00
5	✦	▷ David Crawford	278 hrs		Cost					$3,800.00	$7,300.00	$2,400.00
6	✦	▷ Joan Higgins	254 hrs		Cost					$6,000.00	$7,860.00	$2,400.00
7	✦	▷ Mike Goren	86 hrs		Cost					$5,880.00	$140.00	
8	✦	▷ Julie Pawlkowski	94 hrs		Cost					$7,360.00	$160.00	
9		▷ Ted Haley	24 hrs		Cost					$1,200.00		
10		▷ Mary Remington	120 hrs		Cost							$8,400.00
					Cost							
					Cost							

5 Click the arrow to the left of *David Crawford* to see which assignments make up his total cost by month.

Figure 62.

Total cost for David Crawford per month, per assignment

	Resource Name	Cost	Details	Sep	Oct	Nov	Dec
5	▲ David Crawford	$13,900.00	Cost	$3,800.00	$7,300.00	$2,400.00	$400.00
	Determine current architecture	$2,500.00	Cost	$2,400.00	$100.00		
	Assess processes on the server	$1,000.00	Cost	$1,000.00			
	Complete architecture draft	$400.00	Cost	$400.00			
	Send out prep packet	$800.00	Cost		$800.00		
	Conduct pre-interviews	$400.00	Cost		$400.00		
	Conduct session	$800.00	Cost		$800.00		
	Prepare draft document	$2,400.00	Cost		$2,400.00		
	Send out draft and review with key sponsors	$2,400.00	Cost		$2,400.00		
	Finalize additional session scope	$1,600.00	Cost		$400.00	$1,200.00	
	Communicate sessions to necessary attendees	$400.00	Cost			$400.00	
	Conduct requirements sessions	$800.00	Cost			$800.00	
	Circulate for comments	$400.00	Cost				$400.00

6 Save and close your project.

8.4 Constraints

Microsoft Project 2016 provides tools you can use to influence when project tasks occur. These tools provide the flexibility to adjust the project schedule more efficiently, which is required to support often-changing business requirements. This lesson will demonstrate how to apply constraints that limit the flexibility of task scheduling. It will also demonstrate how to set deadline dates that warn you when the project schedule has slipped to an unacceptable degree.

If you follow the logic of this course in developing a project plan, the only date you will have entered at this point is the project start date. If you want to change the project start date or switch to project finish date scheduling, this is the best time to do so. Your entire project schedule, based on durations and dependencies, will simply move across the Gantt Chart calendar presentation without change. Constraints limit your ability to relocate the project plan in time because they "lock" tasks to dates.

Applying Constraints to Tasks in a Project Scheduled from the Project Start Date

Based on the project start date, task durations, and task dependencies, Microsoft Project determines the start and finish dates for each task in the plan.

But some tasks in your plan may be tied to specific dates. For example, if the delivery of a piece of hardware or some other product from an outside company occurs on a specific date, any work using that equipment must consider the delivery date. Similarly, a new employee can't begin work on project tasks until they actually join the company. You can indicate these schedule-related situations by applying a constraint to the task.

Task constraints are used when you want to make sure that a task starts or finishes on, by, or no earlier than a particular date. By default, Microsoft Project 2016 schedules all tasks to start as soon as possible (when scheduling from a project start date). You can select specific limits on any task you feel needs a different schedule constraint.

In general, schedule flexibility is the project manager's friend because external events will impact the schedule once a project starts. Task constraints are defined as flexible (soft constraints) or inflexible (hard constraints). Microsoft Project is designed to use a flexible constraint when it has a choice. The flexibility of the constraint varies depending on whether you are scheduling your project from a start date or from a finish date.

An example of a flexible constraint when you are scheduling from a start date is the Start No Earlier Than (SNET) constraint. The task cannot start earlier than the constraint date but, based on the scheduling of the predecessor tasks, it could start later.

While constraints are required for some tasks, it is common for new Microsoft Project users to inadvertently set constraints when they don't mean to. For example, if you set a start date for a task, you are applying a SNET constraint.

Microsoft Project 2016 will not automatically apply an inflexible constraint to a task. The practical result of an inflexible constraint is to override the logical relationships you established between tasks. If the Planning Wizard message options are left turned on, Microsoft Project will warn you that applying an inflexible constraint could cause a scheduling conflict. In some situations this is helpful because Microsoft Project will alert you before a constrained task is automatically re-scheduled.

The following table displays the behavior of a constraint when you are scheduling from a start date.

Constraint	Type	Constraint behavior when you are scheduling from a project start date
As Soon As Possible (ASAP)	Flexible	Default constraint for a new task if no dates are entered; starts on day one of the project if there are no predecessors; if a task does have predecessors, the dependency will drive when the task can start
As Late As Possible (ALAP)	Flexible	Always finishes the task on the project finish date; rarely used
Finish No Earlier Than (FNET)	Flexible	Finishes the task on or after the date that you entered; if the task has no predecessor, the task will finish on the date you selected. The finish date can be driven to a later date based on the predecessor(s). FNET is the default constraint type assigned by Microsoft Project when you select a finish date for a task. Microsoft Project applies this flexible constraint so that it preserves the ability of the scheduling engine to automatically schedule the task finish to a later date.
Start No Earlier Than (SNET)	Flexible	Starts the task on or after the date that you entered; if the task has no predecessor, the task will start on the date you selected. The start date can be driven to a later date based on the predecessor(s). SNET is the default constraint type assigned by Microsoft Project when you select a start date for a task. Microsoft Project applies this flexible constraint so that it preserves the ability of the scheduling engine to automatically schedule the task start to a later date.
Finish No Later Than (FNLT)	Inflexible	Finishes the task on or before the date that you entered; if a task does have predecessors, the dependency will drive when the task can start unless the predecessor attempts to move the task beyond the planning constraint date. In this situation, you will be alerted to a scheduling conflict if the Planning Wizard is activated.

Constraint	Type	Constraint behavior when you are scheduling from a project start date
Start No Later Than (SNLT)	Inflexible	Starts on day one of the project if there are no predecessors; if a task does have predecessors, the dependency will drive when the task can start unless the predecessor attempts to move the task beyond the planning constraint date. In this situation, you will be alerted to a scheduling conflict if the Planning Wizard is activated.
Must Finish On (MFO)	Inflexible	Task cannot finish any earlier or later than the indicated date; if the task has a predecessor, the predecessor cannot indicate the finish date of the task. Instead, the Planning Wizard will alert you of a scheduling conflict.
Must Start On (MSO)	Inflexible	Task cannot start any earlier or later than the indicated date; if the task has a predecessor, the predecessor cannot indicate the start date of the task. Instead, the Planning Wizard will alert you of a scheduling conflict.

Entering Task Constraints

The default constraint for new tasks will be set according to the *Schedule from* option selected in the **Project Information** dialog box as shown in the following figure.

Figure 63.

Schedule from options

If you choose to schedule from the *Project Start Date,* the default constraint for new tasks will be *as soon as possible.* If you choose to schedule from the *Project Finish Date*, the default constraint for new tasks will be *as late as possible.*

Once these constraints are set (according to the defaults described above), you can change them to suit how you wish certain tasks to behave as the Microsoft Project scheduling algorithms automatically update the schedule, which occurs each time a schedule is changed. Microsoft Project will also set some constraints automatically, based on user input.

If you enter a start or finish date into Microsoft Project, there's a good chance that you are also setting a soft constraint (SNET or FNET), as follows:

❑ If you schedule from the *Project Start Date* and you enter a task start date, Microsoft Project will change your constraint from ASAP to SNET (i.e. a "soft" constraint from scheduled start).

❑ If you schedule from the *Project Start Date* and you enter a task finish date, Microsoft Project will change your constraint from ASAP to FNET (i.e. a "soft" constraint from scheduled finish).

Once these constraints are set, the operation of Microsoft Project's scheduling algorithms may confuse you if you do not know that these constraints have been set. Because many Microsoft Project users don't notice or understand why this scheduling behavior is happening, the constraint field in Microsoft Project is widely misunderstood and often avoided because of fear of unpredictable behavior.

The hard constraints—*Start No Later Than*, *Finish No Later Than*, *Must Start On* and *Must Finish On*—can only be set by the end user. Hard constraints cause even more unpredictable behavior when set, which is why Microsoft Project does not automatically set these constraints for you.

The best way to handle task constraints' effects (or non-effects) on task scheduling behavior is to take the time to familiarize yourself with this feature of Microsoft Project.

Setting Task Constraints

In this exercise, the team assigned to create a project plan has to wait until all the management review comments have been received; if they start the task before the comments are in, they will undoubtedly have to throw out any completed work and repeat it. In a case like this, starting early will actually waste effort, not save time, so we want to make sure the task information in the plan reflects this practical constraint.

👈 This exercise uses the file **ProjectScheduling.mpp**. Be sure this file is open before beginning.

1 Go to the task *Create project plan* (ID 4) and enter a Start date of "10/26." You should be prompted with a dialog box that with an option to *Move the task, keep the link*. The Planning Wizard presents this question because you are moving a linked task to a later date. The Microsoft Project scheduling engine had set the finish date set to 11/6 based on the default constraint of "As early as possible" and the end of its predecessor task.

Figure 64.

Planning Wizard
constraint
warning

2 Click *OK*.

3 Notice the icon that appears in the Indicator field for Task 4—a calendar icon with a blue square [⊞]. Hover your mouse pointer over it to read the note.

Figure 65.

Constraint
indicator
message

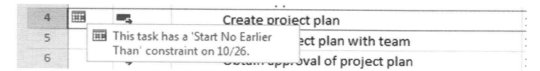

4 Double-click the task *Create project plan* (ID 4). You will be presented with the **Task Information** dialog box.

5 Click the *Advanced* tab.

4 You will see that Microsoft Project automatically set the *Constraint type* to *Start No Earlier Than*. Also, the *Constraint date* was automatically set to 10/26. Your dialog box will resemble the following:

Figure 66.

Viewing
SNET
constraint in **Task
Information**

7 Look at the Gantt Chart to see what appears to be a lag between Tasks 3 & 4. The gap between these tasks are a result of the SNET constraint you set by entering a different start date than what the scheduling had calculated.

Overriding a Task Dependency with a Hard Constraint

8 Double-click the task *Conduct session* (ID 16). You will be presented with the **Task Information** dialog box.

9 Click the *Advanced* tab.

10 From the *Constraint type* dropdown list, select *Finish No Later Than*.

11 From the *Constraint date* dropdown calendar, select *December 12* of next year. You have indicated that the task *Conduct session* must finish on or before December 12.

12 Click *OK*. You will see the **Planning Wizard** dialog box:

Figure 67.

Planning Wizard alert

13 Microsoft Project is alerting you to a potential scheduling conflict that has occurred because *Conduct session* is linked to another task. Click the *Continue. A Finish No Later Than constraint will be set* option button.

14 Click *OK*. Notice the new icon in the Indicator column for *Conduct session*—a small calendar with one red square [⊞]. This icon indicates the task constraint is inflexible.

15 Increase the duration of *Conduct pre-interviews* (ID 15) from 6 days to 10 days. Allow the schedule conflict and click *OK*. What happens to the link between *Conduct pre-interviews* and *Conduct session*?

Figure 68.

Schedule conflict caused by an inflexible constraint

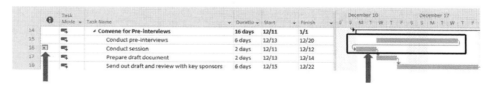

16 Notice the schedule conflict in the visual overlap (inside the rectangle) between *Conduct pre-interviews* and *Conduct session*.

17 Save your project.

Setting and Clearing Constraints Using a Split Window

This exercise continues the use of **ProjectScheduling.mpp**. Ensure this file is open before beginning, or open **ProjectScheduling_Inst1.mpp**.

1 Select *Create Statement of Work* (ID 2). From *Task:Properties* click
 the *Details* icon. Your screen will resemble the following:

Figure 69.

Gantt Chart and
Task Details
Form

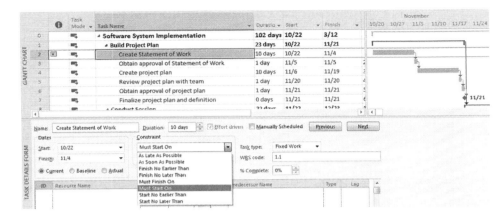

2 From the *Constraint* dropdown list in the bottom half of your screen,
 select *Must Finish On* for Task 2 and click *OK*. The button face will
 change from *OK* to *Previous*. If you do not assign a constraint date,
 Microsoft Project uses the already calculated date.

3 In the top pane, select the task *Create project plan* (ID 4). Recall that
 we assigned a SNET constraint to it, but then decided it really was
 unnecessary.

4 To remove the constraint, if it is not already removed, select *As Soon
 As Possible* from the *Constraint* dropdown list in the bottom pane.
 Click *OK*.

5 Double-click the window split bar to remove the split.

Clearing Constraints for Multiple Tasks

6 Make sure you are in the Gantt Chart view.

7 Select the *Task Name* column by clicking the column header.

8 From *Task:Properties* click the *Information* button. You will be
 presented with the following dialog box:

Figure 70.

**Multiple Task
Information**
dialog box

9 Click the *Advanced* tab (if necessary).

10 Select *As Soon As Possible* from the *Constraint type* dropdown list.

11 Click *OK*. Notice that any remaining task constraints have been cleared.

12 Save your project.

Deadline Dates

From time to time you may want to track a deadline for an individual task without restricting the schedule with a constraint. Microsoft Project 2016 enables you to establish a deadline date for a task and shows an indicator if the task finishes after its deadline as the project file is updated.

 This exercise continues the use of **ProjectScheduling.mpp**. Be sure this project is open before beginning, or open **ProjectScheduling_Inst2.mpp**.

1 Confirm that you are in the *Task* tab and Gantt Chart view.

2 Double-click the task *Finalize project plan and definition* (ID 7). You will be presented with the **Task Information** dialog box.

3 Click the *Advanced* tab.

4 From the *Deadline* dropdown calendar select *11/10*.

5 Click *OK*. A deadline of 11/10 is set for *Finalize project plan and definition*, and a green arrow appears beyond the Gantt bar for the task.

6 For the task *Create project plan* (ID 4), increase the duration from 5 to 15 days. Since the finish date for *Finalize project plan and definition* now extends past the deadline date, an icon appears in the Indicator column alerting you to this information and the deadline arrow in the Gantt Chart graphic moves left of the milestone diamond.

Figure 71.

Deadline alert
icon in the
Indicator column

An Alternative to Deadline Dates

While deadline dates can be useful, the little red diamond you receive as a warning is easily overlooked, especially if the task is off the screen. There is another more effective way to accomplish the same thing.

7 Scroll to the task you are concerned about: Task 33 (*Circulate for comments*). Click in the next empty *Task Name* cell, and add a new task: *Target finish date* with a duration of 0 days. Recall that a duration of 0 makes a task a milestone.

8 Link Task 33 finish-to-start with the new milestone Task 34, which will be the trigger for our alert mechanism.

9 Assign a *Must Finish On* constraint to the new milestone task, accepting the default constraint date of 3/4/14.

10 Press *F5* to see the **Go To** dialog box.

11 Enter "0" in the *ID* field and click *OK* to return to Task ID 0. Notice that the task we are interested in, Task 33, is off the screen. Increase the duration of Task 2, *Create Statement of Work*, to 11 days. What is the result?

Figure 72.

Planning Wizard
alert

The Planning Wizard message not only tells you that something is happening, it tells you specifically where to look: "...Task 33 of" Select *Continue. Allow the scheduling conflict.* to allow the change, then *F5* until Task 33 is displayed to see the effect.

12 Save and close your project.

8.5 Resource and Assignment Review Exercise

If you are not working in the enterprise environment, connected to Project Server, this exercise will review how you will handle exercises manually. If you will be working in the enterprise environment, these functions will be performed by the Project Server administrator unless your project uses local resources.

 This exercise uses **MeetingTasks.mpp** which you created at the end of the previous chapter. If you did not do that exercise, you can use **MeetingTasks_Inst1**. Ensure the appropriate file is open before beginning.

1 Switch to the Resource Sheet view and enter the following names and resource information:

Name	Initials	Group	Max. Units
Vice President	VP	Management	100%
Office Manager	OM	Management	100%
Administrative Assistant	AA	Office Staff	200%
Intern	IN	Office Staff	100%

2 Assign the resources to tasks as listed below, keeping task durations unchanged:

Task	Resource(s)
Schedule conference date	Vice President, Office Manager
Reserve conference center	Intern
Book keynote speaker	Office Manager
Develop letter	Administrative Assistant, Intern
Get corporate approval	Vice President

Task	Resource(s)
Plan food with caterer	Administrative Assistant
Print catering menu	Intern

3 Enter the following cost information on the resource sheet:

Resource	Standard rate	Overtime rate
Vice President	$75,000/year	--
Office Manager	$45,000/year	--
Administrative Assistant	$25/hour	$37.50/hour
Intern	$15/hour	$22.50/hour

4 Effective April 1, the intern resource will have a pay increase of 4.9%
 for both standard and overtime rates. Prepare your project plan to
 account for this increase. Hint: see the *Costs* tab in the **Resource
 Information** dialog box for steps 4 and 5

5 What is the total forecast cost for your project?

6 Save and close your project.

End of Chapter Quiz Questions

1. What are the three resource types? _____, _____, & _____.

2. Which type of resource is not consumed by the project? _____ _____

3. What's an example of a case when it is reasonable to assign a generic resource at more than 100%?

 ┌───┐
 │ │
 │ │
 │ │
 │ │
 └───┘

4. How do you change a resource to generic from the Resource Sheet?

 ┌───┐
 │ │
 │ │
 │ │
 │ │
 └───┘

5. What does checking the *Budget* checkbox from the **Resource Information** dialog (*General* tab) allow you to do?

6. What's the danger of adding a name directly to the Resource Name field in the Gantt Chart Entry Table or in the **Assign Resources** dialog box?

 ┌───┐
 │ │
 │ │
 │ │
 └───┘

7. One of your resources has just informed you he will be on vacation a week when you have him/her scheduled to work on a task. How would you update his calendar to reflect the fact that s/he will not be available?

 ┌───┐
 │ │
 │ │
 │ │
 └───┘

8. What does the Team Planner view allow you to see and how does it work?

```

```

9. What is the recommended task type, if your resource demand and project budget are based on labor estimates? _____

10. What organizations most commonly use fixed work as the default task type and why?

```

```

11. True or False: When work is fixed, Microsoft Project won't change the work estimate, and you cannot modify the specific work value for a task.

12. You are renting a piece of equipment for a few days, and therefore the resources using that equipment must complete the work during that time. What task type would be the best one to use in this scenario? _____

13. If you assign two resources to an effort-driven task, what happens to the duration? What if it is not an effort-driven task?

```

```

14. True or False: All fixed work tasks behave as effort-driven tasks.

15. The default task type selected by Microsoft is:
 a. Fixed work
 b. Fixed duration
 c. Fixed units
 d. None of the above

16. What do Smart Tags do?

17. Which view lists tasks and the resources assigned to each one? _____

18. Fill in the blank: Microsoft Project calculates basic cost calculations at the _____ level.

19. What formula does Microsoft Project follow to calculate assignment cost?

20. What formula does Microsoft Project follow to calculate task cost?

21. Is it possible for a resource to have different costs depending on the roles and/or tasks they are performing in Microsoft Project? If so, how?

   ```

   ```

22. Up to how many separate rates can each resource have? _____

23. How can you apply the Cost Table to a view?

24. How can you display a high-level outline of your plan?

25. Microsoft Project determines the start and finish dates for each task in the plan based on which of the following?
 a. Project start date
 b. Task durations
 c. Task dependencies
 d. All of the above

26. Which of the following constraints are inflexible?
 a. As Late As Possible
 b. Finish No Earlier Than
 c. Start No Later Than
 d. Start No Earlier Than

27. Which constraint type starts on day one of the project if there are no predecessors? Is this flexible or inflexible? _____; _____

28. With which constraint type, can tasks not finish any earlier or later than the indicated date? Is this flexible or inflexible? _____; _____

29. How do you set the constraint type and date of a task?

+---+
| |
| |
| |
| |
+---+

30. True or false: A hard constraint will override a task dependency.

31. Explain an alternative to deadline dates that provides more dramatic alerts.

+---+
| |
| |
| |
| |
+---+

chapter 9

Using Microsoft Project 2016 to Optimize the Plan

- Identifying the Critical Path

- Adding Recurring Tasks and Using Task Calendars

- Managing Resource Workloads and Resolving Resource Over-Allocations

- Setting the Project Baseline

- Communicating the Project Plan (Introduction)

- Optimizing the Plan Review Exercise

Learning Objectives for this Chapter

At the end of the chapter, the reader should be able to:

- Understand and identify the project's critical path
- Use the appropriate views to analyze the critical path
- Set up recurring tasks
- Define and use task calendars
- Review resource workloads and resolve resource over-allocations
- View, set, and clear the project baseline and know how to set multiple baselines (interim plans)
- Take a picture of the project Gantt Chart

Completing the Plan

The planning steps covered up to this point will help you produce a reasonable first draft of the project plan, but it's generally necessary to refine the plan before the project actually begins. Several of the steps may be repeated as the plan is optimized—resources may be added to meet the target end date, estimates may be adjusted as resource skills or roles are converted to real names, new tasks may be discovered as details are filled in, links may change to accommodate other schedule constraints, and assignments may shift to load level the plan. Each of these changes can force the project manager to repeat the steps of planning until a realistic plan is built—a process so common that PMI refers to this progressive elaboration as a fundamental defining characteristic of a project.

The work plan and schedule are not optimized until the scope, schedule, and resources have been configured to meet the project objectives.

9.1 Identifying the Critical Path

Network Diagram

The critical path is defined as the series of tasks that must be completed on schedule in order for a project to finish on schedule. Each task on the critical path is called a critical task. Tasks that are on the critical path have the minimum level of slack (usually 0 days). In other words, the task can be delayed for 0 days before it will delay the finish date of the project.

In the following exercise, we will explore how we can modify the Gantt Chart view to see which tasks are on the critical path in a project.

This exercise uses the file **CriticalPath.mpp**. Be sure this project is open before beginning.

1 Go to *File:Options* to view the **Project Options** dialog, and then click *Advanced* in the sidebar. Scroll to the bottom and note the *Tasks are critical if slack is less than or equal to* option. Ensure this is set to *0* days and click *OK*.

Figure 73.

The **Project Options** dialog box

2 As explained in Note 3 of the *Selecting a View* heading of Section 3.5, apply the *Schedule* table to see the total slack for the tasks in this project. To do so, from *View:Data* click the *Tables* dropdown list and select *Schedule*. Note that the last column shows the total slack for each task.

Figure 74.

Total slack calculation that defines the critical path

3 From *View:Data* select *Critical* from the *Filter* dropdown list. Only critical tasks in your project will now appear. Note: Look at the ID numbers of these tasks to see that not all tasks are displayed.

Figure 75.

Identifying the
critical path
using the
Critical filter

4 The Network Diagram view displays a node for tasks, along with
 schedule information and connecting arrows to show the relationship
 and sequence of activities. To see this view, from *View:Task Views*
 click the *Network Diagram* icon []. Your screen will resemble the
 following:

Figure 76.

Network
Diagram view

5 Critical tasks can also be identified in the Gantt Chart. Reapply the
 Gantt Chart view, remove the *Critical* filter (so you again see all tasks
 in the project), and from *Format:Bar Styles* select the *Critical Tasks*
 checkbox.

Your screen will resemble the following:

Figure 77.

Critical tasks formatted with red bars in the Gantt Chart

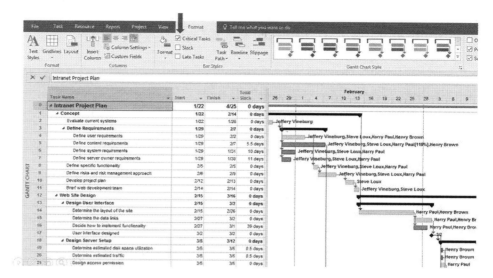

6 Scroll through the tasks in the plan to see which tasks appear with red Gantt bars, indicating they are on the critical path. What is the current estimated finish date for the project?

7 Uncheck the Critical Tasks checkbox. Note the total slack for Tasks 5, 6, and 7. Recall that the total slack can be seen by applying the schedule table to the Gantt Chart.

8 Link Task 4 to Task 5. (Task 4 should be the predecessor). Note the change to the total slack for Task 5.

9 Link Task 5 to Task 6. (Task 5 should be the predecessor). Note the change to the total slack for Task 6.

10 Link Task 5 to Task 7. (Task 5 should be the predecessor). Note the change to the total slack for Task 7.

11 Save and close your project.

The critical path is constantly calculated by Microsoft Project and can change as tasks are modified or updated. The Tracking Gantt Chart includes the critical path by default. See the *Viewing Baseline Information* heading of Section 9.4 to learn more.

9.2 Adding Recurring Tasks and Using Task Calendars

A recurring task is one that occurs more than once in a project on some kind of regular schedule, for example a bi-monthly status meeting, a weekly on-site visit, or a monthly report. Once the initial project schedule has been developed, you may want to add these types of tasks to your plan. Microsoft Project 2016 helps you to define and create several tasks with one dialog box for when you want to create a recurring event.

☞ This exercise uses the file **RecurringTask.mpp**. Be sure this project is open before beginning.

1 Confirm that you are in the *Task* tab with the Gantt Chart view.

2 Select *Build Project Plan* (Task ID 1), and from *Task:Insert* use the *Task* dropdown list to select *Recurring Task*. You will be presented with the **Recurring Task Information** dialog box.

Figure 78.

Recurring Task Information dialog box

3 In the *Task Name* field, type "Status meeting."

4 In the *Duration* field, enter "1h."

5 In the *Recurrence pattern* section, confirm the (default) *Weekly* option is selected.

6 In the *Recurrence pattern* section, select the *Monday* checkbox.

7 Do not change the *Range of recurrence* dates. (By default, it's set from the current project start date to project finish date).

8 From the *Calendar* dropdown list, select *Standard*. This tells Microsoft Project to schedule the meetings according to the working dates in that calendar (the project calendar for this exercise).

9 Click the checkbox for *Scheduling ignores resource calendars*. This selection will maintain the status meeting schedule without checking against every resource calendar.

10 Click the *OK* button. Your screen will resemble the following:

Figure 79.

New recurring
task

11 Place your mouse pointer over the new icons in the *Information* column to see their meaning.

12 Ensure the summary task *Status meeting* is still selected. From *Resource:Assignments* click *Assign Resources* to open the **Assign Resources** dialog box. Assign *Bernie Frazer*, *David Crawford*, *George Brody*, and *Joan Higgins* to the summary task. Your screen will resemble the following:

Figure 80.

Recurring task
assignments

13 In the **Assign Resources** dialog box, click *Close*. Click the arrow next to the *Status meeting* summary task to see the summary recurring task.

Figure 81.

Summary task for
weekly recurring
status meetings

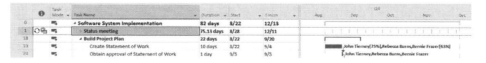

Notice that the resources are assigned to all the individual meetings, even though you assigned them to the summary task. Separate resource assignments can also be made to individual recurring tasks, but assigning a core team to the summary task is a quick way to populate the recurring tasks with resources. Recurring tasks are the only summary tasks that show this behavior.

It is always possible to assign resources to summary tasks, but ordinarily this is not recommended since the resources are not automatically assigned to the subtasks under the summary task.

14 Click the arrow next to the *Status meeting* summary task to hide the individual meetings, and save your project.

Adding Occurrences to a Recurring Task and Adding Resource Assignments to Them

📂 This section continues the use of **RecurringTask.mpp**. Ensure this file is open before beginning, or open **RecurringTask_Inst1.mpp**.

As your project progresses, you may encounter a situation that extends the project end date. In those situations, any recurring tasks that have been used to schedule status reporting, actuals tracking, or team meetings will need additional occurrences added to ensure that they remain active until your project's new finish date.

You have just been told that your project will be extended by four weeks because the client has increased the scope of work. The recurring task *Status Meeting* (ID 1) was set up to run to the original finish date of the project so now needs to be extended.

1 Double-click *Status meeting* (Task ID 1) to view the **Recurring Task Information** dialog box.

2 Select the box for *End after... occurrences*. Increase the occurrences from "16" to "21" and click *OK*.

3 Click the arrow to the side of *Status meeting* to see all of the status meetings, including the four new ones.

Remember that you still need to assign resources to the new meetings. Chances are you will want to assign the same resources to the new tasks as were assigned to the original ones. There are two easy ways to accomplish this:

❏ Highlight each of the new occurrences, and use the **Resource Assignment** dialog box to assign the resources to the new tasks.

❏ Use the *Fill Handle* to copy the *Resource Names* column for the new occurrences. We will use this approach in this lesson.

4 From *View:Task Views* ensure the Gantt Chart view is selected, and from *View:Data* use the *Table* dropdown list to confirm the *Entry Table* is applied. Expand the *Status Meeting* summary task by clicking the arrow next to the summary task name. Then, scroll to the last column of the *Entry Table* called *Resource Names*, and click the *Resource Names* column header and drag its column to the left until it is next to the *Task Name* column.

5 Using your mouse pointer, click in the cell of the *Resource Names* column for the last occurrence that had resources assigned (adjacent to *Status meeting 16*). Then, use the *Fill Handle* (the small black square in the lower right-hand corner of the cell) to drag the column down, highlighting all cells for new recurring tasks with no resources assigned.

Figure 82.

Fill Handle

Status meeting 16 | Bernie Frazer,David Crawford,George Brody

The resource assignments will be copied to the new tasks, and your screen will resemble the following:

Figure 83.

New task assignments

Status meeting 16 | Bernie Frazer,David Crawford,George Brody
Status meeting 17 | Bernie Frazer,David Crawford,George Brody
Status meeting 18 | Bernie Frazer,David Crawford,George Brody
Status meeting 19 | Bernie Frazer,David Crawford,George Brody
Status meeting 20 | Bernie Frazer,David Crawford,George Brody
Status meeting 21 | Bernie Frazer,David Crawford,George Brody

You may have noticed one other result of adding these tasks: the critical path went away! All the tasks that were red have turned blue, meaning they are non-critical. It's not unusual for Microsoft Project users to complain, "My project has no critical path," but there is always a critical path somewhere.

6 Use the *Go to selected task* button (or scroll) to view the Gantt Chart bar for *Status Meeting 21*. Notice anything different about it?

Microsoft Project uses durations and dependencies to calculate the project schedule, but it also uses dependencies to identify paths in a project. All unlinked tasks are considered to be separate, stand-alone paths, and as far as Microsoft Project can tell, *Status Meeting 21* is the only thing controlling the end date of the project. If you remove the four new status meetings by resetting the number of occurrences to 16, the original critical path will reappear.

What can be learned from this? Don't underestimate the importance of logical links between tasks, and make sure there are no unlinked tasks after the finish date of the *real* tasks in the project.

7 Save and close your project

9.3 Managing Resource Workloads and Resolving Resource Over-allocations

Resources are the people, equipment, and materials (and sometimes money) essential to the completion of tasks. Resource assignment allows you to indicate which people and/or things are necessary for which tasks. Microsoft Project 2016 allows you to create a project schedule with or without assigning resources to individual tasks, but assigning resources is a critical feature for enterprise project management.

It's a good idea to check availability before assigning people to tasks, but in the process of assigning people to project tasks, it is easy to assign them to more hours than they have available on a given day—this is known as *over-allocation*. It's especially easy to over-allocate people when they are working on multiple projects with multiple project managers who may not be aware of each other's plans. This is one of the valuable features of the resource pool approach discussed in Section 10.3: *Enterprise Resource Management*.

What can an individual project manager do about over-allocations within his or her own project?

Viewing Resource Workloads and Task Assignments

Microsoft Project 2016 doesn't stop you from over-allocating a resource, but it does enable you to identify over-allocations and under-allocations. When a resource is over-allocated, Resource views display the resource name in bold, red text with a Leveling indicator [◆]. Microsoft Project considers a resource over-allocated if that resource is assigned to more than 8 hours of work on any given day in the project (assuming 100% maximum units and 8 hours per working day).

🗁 This exercise uses the file **ResourceWorkload.mpp**. Be sure this project is open before beginning. Note: This exercise uses basic navigational concepts outlined in Section 3.3: *Navigating in Microsoft Project Views*.

1 From *Task:View* select the Resource Usage view. Your screen will resemble the following (you may need to click the first task below *John Tierney* and click the *Scroll to Task* icon to get this exact view):

Figure 84.

Resource
Usage view

2 Select the resource *George Brody* (ID 4). Note that his name is displayed in bold, red text to indicate his over-allocation. Move your mouse pointer over the icon in George Brody's Indicators column to read the over-allocation message.

3 From *View:Split View* click *Details*, and from the dropdown list select *More Views…*. In the **More Views** dialog box, select *Resource Allocation* and click *Apply*. You may also want to zoom out to a weekly or monthly view (*View:Zoom:Timescale* drop down)

4 All of George Brody's task assignments will appear in the bottom pane, the Leveling Gantt view. Select George's name in the upper pane, and in *Task:Editing* click *Scroll to Task* to see George's first set of tasks.

Figure 85.

Resource
Allocation
view

Notice that on the week of 9/24 George is scheduled to do 72 hours' work—flagged as an over-allocation—and the week of 10/8 is not much better.

5 With *George Brody* selected in the top pane, click the *Next Overallocation* button [▦] (found in *Resource:Level*). This button will move you down the resource list and across the timescale into the future to help you locate individual over-allocations.

6 Again, select *George Brody* and click *Scroll to Task* to return to the week of 9/24 (current year). Inspection of the bottom frame reveals the problem. As you can see, George has two tasks scheduled simultaneously on that week, one at 32 hours and another at 40 hours.

Figure 86.

George's over-allocation on 9/24

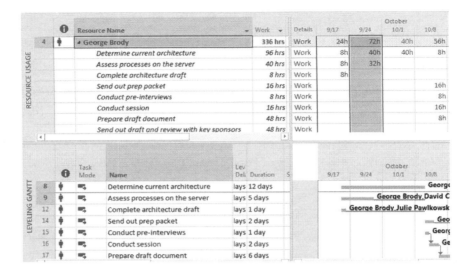

The Leveling Gantt in the bottom pane displays all the tasks the selected resource in the top pane is assigned to. All tasks are displayed with blue Gantt bars, and a task's slack is represented as a thin line to the right of the task bar. If you click on a different resource in the upper pane, all of the tasks assigned to that resource will be displayed in the bottom pane.

7 Save your project.

Resolving Resource Over-allocations

Microsoft Project 2016 provides an automatic resource leveling function that can help deal with these problems.

However, this function may not entirely resolve the over-allocations in your project and may lead to schedule changes you do not want. This tool is very powerful but quite often misunderstood. It is not a magic button; automatic leveling can only resolve resource over-allocations by delaying tasks in the plan until a resource is no longer over-allocated. For example, if a resource is scheduled to work on two tasks today for a total of 16 hours, the automatic leveling function would delay the second task until tomorrow to resolve the over-allocation. That is not always realistic.

Note: Resource leveling can also accelerate scheduled work if resources have early availability.

📂 This exercise, which explores Microsoft Project's leveling function, continues use of the file **ResourceWorkload.mpp**. Be sure this project is open before beginning, or open **ResourceWorkload_Inst1.mpp**.

1 What is the current finish date for this project? (See the finish date of the project summary task, Task 0)

2 From *Resource:Level* click the *Leveling Options* icon [▤]. You will be presented with the **Resource Leveling** dialog box.

Figure 87.

Resource Leveling dialog box

Although the leveling function in Microsoft Project can be set to *Automatic*, the result is that Microsoft Project continuously re-calculates and reschedules every task every time a resource becomes over-allocated by any amount of time! Using the default *Manual* setting allows you to control when and how Microsoft Project applies the leveling calculations.

Note that the leveling options enable you to resolve over-allocations by evaluating a specified time period. The time periods that Microsoft Project can evaluate are:

❑ Minute by Minute

❑ Hour by Hour

❑ Day by Day

❑ Week by Week

❑ Month by Month

By specifying a block of time in which to look for over-allocations, Project evaluates the selected block of time *before* it performs leveling calculations. Resources are considered over-allocated and will be leveled if the total assigned work exceeds the total work hours for the selected block of time.

For example, if a resource has two 8-hour tasks scheduled to begin at 8:00 AM on the same day, and you choose to look for over-allocations on a day-by-day basis, one task will be delayed until the next day so that there is no over-allocation on the first day. If, however, you choose to look for over-allocations on a week-by-week basis, the scheduled tasks will not be affected because they do not exceed the amount of work the resource can perform in a week (typically 40 hours, as set in *File:Options:Schedule*).

3 In the **Resource Leveling** dialog box, accept the option to look for resource over-allocations on a *Day by Day* basis. Note that the *Level only within available slack* box is not checked by default, so Microsoft Project is set up to level critical tasks as well. Now click the *Level All* button.

4 Did the leveling resolve the resource over-allocations? What is the new estimated project finish date?

5 From *Resource:Level* click *Clear leveling*.

6 Once again, from *Resource:Level* select *Leveling Options*, but this time select *Level only within available slack* in the **Resource Leveling** dialog box before clicking *Level All*. When you receive the alert shown in the following figure, it is generally best to stop leveling, resolve the issue, and then level again. For our exercise, however, click *Skip All*.

Figure 88.

Resource
leveling alert

7 Did the leveling resolve the resource over-allocations? What is the project finish date?

The resource leveling function is often used as a negotiating tool. You can present both options for a management decision—"With the resource currently assigned I can complete the project by this date: ____, while with additional resources, I can complete it on this date: ____." For example, when you leveled without changing the finish date (*Level only within available slack*), George Brody's over-allocation couldn't be completely fixed. If you scroll through the view, you'll see that from October 3-9 George is still over-allocated. The Leveling Gantt shows why; George has two tasks that can't be moved: *Determine current architecture* and *Assess processes on the server* because *Determine current architecture* is a critical task. It's much more convincing to be able to say—and show—"I need someone who could replace George on *Assess processes on the server* beginning October 3."

As it happens, Ted Haley is available and has the skills necessary for this task.

8 Clicking *Level All* will also level all resources without opening the **Resource Options** dialog box (by using the current Leveling options that are already preset). To level a specific resource, from *Resource:Level* click the *Level Resource* icon. Then, from the **Level Resource** dialog box, select the desired resource and click *Level Now*.

Figure 89.

Using the **Level Resources** dialog to level George Brody's assignments

9 Once you review your results, click *Clear Leveling*.

10 Now display the Resource Usage view in full screen mode (i.e. remove the lower pane view). Click to select the assignment *Assess processes on the server* under *George Brody* and drag it downward until it moves to *Ted Haley*. You will need to collapse the assignments for *David Crawford, Joan Higgins, Mike Goren,* and *Julie Pawlkowski* so you can see Ted Haley's assignments. During the move, your screen will resemble the following.

Figure 90.

Collapsing assignments

		Resource Name	Work	Add New C	Details	9/17	9/24	10/1	10/8	10/15	10/22
4		▲ George Brody	296 hrs		Work	16h	40h	40h	56h	40h	40h
		Determine current architecture	*96 hrs*		Work	8h	40h	40h	8h		
		Complete architecture draft	*8 hrs*		Work	8h					
		Send out prep packet	*16 hrs*		Work				16h		
		Conduct pre-interviews	*8 hrs*		Work				8h		
		Conduct session	*16 hrs*		Work				16h		
		Prepare draft document	*48 hrs*		Work				8h	40h	
		Send out draft and review with key sponsors	*48 hrs*		Work						40h
		Finalize additional session scope	*32 hrs*		Work						
		Communicate sessions to necessary attendees	*8 hrs*		Work						
		Document minutes from sessions	*8 hrs*		Work						
		Circulate for comments	*8 hrs*		Work						
5		▷ David Crawford	278 hrs		Work	24h	52h	2h	48h	40h	40h
6		▷ Joan Higgins	254 hrs		Work	24h	52h	2h	32h	40h	40h
7		▷ Mike Goren	86 hrs		Work	24h	60h	2h			
8		▷ Julie Pawlkowski	94 hrs		Work	32h	60h	2h			
9		▲ Ted Haley	64 hrs		Work	24h	40h				
		Assess processes on the server	*48 hrs*		Work	8h	32h				
		Assess printer hardware	*16 hrs*		Work	8h	8h				

11 Save your project.

It is not uncommon for automatic leveling to fail to resolve all resource over-allocations or results in unacceptable schedule changes. In these cases, you will need to resolve the resource conflicts manually so that you can dictate where and how adjustments are made. We will review a technique that we call "task leveling" later in this section.

The following techniques can be used to resolve resource over-allocations:

❑ Increase the maximum units of the resource

❑ Reschedule the task that has created the over-allocation

❑ Add overtime

❑ Adjust task dependencies or constraints

❑ Remove the resource if it isn't mandatory to the task

❑ Replace the over-allocated resource with an under-allocated resource

❑ Make calendar adjustments to extend the working days and hours for the project or resource

❑ Decrease the amount of work assigned to the resource.

Of course some of these options are more practical than others. The two most commonly used methods are rescheduling the work and replacing the resource. Of these, at this point in the course, Microsoft Project can realistically only use one: reschedule the task that has created the over-allocation.

All other options require human judgment and communication and negotiation. Microsoft Project's real value is in allowing the project manager to easily find where schedule impossibilities exist.

If Microsoft Project gave us the ability to view allocations across all projects the resource was assigned to, it could help eliminate the multiple scheduling problems that lead to many over-allocations. Fortunately, Microsoft Project does provide us with that capability, as we'll see shortly.

Task Leveling versus Resource Leveling

When building your project plan and assigning resources to it, one way to avoid resource over-allocation is to ensure that resources are available as they are assigned to a task. This technique is referred to as task leveling.

In this exercise we will build a view that allows you to see resource allocation to a task in relationship to all other tasks to which that resource is assigned.

☞ This exercise continues use of the file **ResourceWorkload.mpp**. Be sure this project is open before beginning, or open **ResourceWorkload_Inst2.mpp**.

1 From *View:Resource Views* click the *Other Views* dropdown list and select *More Views*. In the **More Views** dialog box, click *New*. You will see the **Define New View** dialog box.

Figure 91.

Define New View dialog box

2 Select the *Combination view* option and click *OK* to see the **View Definition** dialog for the project.

Figure 92.

View Definition dialog box

3 Type "My Task Leveling" in the *Name* field. From the *Primary View* dropdown, select *Task Usage*. From the *Details Pane* dropdown, select *Resource Usage*. Ensure the *Show in menu* option is selected and click *OK*. When the **More Views** dialog again appears, click *Apply*. Your new view will appear on the screen.

Figure 93.

My Task Leveling view

4 In the upper pane, select the task *Determine current architecture* (Task 8).

5 In the upper pane, under *Determine current architecture*, select *George Brody*. Note that all tasks to which George is assigned are displayed in the lower pane.

6 In the upper pane, click on *David Crawford*. Note that all tasks to which David is assigned are displayed in the lower pane.

7 Click on *Joan Higgins*. Note that all tasks to which Joan is assigned are displayed in the lower pane.

8 Click on *Mike Goren*. Note that all tasks to which Mike is assigned are displayed in the lower pane.

9 Save and close your project.

Note: This view can be used to identify resource over-allocations within a single task as well as across all other tasks. In order to resolve over-allocations you can use the resource assignment techniques outlined earlier in this section to manually adjust resource assignments.

9.4 Setting the Project Baseline

The project baseline represents your expectations for the project. When you track actual project progress, you can use the baseline to compare your original plan for the project with the actual results—which tasks started earlier or later than planned, exceeded their original budget, took longer than planned, and so on. You may be able to use this information to prevent problems on future projects and make better time and budget estimates.

After you finish building your plan, but before you begin to execute it, you are ready to set a baseline. After you save a baseline plan and begin updating your schedule, you may want to periodically save an interim plan, a snapshot of the evolving project plan at a time of your choice. For example, on a project lasting longer than a year, you might decide to save an interim plan on a quarterly basis, either for your own information or for reporting purposes. You can save up to ten (10) interim plans for each schedule. Since interim plans contain start and finish dates only, they help you to compare changes in the scheduled dates of tasks, useful for analyzing the accuracy of your scheduling estimates and for determining when your schedule began to get off track.

Baselining, therefore, refers to the concept of capturing the original estimate for your project. Before a project is baselined, you have what's known as the *current estimate* for work, cost, start, finish, and duration. But the baseline values for these fields remains blank until you ask Microsoft Project to capture a baseline, as noted in the following figure:

Figure 94.

Before baselining

Current Estimate	Field Content	Baseline (original estimate)	Field Content
Work	8h	Baseline Work	0h
Cost	$800	Baseline Cost	$0
Start	11/5	Baseline Start	NA
Finish	11/9	Baseline Finish	NA
Duration	5d	Baseline Duration	0d

Once you capture a baseline for your project, the current estimate values for work, cost, start, finish, and duration are copied into the baseline fields as displayed in the following figure. In this way, you're able to use Microsoft Project to set a foundation for comparing work, cost, start, finish, and duration values to the baseline as your project progresses.

Figure 95.

After baselining

Current Estimate	Field Content	Baseline (original estimate)	Field Content
Work	8h	Baseline Work	8h
Cost	$800	Baseline Cost	$800
Start	11/5	Baseline Start	11/5
Finish	11/9	Baseline Finish	11/9
Duration	5d	Baseline Duration	5d

Applying the Baseline Table

📁 This exercise uses the file **SetBaseline.mpp**. Be sure this project is open before beginning.

Microsoft Project 2016 allows you to view baseline data by applying the Baseline Table.

1 From *View:Data* use the *Tables* dropdown arrow to select *More Tables*.

2 From the **More Tables** dialog, click *Baseline* and then *Apply*. Your screen will resemble the following:

Figure 96.

Baseline table applied prior to setting the initial baseline

	Task Name	Baseline Dur.	Baseline Start	Baseline Finish	Baseline Work	Baseline Cost
0	Software System Implementation	0 days	NA	NA	0 hrs	$0.00
1	Build Project Plan	0 days	NA	NA	0 hrs	$0.00
2	Create Statement of Work	0 days	NA	NA	0 hrs	$0.00
3	Obtain approval of Statement of Work	0 days	NA	NA	0 hrs	$0.00
4	Create project plan	0 days	NA	NA	0 hrs	$0.00
5	Obtain approval of project plan	0 days	NA	NA	0 hrs	$0.00
6	Finalize project plan and definition	0 days	NA	NA	0 hrs	$0.00
7	Define System Environment	0 days	NA	NA	0 hrs	$0.00
8	Determine current architecture	0 days	NA	NA	0 hrs	$0.00
9	Assess processes on the server	0 days	NA	NA	0 hrs	$0.00
10	Assess printer hardware	0 days	NA	NA	0 hrs	$0.00
11	Communicate with integrator	0 days	NA	NA	0 hrs	$0.00
12	Complete architecture draft	0 days	NA	NA	0 hrs	$0.00
13	Conduct Session	0 days	NA	NA	0 hrs	$0.00
14	Send out prep packet	0 days	NA	NA	0 hrs	$0.00
15	Conduct pre-interviews	0 days	NA	NA	0 hrs	$0.00
16	Conduct session	0 days	NA	NA	0 hrs	$0.00
17	Prepare draft document	0 days	NA	NA	0 hrs	$0.00
18	Send out draft and review with key sponsors	0 days	NA	NA	0 hrs	$0.00

Note: The baseline fields for the project plan displayed in the preceding figure reflect the uninitiated values that we would expect to see when a project has not yet been baselined.

Project Management Using Microsoft Project 2016

Setting the Project Baseline

3 From *Project:Schedule* click the *Set Baseline* icon [] and choose *Set Baseline*.... You will be presented with the following dialog box:

Figure 97.

Set Baseline
dialog box

4 Ensure that both the default *Set Baseline* button and the default *Entire project* options are selected, and click *OK*. Your screen will resemble the following:

Figure 98.

Results of setting
a new baseline

	Task Name	Baseline Dur.	Baseline Start	Baseline Finish	Baseline Work	Baseline Cost
0	**Software System Implementation**	**77 days**	**8/22**	**12/6**	**1,821 hrs**	**$182,000.00**
1	**Build Project Plan**	**22 days**	**8/22**	**9/20**	**468 hrs**	**$46,800.00**
2	Create Statement of Work	10 days	8/22	9/4	180 hrs	$18,000.00
3	Obtain approval of Statement of Work	1 day	9/5	9/5	24 hrs	$2,400.00
4	Create project plan	10 days	9/6	9/19	240 hrs	$24,000.00
5	Obtain approval of project plan	1 day	9/20	9/20	24 hrs	$2,400.00
6	Finalize project plan and definition	0 days	9/20	9/20	0 hrs	$0.00
7	**Define System Environment**	**22 days**	**9/6**	**10/7**	**544 hrs**	**$54,400.00**
8	Determine current architecture	12 days	9/6	9/23	296 hrs	$29,600.00
9	Assess processes on the server	5 days	9/24	9/30	120 hrs	$12,000.00
10	Assess printer hardware	2 days	10/1	10/2	64 hrs	$6,400.00
11	Communicate with integrator	2 days	10/3	10/4	16 hrs	$1,600.00
12	Complete architecture draft	1 day	10/7	10/7	48 hrs	$4,800.00
13	**Conduct Session**	**16 days**	**10/8**	**10/29**	**424 hrs**	**$42,400.00**
14	Send out prep packet	2 days	10/8	10/9	64 hrs	$6,400.00
15	Conduct pre-interviews	1 day	10/8	10/8	24 hrs	$2,400.00
16	Conduct session	2 days	10/10	10/11	48 hrs	$4,800.00
17	Prepare draft document	6 days	10/14	10/21	144 hrs	$14,400.00
18	Send out draft and review with key sponsors	6 days	10/22	10/29	144 hrs	$14,400.00

Note that the baseline values have been updated to reflect the values of the current estimated fields.

5 Save your project.

Viewing Baseline Information

By default, Microsoft Project does not include the baseline data in the Gantt Chart view. However, you do have several options to view and use baseline information.

 This exercise continues to use the file **SetBaseline.mpp**. Be sure this project is open before beginning, or open **SetBaseline_Inst1.mpp**.

Microsoft Project 2016 allows you to view a statistical summary of your project, including baseline data, through the **Project Information** dialog box.

1 From *Project:Properties* click the *Project Information* icon to access the **Project Information** dialog box.

2 Click the *Statistics* button. You will be presented with the following dialog:

Figure 99.

Project Statistics for **SetBaseline.mpp**

	Start	Finish
Current	8/22	12/6
Baseline	8/22	12/6
Actual	NA	NA
Variance	0d	0d

	Duration	Work	Cost
Current	77d	1,821h	$182,000.00
Baseline	77d	1,821h	$182,000.00
Actual	0d	0h	$0.00
Remaining	77d	1,821h	$182,000.00

Percent complete:
Duration: 0% Work: 0%

3 Click *Close.*

Another common method of looking at baseline data for the schedule is to apply the Variance Table to your project.

4 Make sure you are in the Gantt Chart view. From *View:Data* click the *Tables* icon.

5 From the list of available tables, select *Variance*. Your screen will resemble the following:

Figure 100.

Variance Table applied, showing the schedule baseline dates

	Task Mode	Task Name	Start	Finish	Baseline Start	Baseline Finish	Start Var.	Finish Var.
0		◢ Software System Implementation	8/22	12/6	8/22	12/6	0 days	0 days
1		◢ Build Project Plan	8/22	9/20	8/22	9/20	0 days	0 days
2		Create Statement of Work	8/22	9/4	8/22	9/4	0 days	0 days
3		Obtain approval of Statement of Work	9/5	9/5	9/5	9/5	0 days	0 days
4		Create project plan	9/6	9/19	9/6	9/19	0 days	0 days
5		Obtain approval of project plan	9/20	9/20	9/20	9/20	0 days	0 days
6		Finalize project plan and definition	9/20	9/20	9/20	9/20	0 days	0 days
7		◢ Define System Environment	9/6	10/7	9/6	10/7	0 days	0 days
8		Determine current architecture	9/6	9/23	9/6	9/23	0 days	0 days
9		Assess processes on the server	9/24	9/30	9/24	9/30	0 days	0 days
10		Assess printer hardware	10/1	10/2	10/1	10/2	0 days	0 days
11		Communicate with Integrator	10/3	10/4	10/3	10/4	0 days	0 days
12		Complete architecture draft	10/7	10/7	10/7	10/7	0 days	0 days

Note that variance values (start variance and finish variance) are set to zero immediately after setting the baseline. We will cover this topic in greater detail in Section 14.1: *Variance Analysis*.

By default, the Gantt Chart provides a visual display of planned tasks and their assigned resources. The Tracking Gantt displays baseline data along with the current plan and actual results.

6 From *View:Task Views* click the *Gantt Chart* icon dropdown and
 select *Tracking Gantt*. Your screen will resemble the following:

Figure 101.

Tracking Gantt
view with a
weekly timescale

The gray bars represent the baseline plan, while the red and blue bars
represent the critical and non-critical tasks in the *current* plan. As the plan
evolves during the project, the red and blue bars will move; the gray bars will
remain unchanged.

7 Save your project.

Multiple Baselines

Microsoft Project 2016 includes a multiple baseline feature, which allows you
to save all baseline fields up to a total of eleven (11) times for each project.
The **Save Baseline** dialog box has a dropdown list for each of the eleven
baselines, and the **Clear Baseline** dialog box has the same dropdown list.
When a baseline is saved, a date stamp is also stored with the baseline and
is displayed in the dialog box for future reference.

Following is the **Save Baseline** dialog showing the date stamp for the initial
baseline:

Figure 102.

Date-stamped
baseline with ten
additional
baselines

As in previous versions of Microsoft Project, summary task baseline data is, by default, not updated when you choose to save a new baseline for selected subtasks. However, you now have the option to rollup subtask baseline updates to summary tasks when saving a baseline for selected tasks. These options are shown in the following figure:

Figure 103.

Rollup
baselines
options

These multiple baseline fields also let you choose which baseline you want to use in earned value calculations. The selection is made in *File:Options:Advanced* under *Earned Value options for this project*. The *Baseline for Earned Value calculation* option in this section allows you to choose which baseline should be used in calculations.

Capturing Interim Plans

📁 This exercise continues to use the file **SetBaseline.mpp**. Be sure this project is open before beginning, or open **SetBaseline_Inst2.mpp**.

1 From *Project:Schedule* click the *Set Baseline* icon and select *Set Baseline...*. You will be presented with the **Set Baseline** dialog box.

2 Select the *Set interim plan* option button. Your dialog box will resemble the following:

Figure 104.

Set interim plan
option selected

3 Accept the default *Entire project* option and click *OK*. The *Start* and
 Finish values for the current plan tasks will be copied into the *Start1*
 and *Finish1* fields. Your interim plan is set. These fields can be used
 as the parameters for a new bar with a different appearance if you
 want to show the snapshot on the Gantt Chart for reporting purposes.
 We will describe how to do this in Section 15.1: *Communication
 Options.*

4 Open the **Set Baseline** dialog box again and click the dropdown arrow
 on the *Copy* selector. Your dialog box will resemble the following:

Figure 105.

*Set interim
plan: Copy*

These options allow you to move one baseline to another or convert a
baseline to an interim plan. Baselines contain a complete set of project data
fields, including start and finish, duration, work, and cost. Interim plans, on
the other hand, contain only start and finish dates for the tasks in the plan.

Also, selected tasks can be saved into a specified baseline. This technique
can be used to support rolling wave planning, where detailed plans are
constructed only for a limited timespan.

5 Click *Cancel* to close the **Set Baseline** dialog box.

Clearing a Baseline

6 From *Project:Schedule* click the *Set Baseline* icon and choose *Clear
 Baseline*. You will be presented with the following dialog box:

Figure 106.

Clear Baseline
dialog box

7 Accept the default *Clear baseline plan* option button selection.

8 Accept the default *Entire project* option button selection.

9 Click *OK*. Your baseline is cleared.

Figure 107.

Cleared baseline

	Task Name	Baseline Dur.	Baseline Start	Baseline Finish	Baseline Work	Baseline Cost
0	◢ Software System Implementation	0 days	NA	NA	0 hrs	$0.00
1	◢ Build Project Plan	0 days	NA	NA	0 hrs	$0.00
2	Create Statement of Work	0 days	NA	NA	0 hrs	$0.00
3	Obtain approval of Statement of Work	0 days	NA	NA	0 hrs	$0.00
4	Create project plan	0 days	NA	NA	0 hrs	$0.00
5	Obtain approval of project plan	0 days	NA	NA	0 hrs	$0.00
6	Finalize project plan and definition	0 days	NA	NA	0 hrs	$0.00
7	◢ Define System Environment	0 days	NA	NA	0 hrs	$0.00
8	Determine current architecture	0 days	NA	NA	0 hrs	$0.00
9	Assess processes on the server	0 days	NA	NA	0 hrs	$0.00
10	Assess printer hardware	0 days	NA	NA	0 hrs	$0.00
11	Communicate with integrator	0 days	NA	NA	0 hrs	$0.00
12	Complete architecture draft	0 days	NA	NA	0 hrs	$0.00
13	◢ Conduct Session	0 days	NA	NA	0 hrs	$0.00
14	Send out prep packet	0 days	NA	NA	0 hrs	$0.00
15	Conduct pre-interviews	0 days	NA	NA	0 hrs	$0.00
16	Conduct session	0 days	NA	NA	0 hrs	$0.00
17	Prepare draft document	0 days	NA	NA	0 hrs	$0.00
18	Send out draft and review with key sponsors	0 days	NA	NA	0 hrs	$0.00

10 Save and close your project.

Protect-Saved Baselines

In Microsoft Project 2016, Project Server administrators have the option to lockdown a user's ability to save baselines. Once an agreed-upon baseline has been reached, an organization can prevent a project manager from changing that baseline. This feature is invoked and controlled via the Global Permissions setting for each group (or in the security template for each group). Note: Global permission settings are controlled through Project Web App by a Project Server administrator.

9.5 Communicating the Project Plan (Introduction)

Because communication management is a critical part of the project management process, Microsoft Project 2016 includes a variety of tools to support communication with internal and external clients. This section documents a method of sharing a project plan with team members or clients who do not have Microsoft Project.

Taking a Picture of Your Gantt Chart

One way to use the communication power of the Gantt Chart view is to photograph it and send the picture as part of another document (e.g. e-mail, webpage, PowerPoint).

🗁 This exercise uses the file **Communication.mpp**. Be sure this project is open before beginning.

1 From *Task:Clipboard* click the *Copy* dropdown and select *Copy Picture*. You will be presented with the **Copy Picture** dialog box. This tool allows you to make a copy of the task or resource information that is currently visible (without the ribbon or any surrounding control). This copy can then be pasted or inserted into another application.

Figure 108.

Copy Picture
dialog box

2 The *Render image: For screen* option copies the Microsoft Project view as an image with a resolution best for viewing on a screen, such as in PowerPoint. *Render image:For printer* copies in a resolution best for printing. *Render image: To GIF image file* saves the image as a separate picture file, which can be manipulated in a variety of ways or e-mailed as an attachment.

3 In the *Render image* area of the dialog box, click *For printer*.

4 In the *Copy* area of the dialog box, check *Selected rows*.

5 In the *Timescale* area of the dialog box, select *As shown on screen*.

6 Click *OK*. Except for a brief appearance of the hourglass icon, nothing appears to happen.

7 Launch Microsoft Word and open a blank document. In the new Word document that appears, select *Edit:Paste* (or use "Ctrl-V"). A picture of your Gantt Chart will be inserted into your Word document.

8 Exit Word, discarding the new document. Save and close your project.

9.6 Optimizing the Plan Review Exercise

1 Open the file **PlanOptimization.mpp**.

2 Display critical path information using the Gantt Chart.

3 Apply the Resource Allocation view.

4 Select *Julie Pawlkowski*. In which month is Julie over-allocated? ***September***

5 What is the current finish date for the project? ***1/30***

6 Try to resource level *Julie Pawlkowski* within the available slack.

7 Did this resolve the over-allocation for Julie? ***No***

8 What about the other resources? ***If you choose to level only Julie, other resources will not be effected.***

9 Did the project finish date change? ***No. Some of Julie's tasks were rescheduled to a later date, but because you leveled within available slack, by definition the critical path does not change, so the project finish date will not change.***

9 Apply the Gantt Chart view.

10 Insert a weekly task, *Review plan and make adjustments,* to occur every Thursday with a duration of one hour, starting after the Task 6 milestone and repeating to the end of the project.

11 Set and display a baseline for the project.

12 Save and close your project.

End of Chapter Quiz Questions

1. Fill in the blank: The work plan and schedule are not optimized until the _____, _____, & _____ have been configured to meet the project objectives.

2. What is the critical path and what are critical tasks?

3. Which of the following does the Network Diagram view display?
 a. Tasks
 b. Schedule information
 c. Connecting arrows displaying relationship and sequence of activities.
 d. All of the above

4. How do you create a recurring task?

5. Is it possible to assign resources to summary tasks? Is it recommended?

6. What is over-allocation?

7. True or False: Microsoft Project 2016 stops you from over-allocating a resource.

8. When does Microsoft Project 2016 consider a resource over-allocated?

9. What does the Leveling Gantt view display?

```
┌─────────────────────────────────────────────────────┐
│                                                       │
│                                                       │
│                                                       │
│                                                       │
└─────────────────────────────────────────────────────┘
```

10. How does the automatic resource leveling function provided by Microsoft Project 2016 help deal with resource allocation problems?

```
┌─────────────────────────────────────────────────────┐
│                                                       │
│                                                       │
│                                                       │
│                                                       │
│                                                       │
│                                                       │
│                                                       │
└─────────────────────────────────────────────────────┘
```

11. Fill in the blank: Resources are considered over-allocated and will be leveled if the total assigned work exceeds the total _____ _____ for the selected block of time.

12. What can you do if automatic leveling cannot resolve the over-allocation or if it results in unacceptable schedule changes?

13. What are some techniques that can be used to resolve resource over-allocations manually (select 5)?
 - Increase the maximum units of the resource
 - Reschedule the task that has created the over-allocation
 - Add overtime
 - Adjust task dependencies or constraints
 - Remove the resource if it isn't mandatory to the task
 - Replace the over-allocated resource with an under-allocated resource
 - Make calendar adjustments to extend the working days and hours for the project or resource
 - Decrease the amount of work assigned to the resource

14. What is task leveling?

```
┌─────────────────────────────────────────────────────┐
│                                                       │
│                                                       │
│                                                       │
└─────────────────────────────────────────────────────┘
```

15. How do you create a new Resource view?

```
┌─────────────────────────────────────────────────────────────────────┐
│                                                                       │
│                                                                       │
│                                                                       │
│                                                                       │
│                                                                       │
└─────────────────────────────────────────────────────────────────────┘
```

16. What is the project baseline and what can it be used for?

```
┌─────────────────────────────────────────────────────────────────────┐
│                                                                       │
│                                                                       │
│                                                                       │
│                                                                       │
│                                                                       │
└─────────────────────────────────────────────────────────────────────┘
```

17. When should you baseline?

18. Up to how many interim plans can you save? _____

19. Fill in the blank: Baselining refers to the concept of capturing the _____estimate for your project.

20. How do you apply the Baseline Table in Microsoft Project 2016?

21. How do you set the project baseline?

```
┌─────────────────────────────────────────────────────────────────────┐
│                                                                       │
│                                                                       │
│                                                                       │
└─────────────────────────────────────────────────────────────────────┘
```

22. How can you see a statistical summary of your project information?

```
┌─────────────────────────────────────────────────────────────────────┐
│                                                                       │
│                                                                       │
│                                                                       │
└─────────────────────────────────────────────────────────────────────┘
```

23. Which view displays baseline data along with the current plan and actual results?

24. How many baselines can be saved using the multiple baseline feature? _____

25. How can you choose which baseline you want to use in earned value calculations?

[blank box]

26. How do you capture an interim plan?

[blank box]

27. What is the difference between baselines and interim plans?

[blank box]

28. What is an example where saving selected tasks into a specified baseline can be useful?

29. How do you clear a baseline?

[blank box]

30. What does the Render Image functionality do and what are the different rendering options?

[blank box]

part
IV

Enterprise Project Management

chapter 10

Creating Enterprise Projects

- How Microsoft Project 2016 Communicates with Project Server 2016

- Publishing a Project to Microsoft Project Server 2016

- Enterprise Resource Management

- Inter-Project Dependencies

- Program Management

- Managing Multiple Projects Review Exercise

 Learning Objectives for this Chapter

At the end of the chapter, the reader should be able to:

- Understand how Microsoft Project Professional communicates with Project Server
- Save and publish an enterprise project to Microsoft Project Server
- Build a project team using enterprise resources
- Open an enterprise project in Read and Write file access modes
- Use Project Web App (PWA) to publish a project
- Create a new project from a Project Server template
- Safely save and close an enterprise project
- Save an offline copy of an enterprise project and check it back into Microsoft Project Server
- Define and view inter-project dependencies
- Use multiple projects to define a program (master schedule)

\mathcal{E}verything we have discussed so far was focused on an individual project manager preparing an individual project plan at her or his desktop. Of course in most organizations there are multiple project managers managing multiple projects using shared resources. In this chapter, we will explore the Microsoft Project 2016 features designed for managing multiple projects using a common set of resources belonging to the entire organization. To do so, we will have to first describe how Microsoft Project 2016 interacts with Project Server 2016, which provides the needed enterprise project management features.

10.1 How Microsoft Project 2016 Communicates with Project Server 2016*

*All references to Project Server 2016 can be substituted with the term "Project Online" if you are using Microsoft Project Professional connected to the Microsoft Office 365 hosted environment)

Microsoft Project is no longer a single "one size fits all" product. Microsoft Project 2016 Professional works with Project Server 2016 to provide tools to manage resources and analyze organization-wide project performance. This is referred to as enterprise project management (EPM), since projects on the server belong to the entire organization, not a single project manager.

Microsoft Project Professional supports collaboration and reporting with the option to use the web-based application Project Web App, which allows users to view information and report progress using a web-browser rather than working through Microsoft Project itself.

Earlier in the course we described the high-level architecture of the entire system; now we'll focus on important details of how Microsoft Project and Project Server work together. Project Web App will be covered later, in Chapters 12 and 13.

When Microsoft Project 2016 first connects with Project Server 2016, any formatting elements (views, tables, filters, etc. shown in the organizer) not in the Global.mpt are automatically downloaded from the server to the local computer. Microsoft Project 2016 is a "thick client"—that is, all the information needed to create project views is held locally. Data moves back and forth from Microsoft Project to Project Server when you are working, and much of this is buffered so that your work is not slowed down during this movement.

There are significant differences between projects created and stored locally and projects that have been published to Project Server, as summarized in the following figure.

Figure 109.

Projects created in Microsoft Project can be stored locally and/or stored on Project Server 2016.

Microsoft Project

1. Project
2. Global.mpt
3. Manual resource entry
4. Format, .mpp

Microsoft Project Server

1. Enterprise Project
2. Enterprise Global
3. Enterprise Resource Pool
4. SQL Database
 (MOLAP Analysis)

A project created and stored locally is simply referred to as "a project"; once published, it is referred to as "an enterprise project" to reflect the fact that it is part of a group of projects belonging to the entire organization. Local projects use the formatting instructions contained in the Global.mpt, while Project Server stores additional formatting elements in the Enterprise Global. These elements are automatically downloaded as described above.

Local projects require some form of manual resource entry since each project usually has its own unique resources; enterprise projects can take advantage of the enterprise resource pool in Project Server, which allows resource tracking and analysis across multiple projects.

Local projects are stored as .mpp files by default; the project data sent to Project Server is stored in a SQL database, which allows the use of Microsoft's proprietary Multidimensional Online Analytical Processing (MOLAP) tools to combine and manipulate data from all projects in Project Server. It's interesting to note that there are up to five (5) versions of the project data stored on the server in different SQL Server tables:

❏ **Working** (or Draft) – This is the first and minimum version of the project data. It is what is created and updated every time you save an enterprise project.

❏ **Published** – This is the version that is created and updated every time you publish a project. You will notice that when you publish a project, you will be prompted to save it first. This is to ensure that the published version is never more advanced (more recently updated) than the working version.

❏ **Reporting** – The SQL Server data model for the working and published versions is very complicated and not suitable for reporting or general data retrieval, so the Reporting version uses a much more straightforward data model that is more easily understood. It is updated automatically every time the published version is updated.

❏ **MOLAP** (or OLAP) – This is described above. It contains a de-normalized version of all published project data that is recreated in batch mode as specified by the administrator.

❏ **Archived** – This contains a saved version of the published project data from which a project can be restored. This is a way of erasing a project from the list of displayed projects without completely losing the data in case it needs to be restored.

This chapter will focus on creating and staffing enterprise projects. The analytical tools will be covered separately.

10.2 Publishing a Project to Microsoft Project Server 2016

As we covered earlier, a Microsoft Project file that has been created locally is not an enterprise project. The enterprise designation is restricted to the set of projects that have been published to Project Server. Executives and resource managers can use these to track resource and financial management issues related to projects organization-wide. In the Microsoft Project 2016 environment, projects must be enterprise projects for collaboration with the team or analysis of the portfolio of projects.

There are four different ways to generate enterprise projects: creating a new project on the server, creating a new project from a server-based template, saving an existing project to Project Server, and using the Import Project Wizard.

Setting Up Access to Project Server from Project Professional

To connect to Project Server for the first time, you will need to set up an account to log into Project Server from Microsoft Project Professional.

1 From *File:Info* click the dropdown arrow by the *Manage Accounts* icon and click *Configure Accounts*.

Figure 110.

Configuring access to Project Server from Microsoft Project Professional

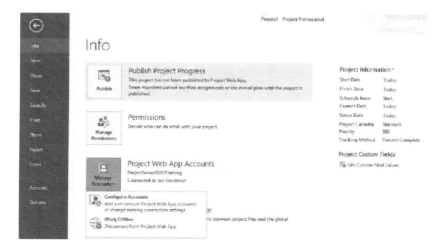

- ❏ If you are logged into a Windows Server Domain, your screen will resemble the figure above, and you will be presented with a dropdown menu option to *Configure Accounts* or *Work Offline*. Select *Configure Accounts* to access the **Project Web App Accounts** dialog box.

- ❏ If you are not logged into a Windows Server Domain, you must click the *Manage Accounts* icon to see the **Project Web App Accounts** dialog box, as in the following figure:

Figure 111.

Project Server/PWA Accounts dialog box

2 Click *Add* to see the **Account Properties** dialog box.

Figure 112.

Account Properties dialog box

3　In the **Account Properties** dialog box, enter an *Account Name*, such as "Office 365 for Project 2016".

4　In the **Account Properties** dialog, enter a Project Server or Office 365 URL. Note: you may need to contact your Project Server or Office 365 administrator for this information.

5　Select the *Set as default account* option if you want Microsoft Project to automatically log in to the server each time you start Microsoft Project.

6　Click *OK* to close the **Account Properties** dialog box and *OK* again to add the new Project Server account.

7　Now, when you login to Microsoft Project Server, your new Project Server account will appear as an option in the *Profile* dropdown list. All you will have to do is select this option and click *OK* to connect to Project Server. Note: If you'd like to work offline (not connected to Project Server), click the *Work Offline* button.

Figure 113.

Login prompt when launching Microsoft Project Professional

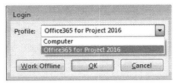

Creating a New Enterprise Project

When you are working online, it is best to save new projects to Project Server.

📂　Launch Microsoft Project 2016 and connect to a valid Project Server account before beginning this exercise.

1　From the introductory screen, click *Blank project* to create a new project plan. The new project will open in the Gantt Chart view with the Timeline displayed above. Your screen will resemble the following:

Figure 114.

New Project With Gantt Chart and Timeline view

2 From *Project:Properties* click the *Project Information* icon to see the **Project Information** dialog box for this new project. Note that this is where you would enter values for enterprise custom fields. Set a new project start date and click *OK* to return to the project.

Figure 115.

Project Information dialog showing the configured enterprise custom fields

3 From the *File* tab, click *Save* and, in the resulting screen, click the *Save* button under the *Project Web App* icon:

Figure 116.

Save button *after* clicking *Save* in the *File* tab

4 You will now see the **Save to Project Web App** dialog box.

Figure 117.

Save to Project Web App dialog box

5 Give the project a descriptive name (notice you have another opportunity to select or change values for any enterprise custom fields) and click *Save* to save the project.

After the project is saved to the server, you will see the project name at the top of your screen as usual.

Figure 118.

Project name

6 From the *File* tab, click *Open* and then click the *Project Web App* icon [🖥]. Finally, click *Browse* to see the list of enterprise projects on Project Server, including your new project (as shown in the following figure). Notice that your project is flagged as *Working*, rather than *Published*.

Figure 119.

Open
dialog box

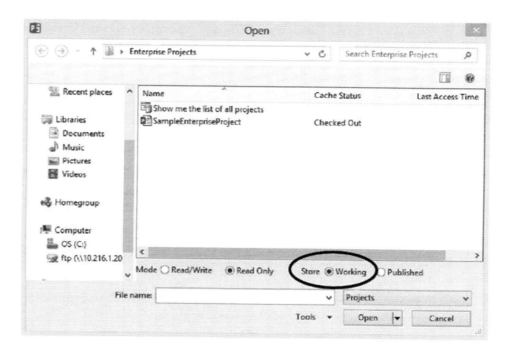

The *Working* option allows you to put projects on the server without sending any information to Project Web App, where it becomes available to team members and executives; however, Project Server administrators can see the file and open it in Read-Only mode. Some project managers prefer not to post a project in this blank state, and so they use the Save As method (described in the following section) after completing the project task list.

You can now begin creating a task list and converting your WBS to a schedule as you did before. When you save changes, the server-based project will be updated but will remain a working draft.

7 Click *Cancel* to close the **Open** dialog box and close your newly created file. You will be prompted to check your file in.

Figure 120.

Project check in prompt

8 Click *Yes* to check your file in prior to closing it.

Creating a New Project with the Save As Method

If a local project is opened and changed, the *Save* command keeps those changes in the .mpp file. Similarly, if a server-based project is changed, those changes are saved to the Server database automatically. To move from a local copy to Project Server, the *Save As* command is used.

📂 This exercise uses the file **SaveAsDemo.mpp**. Be sure this project is open before beginning and ensure you are connected to Project Server.

1 From the *File* tab click *Save As* and then click the *Project Web App* icon to open the **Save to Project Web App** dialog box.

Figure 121.

Save to Project Web App dialog box

2 Name your project **Demo_MM-DD**, where "MM" is the current 2-digit month and "DD" is the 2-digit day of your birthday.

3 Click *Save*. If your project contains resources, Project Server will check them against the data in the enterprise resource pool when you use the *Save As* method. If it finds a match, you will see a message similar to the following:

Figure 122.

Prompt when there is a resource match

The *Rename* option allows you to keep the resource with your local project but requires that you give the resource a unique name, different from the resource in the enterprise pool. The *Yes* option replaces the local resource with the enterprise version, but only the associated resource information changes—not the name.

Project Server also checks the scheduling of tasks and resources to make sure there is no conflicting data. If there is, you will see an alert.

4 Click *Yes to All*. Another dialog box will warn you that an enterprise standard calendar will be applied, which may change the schedule dates of your project (but not the duration):

Figure 123.

Calendar
warning

5 Click *Yes* to allow the enterprise standard calendar to be applied.

New calendars can be created in Project Server by a Project Server administrator, so you may be able to match the calendar you have used in developing the project with one on the server, and the dates will be the same. Projects can use local calendars, but this option must be set by the Project Server administrator; by default, enterprise standard calendars are required.

6 The saving process will take a minute or two, depending on the speed of your connection with the server and the server's current workload. Once done saving, a progress message will appear at the bottom of the screen.

Figure 124.

Status of
Save process
message

When the process is complete, your project will be renamed **SaveAsDemo[XXX]**.

Creating a New Project in Project Web App

Another method for creating enterprise projects is launched from Project Web App. We'll discuss navigating in this tool more thoroughly in Chapters 12 and 13.

In order to access Project Web App you will need the URL to enter into Internet Explorer. Your Project Server administrator can provide this information to you. Again, this will all be covered in much greater detail in the chapters dedicated to Project Web App.

For now, open Project Web App. You will see your home page.

1 From your Project Web App home page, click the *Projects* link in the sidebar or the *Projects* tile to navigate to the Project Center. From *Projects:Project* click the *New* icon and then click *Enterprise Project* from the dropdown list, which includes any available enterprise project templates.

Figure 125.

New project from PWA Project Center

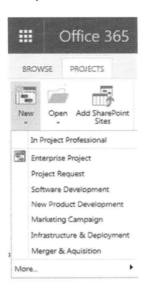

2 You will see a Project Details page, similar to the following:

Figure 126.

New project information entry screen in PWA

Create a new project

Project Request Information

Name *

Description

Business Owner

Project Scope

Business Need Description
Describes the key business
benefits expected from the
project.

Total Benefits

3 Enter the following information:

 ❑ *Name*: "SharePointMigration" Note: If you are in a group training session, add the month and day of your birthday to the end of the project name.

 ❑ *Start Date*: "4/17"

4 Click the *Save* button in the upper-left corner of your screen to save the project.

5 In the Project Schedule page that appears, you will enter new task information by clicking in the *Task Name* field. Note that when you first click in this field, an expanded Project Web App Task toolbar appears at the top of the screen.

Figure 127.

Expanded
toolbar with
Task tab
selected

Note that the Project Web App ribbon is similar in concept to the ribbon in Microsoft Project Professional. By default, the *Task* tab is selected. You may select other tabs on the ribbon such as *Project*, *Page* and *Options*.

In the Project Web App section of this book, we will continue to use the same navigation convention for referencing commands as we did in the Microsoft Project Professional section of this book. For example, to close this project, select the *Project* tab and, in the *Project* group within that tab, click the *Close* icon.

6 Enter the task information specified in the following table. Note that the default fields in Project Web App are the same default fields you find in Microsoft Project Professional: Task Name, Duration, Start, Finish, etc.:

Task Name	Duration	Start	Finish
Design	1m	4/17	5/16
Build	1m	5/17	6/16
Test	2m	6/17	8/16
Deploy	2w	8/17	9/1

7 Drag your mouse to select all four tasks, and from *Task:Schedule* click the *Link the Selected Tasks* icon in the Project Web App ribbon toolbar. This will establish finish-to-start dependencies among the project tasks.

8 Save the project. Your screen will resemble the following:

Figure 128.

Entering task
details

9 From *Project:Project* click *Close*. You will see the **Close** dialog box for
 your project:

Figure 129.

Close dialog
box for
SharePoint
Migration

10 Ensure *Check it in* is selected and click *OK*. You will now see your
 Project Center view, and the new project will be listed in the project
 list and will be available to be opened in Microsoft Project
 Professional.

Figure 130.

Project
Professional
view of project
created in
Project Web
App in read-only
mode

Creating a New Project from a Template

Microsoft Project also allows you to create enterprise projects from templates,
including templates stored on Project Server. For this exercise, ensure you
have Microsoft Project open and you are connected to a valid Project Server
account.

1 From the initial Microsoft Project screen, or from *File:New*, you will
 see several project templates, as well as an option to search online
 for additional templates.

Figure 131.

Project Server
templates
options,
including online
search (circled)

2 Click the *Commercial Construction* template to see more detail about
 that template:

Figure 132.

Selecting the
*Commercial
Construction*
template

3 Enter a *Start Date* of "4/18" for your project, and click *Create*. Your
 project will resemble the following:

Figure 133.

New project
created from
project template

4 From *File:Save As* click the *Project Web App* icon, and then enter
 your project name in the **Save to Project Web App** dialog box.

5 Click *Save* to save your project to Project Server. Close your project.

Creating a New Project Template

Creation of enterprise templates is often the responsibility of administrators or the Project Management Office. If you have permission to create an enterprise project template, open or create a project using the *Save As* method (see Section 5.1: *Creating a New Project*), with one difference: when saving the file, select *Template* instead of *Project* in the **Save to Project Server** dialog box.

1 Ensuring you are connected to a valid Project Server account, click *Blank project* under *File:New*.

2 From *File:Save As* click the *Project Web App* icon and *Save* to access the **Save to Project Web App** dialog box. Enter the template name (for this exercise, type "SoftwareImplementationTemplate") and change the *Type* from *Project* to *Template*. You do not need to provide values for custom fields, even if they are flagged as required fields, since a template will be used to create new projects with different values. Your screen will resemble the following:

Figure 134.

Save to Project Web App dialog box

3 Click *Save*. You will see the **Save As Template** dialog box. You will be asked if you want to discard data that may not be useful in the new projects you will create. Select the data you don't want and *Save* and check the template in.

Figure 135.

Save template options

If your organization has a few major project types, perhaps for different project lifecycle models, and the content of different projects is likely to be different, you will probably check all five boxes on the **Save As Template** dialog box, since you will not want new projects pre-populated with any of the baseline, actuals, costs, etc. On the other hand, if you have a well-structured program where sub-projects are going to be repeated for a number of different deployments, you may want to use the same set of resource rates and fixed costs as you set up in each sub-project. In this case, you would leave those particular data options unchecked.

If you need to change a template, start as though you are going to use it to create a new project. Make changes to the WBS, update task estimates, etc. Save the template using the same name as the original one, again ensuring the *Type* selected is *Template*. This action will effectively update the existing template and any future projects created from the template will use the new information. Of course, any projects created from an earlier version of the template will not be affected by these changes.

Publishing a Project to Project Server 2016

The four methods described previously save new projects in Project Server, but this only creates a working copy, which is not visible to Project Web App users, including team members and executives. To make project plans and assignments visible, a project must be published.

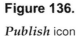 This exercise uses the file **Demo_[MM-DD].mpp**, created earlier in this chapter. Ensure this project is open before beginning, and also ensure the project is checked out (you cannot publish Read-Only files). If you did not perform the previous exercises, you can open and check out **Demo_02-06.mpp**.

Note: It is not possible to publish a project until you have first saved it to Project Server. We have already saved this project to Project Server.

1 From *File:Info* click the *Publish* icon [⬛], as in the following figure:

Figure 136.

Publish icon

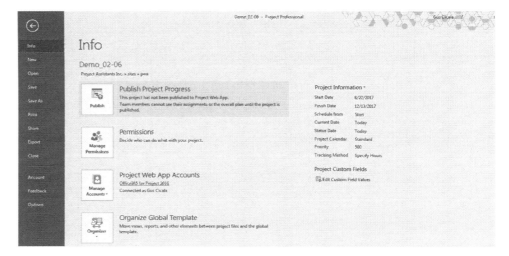

2 An alert may appear, reminding you that the project must be saved; click *Yes* to continue.

3 A dialog box similar to the following will appear, prompting you to create a Project Site for this project:

Figure 137.

New SharePoint site for published project

By default, Windows SharePoint Services creates a unique project site for each published project. This dialog box shows the default settings and gives you an opportunity to change the server used and to make the workspace a sub-workspace of a different project. This workspace provides a "virtual warroom" for the project, a place where a variety of information and tools can be shared with the team.

The project SharePoint site also provides pages for risks, issues, deliverables and document management. We will explore these functions later in this book.

4 Click *Publish*. You will see a description of the status of the publishing job at the bottom of the screen. When the *Publish completed successfully* message appears on the lower status bar in Microsoft Project Professional, the project plan is visible in Project Web App to team members and others with appropriate security permissions.

Safely Exiting Microsoft Project 2016 When Connected to Project Server

It is tempting to simply use *File:Exit* to quit Microsoft Project at the end of a session, but this is not an effective method. Enterprise projects must be checked in individually before you exit Microsoft Project; otherwise, they will be "stranded," or flagged as checked out to you. When you try to open the project again, you will be told you must open it read-only because it's still checked out! This isn't a disaster—you can check in your stranded project through Project Web App—but it is irritating.

1 To avoid this frustration, click *File:Close* for each open project whenever you are closing an enterprise project. If there are no unsaved changes, you will see an alert similar to the following:

Figure 138.

Project
check in
query

 2 Click *Yes* to check in and close the project. If there *are* unsaved
changes, you will see the expanded query shown below. Click *OK* to
save and close the project.

Figure 139.

Save and
check in query

But what if you don't want to check the project in? The project closes and you
can open it again in read/write mode; anyone else with permission to view the
project can open it read-only, not read/write.

Note that when you start Microsoft Project, a blank project (usually **Project1**) is
automatically created. If you are working with other projects, you probably will
not be interested in saving the blank **Project1**. In this case, when you see the
previous **Close** dialog box, select *Discard Changes*.

After closing all projects, you can safely exit Microsoft Project.

Working with Published Projects off the Network

There are times when you will want to work with published files but won't be
connected to the network. Since the *Save as File* button appears in the **Save to
Project Web App** dialog box, it can be tempting to save a published project
locally, but this is not an effective way to work with published projects. Use this
method only to save a working draft or archived copy locally, unconnected to the
project still on the Project Server.

Working Away From the Network

A useful feature in Microsoft Project 2016 is locally caching a copy of the project
which you are working on. In addition to making the process of working off the
network nearly foolproof, it also allows for a speedier interaction with Project
Server. After the original copy of the project (data) is downloaded and cached,
changes only need to be communicated between the server and the client.

1 While connected to Project Server, open **SaveAsDemo[XXX]** created earlier in this chapter (Section 10.2: *Create a New Project with the Save As Method*). Alternatively, you can open and check out **SaveAsDemoJBG.mpp**. Note that once the project opens, you will see a warning above the timeline that indicates the file is currently in read-only mode:

Figure 140.

Read-only mode

2 In order to work with the file, you will need to check it out. To do so, click the *Check Out* button, circled in the preceding figure.

3 From the *File* menu, click *Close*. You will see the **Close** dialog box.

Figure 141.

Close dialog box

4 Ensure the *Keep it checked out* option button is selected in the **Close** dialog box, and click *OK* to close the project.

5 When you are ready to work on your project again, launch Microsoft Project and, in the **Login** dialog box, select the appropriate Project Server *Profile* and click the *Work Offline* button.

Figure 142.

Login to Server to work offline

6 Click *Open Other Projects* (or *File:Open* if you already have a different project opened) at the bottom of the left sidebar. Under the Project Web App heading, click your Project Server Profile name and then click *Browse*. You will see the project you recently closed (in a checked-out status): **Demo_[MM-DD].mpp**.

Figure 143.

List of projects in your cache

Note that the list of projects you see is what is stored on your local machine and not what is stored on Project Server. Those projects are stored in the local cache on your machine. Some of the projects are identified as *Checked Out*. These are projects that you chose not to check in when you closed them during your recent session. The projects that do not appear as checked out are ones you have opened recently and for which you selected the *Check In* option when you closed them.

7 Select your *Checked Out* project (**SaveAsDemo[XXX].mpp**) and open it. Edit the project in some way and again close the project while leaving it checked out. When you reconnect to Project Server and open the project, the data will synchronize automatically. Remember that there is another copy of the project in the database on Project Server. Normally you will update projects while offline. When you connect to the Server and check the project in, the versions between your local cache and the server are synchronized.

8 Now suppose that while you have the project checked out, the Project Server administrator forces a check in of this project to Project Server. The project is now checked in and available to be modified by anyone with proper permissions. Your local machine has the project checked out to you and awaiting check in. What happens when you connect your local machine to Project Server? The Project Server version wins!

Checking In Projects That Have Been Saved Offline

Once you are again connected to the network and able to access Project Server, you can check the projects in that you had checked out while you were working offline.

One method to do this is by opening Microsoft Project Professional in Work Offline mode (see the preceding sub-section, *Working Away from the Network*).

1 Click *Open Other Projects*. Click the *Project Web App* icon and *Browse*. As before, you will see the projects that are checked out (as represented in your local cache).

Figure 144.

Projects that are checked out

2 Select and open one of the checked out projects.

3 At the bottom left of your screen you will see a *Connection* icon []. Click it and select the *Connect to Server* option as in the following figure:

Figure 145.

Connection icon

4 Now click *File:Close*, and you will be prompted to check your project in.

Figure 146.

Project check in prompt

5 Click *Yes* and your project will once again be checked in.

Managing the Local Project Cache

Managing the local project cache is typically handled by the Project Server administrator, but there are some basic features that project managers need to understand. Individual project managers can control aspects of the caching process using a functionality found in *File:Options:Save*. This submenu includes buttons to allow you to view the status of the local project cache as well as change the settings and clean up the cache.

You can view and change the size limit for the cache (although most users will simply let Microsoft Project determine the needed size) and the location where the cache is stored in the *Cache* section of the **Project Options** dialog box, as shown below.

Figure 147.

Cache options

Clicking the *View Cache Status* button opens the **Active Cache Status** window shown in the following figure. The *Status* tab lists all the projects with copies cached locally, the most recent action taken with that project, the date of that action, and whether or not the action succeeded. For unsuccessful actions, the *Errors* tab provides more detail about what happened, which may be useful to the Project Server administrator in helping to correct any problems.

Figure 148.

Cache *Status*
tab

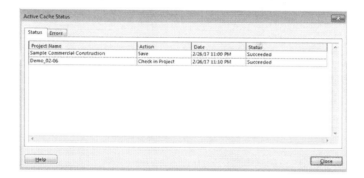

The *Clean Up Cache* button provides details on the cache usage and contents, and it allows you to delete local copies of server-based projects. This button does not affect the project on the server.

Deleting local copies of projects that are no longer needed can save cache space, but this tool can also be used to deal with projects that appear to be checked out but are not listed in the force check in page in Project Web App. Deleting the project from the cache in this situation usually deletes it from the server as well, so you may need to save the project under a different name before clearing it from the cache.

A typical **Clean Up Cache** window is shown in the following figure:

Figure 149.

Cache settings
controls

10.3 Enterprise Resource Management

The enterprise resource pool provides a single place to list all resources that may be available for assignment on projects. Microsoft Project opens enterprise resources when the user opens an enterprise project or checks out one or more enterprise resources.

Projects do not display the entire content of the Enterprise Resource Pool; only resources selected for your project are listed on your Resource Sheet. If additional enterprise resources need to be added, the project manager can use the team builder tool.

But what if an organization wants a functional manager to make the actual assignment to the project team? Project Web App also contains a "build team" function which allows a line manager to designate members of a project team. If the organization chooses to use this approach, project managers will need generic resources as placeholders until the functional manager assigns a specific person to the project team.

Classifying Resources

Classification of resources has become much more sophisticated since the early days of Microsoft Project. Following is a summary of resource classification terminology currently in use:

❑ **Resource Type** – Identifies the kind of activity that is planned or tracked using this resource; options are as follows:

 ❑ Work – Resource assignments have estimated (and actual) work (typically hours of effort) at a specified cost per time period. Units refer to the proportion of time that the resource is assigned to this task.

 ❑ Material – Resource assignments have estimated (and actual) units of consumption at a specified cost per unit (e.g. cubic yards of concrete at $200 per cu yard). Units refer to the number of specified items for the task. There is no work (effort) associated with material resources although under some conditions, the units amount is copied into the work field.

 ❑ Cost – Resource assignments have estimated (and actual) cost amounts for this resource (e.g. consulting fees). There are no units or work associated with cost resources.

❑ **Generic** – This is a Yes/No flag that can be associated with any resource type. A resource flagged as Generic behaves just as the basic resource as far as estimating and scheduling is concerned. However, generic resources are essentially placeholders and so are incapable of carrying out actual work, being consumed as materials, or being charged as costs. Before undertaking an actual task, any assigned generic resources should be replaced with equivalent named resources.

❑ **Local** – This is a Yes/No flag set automatically depending on the source of the resource information. If the resource is derived from the enterprise resource pool, it is an enterprise resource. If it was entered by the project manager in a project, it is a local resource.

❑ **Budget** – This is a Yes/No flag associated with any resource type. A resource flagged as Budget can be assigned only at the project summary level. The purpose of this type of resource is to provide a way of recording a high-level (budget) estimate for the project. The same basic resource types can be applied to budget resources, and you may use a combination of budget resources on a single project to model the various aspects of the project budget. For example, you may have different cost budget resources for capital versus expense and different ones for different general ledger accounts. You may also have different work budget resources for hours of effort by different categories of worker.

Budget resource information is normally applied by using a resource custom field that allows the budget resource information and the "real" resource information to be grouped together in a report. This allows the budget, baseline, actual to date and estimate to completion figures to be seen in the same report.

Using Team Builder

Managers use Team Builder to select resources from the enterprise resource pool before or after a project task plan is built. It can also be used to substitute resources currently assigned in a project plan. You must be connected to Project Server to view enterprise resources. By default, Project Server security allows project managers to view resources and build teams, but the Project Server administrator can change default permissions.

📂 This exercise uses the file **SampleProject.mpp**, the office relocation project we built in the first part of the course. Open this project, or if that file isn't up-to-date with its last associated exercise, you can open **SampleProject_Inst3.mpp**.

1 Save your project to Project Server as **SampleProject_[MM-DD]**, where "MM-DD" represents your month and day of your birthday.

2 From *Resource:Insert* click the *Add Resources* icon [👥₊], and from the dropdown list select *Build Team from Enterprise.*

Figure 150.

Build Team
dialog box

You can use filtering and grouping (discussed in Section 15.2: *Using Tables, Filters, Views, and Groups in Microsoft Project 2016*) to define selection criteria, or you can use the entire list of resources. Enterprise resources are listed in the left side of the dialog box, and generic resources are identified with a blue "head" icon.

Note: In the **Build Team** dialog box, clicking the plus sign next to *Customize filters (optional)* will open a new section of the **Build Team** dialog box that will allow you to filter resources from the overall resource pool. For example, in the following figure the field name is *RBS* (Resource Breakdown Structure), which can be used to select resources from a specific part of the organization, such as a department. In this case, we are filtering for resources from the accounting department.

Figure 151.

Filtering
resources in the
enterprise
resource pool

3 Select the enterprise resources you wish to add to your team, and click *Add* to build the project team as in the following example:

Figure 152.

Project team under construction

4 Click *OK* when you are finished. You will find the selected resources listed in the Resource Sheet view for your project. Switch to the Resource Sheet view.

Figure 153.

Resource Sheet view with added resources

		Resource Name	Type	Material	Initials	Group	Max.	Std. Rate	Ovt.	Cost/Use	Accrue	Base
1		Developer	Work		D		100%	$70.00/hr	$0.00/hr	$0.00	Prorated	Standard
2		Field Searcy	Work		F		100%	$100.00/hr	$0.00/hr	$0.00	Prorated	Standard
3		Gus Cicala	Work				100%	$100.00/hr	$0.00/hr	$0.00	Prorated	Standard
4		Oleg Snurnikov	Work		O	ICC	100%	$100.00/hr	$0.00/hr	$0.00	Prorated	Standard

5 Save your project.

Additional Team Builder Functionality

You can also use Team Builder to remove resources from the project team or to replace one resource with another. Just as before, replace basically changes the resource name and calendar. Team Builder has some other valuable tools:

❑ **Booking** allows you to add resources to the project team while a project is under development and has not yet been approved. By flagging the resource as Proposed, you can reserve the resource's time and make task assignments without sending the assignments to them. If the project is a real one, simply leave the booking value as the default Committed, and assignments can be published to Project Web App.

❏ **Show resource availability** lists the hours of work during a date range. By default, the date range is the project start and end dates. To use this feature, check *Show resource availability*, set the dates (if you don't want the default values), set a minimum availability (optional), and decide whether or not you want to include proposed bookings. Click *Apply* to see the resources that have time available.

❏ **Match** allows you to find resources with the same skill profile as a project resource. This only applies if the Server administrator has defined a skill setting for resources.

❏ **Details** opens the **Resource Information** dialog box for a selected resource in either pane of the Build Team box.

❏ **Graphs** opens a window with a choice of time-phased graphs for selected resources. This can help you identify specifically when a resource is available, since overall availability numbers may not provide the information you need. You can view remaining availability, work, and assignment work graphs for selected resources.

If you need to add local resources to your project team (e.g. for external contractors or materials), always do this by entering their details into the Resource Sheet.

Generic Resources

Microsoft Project 2016 allows you to define generic resources. This is useful when you know the skillset or job title needed for task assignment. Generic resources are often used as placeholders until named individuals can be assigned to specific tasks to replace the generic ones. They are handled much like named work resources, except you cannot create a Microsoft Project Server account or send them assignments via Microsoft Project Server. These resources are often used in project templates or in project planning to support resource planning.

Generic resources can be enterprise resources (that is, they are available for assignment in other projects) or local ones. Generic and local resources are flagged in the **Build Team from Enterprise** dialog box as shown in the following figure:

Figure 154.

Generic and Local resource flags

The Project Server administrator defines whether enterprise resources are generic or not. Another method to determine if a resource is generic is to double-click on a resource in the Resource Sheet to open the **Resource Information** dialog box.

Figure 155.

Resource Information dialog box (with the Generic box circled in black)

10.4 Working with Multiple Projects: Inter-Project Dependencies

Showing an Inter-Project Dependency

If there are logical relationships between tasks in different projects, they can be modeled by creating an inter-project dependency. Consider the scenario where there is a program to install widgets at two sites and completion requires integration testing once the installation at both sites is complete. We have three projects:

❑ *Consolidated Widgets*, which is the overall program plan in which the initial design and final integration testing is managed. This is managed by the program manager who has overall responsibility for the program.

❑ *Widget Installation – Site 1*, which is the project plan in which the widgets at one site are acquired and installed. This is managed by the Site 1 manager who has overall responsibility for Site 1 only.

❑ *Widget Installation – Site 2*, which is the project plan in which the widgets at the other site are acquired and installed. This is managed by the Site 2 manager who has overall responsibility for Site 2 only.

The site installation projects cannot start until the design task in the Consolidated Widgets plan is complete. The integration testing cannot start until both site installations are complete. If all these tasks were in a single project, it would be a simple matter to create dependencies between them. However, because we have different managers for the three projects, they are managed separately. This exercise shows how to build dependencies between tasks in different projects.

🗁 Open Microsoft Project Professional (without connecting to Project Server). This exercise uses the files **ConsolidatedWidgets.mpp**, **WidgetInstallation_Site1.mpp** and **WidgetInstallation_Site2.mpp**. Be sure all of these projects are open before beginning.

1 From *View:Window* click the *New Window* icon []. You will see a
 New Window dialog box similar to the following with a list of all open
 project files:

Figure 156.

New Window
dialog

2 Select *Gantt Chart* from the *View* dropdown list. Then, select
 ConsolidatedWidgets and *WidgetInstallation_Site 1* and click *OK*.
 Both projects will now be displayed in a single window:

Figure 157.

All three Projects
shown in new
window

NOTE

The alphabetic order of the projects in the New Window dialog box
determines their order in the new window. This is not a problem as long
as you remember to create the task links correctly—that is, the order in
which tasks are selected determines the predecessor (link from) and
successor (link to) relationship in Microsoft Project.

3 From *Task:Schedule* click the *Link Tasks* icon to create a finish-to-start dependency from *Plan Installation at Site 1* to *Order Widgets for installation*. Your screen will resemble the following:

Figure 158.

External link between two separate projects

4 Close the temporary project that was used for creating the link between the tasks without saving it. It is not necessary to save this untitled project since we only used it as a temporary device to link the tasks in different projects.

5 From *View: Window* click the *New Window* icon, and this time select only **WidgetInstallation_Site1.mpp**. Notice that the task *Plan installation at Site 1* has been inserted as an external task in this project.

Figure 159.

External task: *Plan installation at Site 1*

6 Now, switch to **ConsolidatedWidgets.mpp** and notice it now contains the external task, as shown in the following figure:

Figure 160.

New external task: *Order widgets for installation*

7 Save **ConsolidatedWidgets.mpp** and **WidgetInstallation_Site1.mpp**.

Note: When you save a project plan with external links, those links to other projects are stored within the project that is linked to it. If the project is not save to Project Server, those links are tracked through the physical file location. Prior to the release of Project Server, the tracking of these links could be challenging if the location or name of the files changed.

When using Project Server, you have the added advantage that Project Server keeps track of the project location, the project name, and the tasks that are linked between projects. This process occurs when you save and publish your project.

8 Close the new project that you created to establish the link between these two projects, without saving it. Again, it is not necessary to save this untitled project since we only used it to link the tasks in different projects.

9 If you wish to keep the master project that you created in the New Window, you can save the file to maintain pointers to the physical locations of the inserted projects. This new file acts like a program plan comprised of subprojects. Try saving the new project and name it **MasterWidgetPlan.mpp** to any location like any other Microsoft Project file.

You also have to save each of the sub-project plans if you want the external links and any other changes to be preserved. You will be prompted to give you the opportunity to save each file.

Figure 161.

Saving the
Master Widget
Plan and the
sub-projects

9 Save and close each project.

NOTE

Links from one project to another must be made to tasks in the projects, not to the project summary tasks. If links are made to a project's project summary task (title), the linked task will not appear in the isolated project. After all, it would have to be Task -1, since the project summary task is Task 0.

The Impact of Changes on Linked Projects

Creating these links between projects shows that changes in one project can impact another. In the widget example, assume that the installation at Site 1 did not go according to plan.

1 This exercise continues the use of **WidgetInstallation_Site1.mpp** from the previous exercise. Alternatively, open **WidgetInstallation_Site1_Inst2.mpp** from your exercise file. Change the duration of *Install Widgets* from "3 days" to "7 days." Save and close this project.

2 Re-open the version of **ConsolidatedWidgets.mpp** used in the previous exercise or open **ConsolidatedWidgets_Inst2.mpp** from your exercise directory. As the project opens, a dialog box similar to the following will open:

Figure 162.

Resolving
updates to
external links

The preceding dialog box shows the impact of changes to an external predecessor of a task in this project. If you highlight the name of the predecessor task, you will see the name of the predecessor project at the bottom of the screen. The detail against the predecessor task shows how the task has changed. In this case, the impact on the successor task (*Order widgets for installation*) is that the finish date would be delayed to 11/7.

As a project manager, you now have several options:

❑ **Accept** – This accepts the change to your project caused by the change to the predecessor project.

❑ **Delete Link** – This removes the dependency on the predecessor task in the other project. In this case, the schedule will ignore any changes to the predecessor task, and different task drivers may apply.

❑ **Close** – This is used to postpone accepting the change for now. You will see the same dialog and prompt every time you open the project until you accept the change or delete the link.

❑ **All** – This selects all the external links, so that accepting or deleting links will apply to all of them. You may consider this option when you have several external predecessor tasks to your project.

3 Click *Close* to close the dialog box, and then close your project without saving changes.

Creating a Consolidated Project

Another way to show inter-project dependencies is to create a consolidated project file—also known as a program file or a master file—to contain a group of related projects. This allows the program manager to observe the plan and progress of all his or her projects in one view without having to create the window every time. Individual project managers can continue to plan and update their projects separately.

If the only goal is to define dependencies between projects, the preceding method works fine; if you want a continually-updating single project window that contains multiple projects, consolidating projects is the better option.

Microsoft Project 2016 allows you to create and publish consolidated projects to Project Server. When you create a consolidated project, Microsoft Project stores links to the projects that have been inserted. When you open a consolidated project, Microsoft Project brings in the information of each of the inserted projects into a consolidated virtual workspace.

Any changes you make to the information in the consolidated workspace can be saved. When you save this information, the changed information still resides within each of the inserted projects.

When you close the consolidated project, you will be prompted to decide whether or not you wish to save the changes. Once the consolidated project is closed, the only information that physically resides within the consolidated project are the links to the inserted projects.

For this exercise, open Microsoft Project and connect to Project Server. Open a new blank project.

1 Set the start date for your new project to be *4/16.*

2 From *File:Info* use the *Project Information* dropdown to select *Advanced Properties.* In the *Title* field enter "AllConsolidatedWidgets." Show the title (project summary task) in your new project.

3 From *Project:Insert* click the *Subproject* icon [⬛], and select **Widget1.mpp** from your exercise directory. Click *Insert.* Widget1 is now displayed as a single row in the **AllConsolidatedWidgets** project.

4 Select the next blank task row in **AllConsolidatedWidgets** and insert the **Widget2.mpp** file into the consolidated project.

5 Finally, select the next blank task row in the **AllConsolidatedWidgets** project, and insert the **Widget3.mpp** file into the consolidated project.

6 Click the arrow [▷] to the left of the **Widget1** project summary task to display the subtasks for the inserted project. Repeat for **Widget2** and **Widget3**. Your screen will resemble the following:

Figure 163.

All
Consolidated
Widgets

7 Save the new project in your exercise directory as **AllConsolidatedWidgets.mpp.**

There are two important features at the bottom of the **Insert Project** window, which appeared when you clicked *File:Insert:Subproject*. The first is that by default, *Link to project* is selected, which means the inserted projects and the consolidated project will change together in real time. For example, if the manager of **Widget 1** makes a change in the plan or updates the project, the change will appear in **AllConsolidatedWidgets**. If you don't want this behavior, clear the *Link to project* check box. The insertion, then, is essentially a cut-and-paste of the project's tasks.

This may seem to be desirable behavior, but communication flows in both directions, meaning the program manager can change any of the widget projects from the consolidated project. Imagine a project manager's frustration if someone else is changing his or her project, especially if this isn't known in advance!

Hence, the second important feature at the bottom of the window: the *Insert* button has a dropdown menu with both *Insert* and *Insert Read-Only* as choices. *Insert Read-Only* makes the communication one-way—the project managers can modify the Widget projects, but the program manager can't. These issues are matters of management policy and preference, but the options exist in Microsoft Project to support either approach.

Figure 164.

Insert Project
options

Publishing a Consolidated Project to Project Server

📂 This exercise continues to use **AllConsolidatedWidgets.mpp** from the
 previous exercise. Alternatively, open **AllConsolidatedWidgets_Inst1.mpp**
 from your exercise directory.

1 From the *File* tab, click *Save As* to see the following screen:

Figure 165.

Save As screen

2 On the right side of this screen, click the *Save* icon to see the **Save to
 Project Web App** dialog box:

Figure 166.

Save to Project Web App dialog box

3 In the *Name* field, enter "AllConsolidatedWidgets" and click *Save*. You should see the warning shown in the following figure. Note: You will only see this warning the first time you try to save this project.

Figure 167.

Warning when saving consolidated projects for first time

Just as with external links (as we learned in the previous section), when you save a master project with inserted projects, the links to those inserted projects are stored within the project that is linked to it. If the inserted projects are not saved to Project Server, those projects are tracked through the physical file location. Prior to the release of Project Server, the tracking of these projects could be challenging if the location or name of the files changed.

When using Project Server, you have the added advantage that Project Server keeps track of the project location and the project name. This process occurs when you save and publish your project.

So, if you want to create a master project on Project Server, the individual projects must be saved to the server first. You can then save the master project to Project Server.

4 Save each of the three inserted projects to Project Server by using the same method we used in steps 2 and 3.

Now, when a project manager opens one of the subprojects and makes a change, the master project is automatically updated.

5 From the *File* menu, click *Close* to close the consolidated project and to check it in. You will be prompted to save changes in the subprojects, as shown in the following figure. Clicking *Yes* means the subprojects will remain checked out (stranded), so it is very important that anyone using the master file clicks *No* or *No to All*, unless the subprojects are meant to be opened in read-only.

Figure 168.

Save published
subprojects
prompt

10.5 Program Management

A group of related projects is called a program. Program managers generally like to be able to see what is going on in all their projects, but they don't generally manage the projects themselves. In earlier versions of Microsoft Project, there were work-arounds that allowed program managers to view current statuses, but they were limited by the fact that master (consolidated) projects tended to be unstable if saved to Project Server. Microsoft Project 2016 offers two different approaches to program management, depending on whether or not the program manager uses Microsoft Project.

Master Projects

As described earlier in this chapter, Microsoft Project 2016 allows you to create a master project and save it to Project Server 2016. Program managers can view the master project to see a cross-section of all their projects. Just as with earlier versions of Microsoft Project, an alternative approach is to open all the projects in the program and combine them in the same window (using the *Window:New Window* command) without saving the master project.

As individual project managers change and update their projects, the master project is updated as well. Reports of various kinds can be prepared from the individual projects or the master program file.

Program Viewing within the Project Center

Another alternative for those interested in a small set of projects is to use Project Web App. Managers who do not wish to use Microsoft Project can still view a subset of the complete portfolio.

The Project Center page in Project Web App lists all the projects the user is allowed to view. These projects can be grouped by any field included in the Project Center view, including a program defining field. If the program manager does not want to use Microsoft Project, this is the easiest way to view related projects side-by-side. In the following example, projects show key performance indicators (KPIs) that display project heath.

Figure 169.

Projects grouped by start date

Project Web App

Project Center

	Project Name ↑	Health Trend	Overall Health	Schedule Health	Budget Health
	ABC Integration ...	↓			
	Apparel ERP Upgrade ...	↓			
	Call Center Upgrade ...	↔			
	Commercial Product Launch Phase 2 ...	↓			
	Construction safety equiqment ...	↔			
	Content Filtering Design and Implementatic...	↔			
	Data Center Relocation ...	↑			
	Demonstration Project ...	↔			
	Dynamics CRM Deployment EMEA ...	↔			
	E-campaign to bloggers ...	↔			
	Employee Retention Tracking System ...	↔			
	Expand raw material acquisition vendor list ...	↔			
	General Ledger (GL) currency update ...	↔			

If the program manager works with Microsoft Project, the manager can highlight several projects and open the related projects together in Microsoft Project all at once by clicking the *Open* button.

All related projects appear in a single window in Microsoft Project as a temporary master project. This master project can be saved to Project Server or used for viewing and communication and then discarded.

Microsoft Project 2016 and Project Server 2016 include a number of tools to help managers work with a subset of projects. But what about senior managers and executives who need information about all the projects in the enterprise? This is where portfolio management comes in, which is outside the purview of this guide.

End of Chapter Quiz Questions

1. What is enterprise project management?

2. What is Project Web App and what does it allow users to do?

3. Where is project data sent on Project Server and why is that significant?

4. What are the five versions of project data?

 _____, _____, _____, _____, & _____.

5. Which of these is updated automatically every time the published version of project data is updated?
 1. Archived
 2. OLAP
 3. Reporting
 4. All of the above

6. What are the four different ways to generate enterprise projects?

 1. _____
 2. _____
 3. _____
 4. _____

7. What is the first thing you will need in order to connect to Project Server for the first time?

8. True or False: When you are working online, it is best to save new projects locally.

9. What is the difference between the *Working* option and the *Published* option in the **Open** dialog?

10. True or False: Projects can use local calendars, but this option must be set by the Project Server administrator.

11. What is the easiest and fastest way to establish finish-to-start dependencies among consecutive project tasks in Project Web App?

12. How do you change a template?

13. When you try to open one of your projects again, you are told that you must open it read-only because it's still checked out, even though you used *File:Exit* to quit Microsoft Project at the end of your previous session. Why is this and what do you need to do differently next time?

14. What are some of the advantages of the "local caching the copy of the project" feature of Microsoft Project 2016?

15. Suppose that while you have a particular project checked out, the Project Server administrator forces a check in of this project to Project Server. Your local machine has the same project checked out to you and awaiting check in. What happens when you connect your local machine to Project Server?

16. What are some of the aspects of the local caching process that project managers can control?

17. Where can you change the size limit and location for the local cache?

18. True or false: Only resources selected for your project are listed on your Resource Sheet in a project.

19. Which tool can the project manager use if additional enterprise resources need to be added? _____

20. What does the "Show resource availability" feature of the Team Builder do?

21. How can you tell if a resource is generic?

```

```

22. Can you link from one project to the project summary tasks of another project? Why or why not?

```

```

23. When is consolidating projects a good option?

```

```

24. How do you insert a subproject into a master project?

25. Fill in the blank: A group of related projects is called a _____.

chapter 11

Monitoring and Controlling – The Project Manager's Functions

- Project Execution – Background

- Tracking with Microsoft Project 2016

- Entering Actual Progress Information

Learning Objectives for this Chapter

At the end of the chapter, the reader should be able to:

- Understand the theory of project execution
- Define the basic information that is utilized to track project progress
- Understand how Microsoft Project calculation options affect tracking of actuals and how Microsoft Project calculates actual work and remaining work
- Use basic features of tracking schedule, work, and cost in Microsoft Project Professional (or Standard)
- Explain the difference between tracking actual progress using %complete versus actual work

\mathcal{T}he project manager's primary functions change once a project has been planned and work is ready to start. Though planning remains necessary throughout project execution to deal with inevitable changes, the most important activities become monitoring project progress and controlling future events by revising the plan to keep the project on course.

11.1 Project Execution – Background

What is Project Control?

All too often, the plan is set aside in favor of "getting some real work done." Effective project control requires that the project manager spend time managing the project using the plan as a road map for the trip. With this map, s/he always knows where the overall project stands during the execution phase. Without a standard for comparison, a project manager cannot understand the meaning of the actuals collected and cannot have any control over the project's future direction.

The baseline plan is the key. A project manager who is actively managing the plan will always know where the project stands in relation to the baseline. In this chapter, we will begin to take a more in-depth look at what it means to be *in control*.

Figure 170.

Elements
of control

Progress Tracking

A very important part of the monitoring activity is tracking—that is, the process of collecting progress information from the project team and entering it into the work plan. The information that is gathered should be accurate and should come from all project resources on a regular basis.

Tracking is often referred to as *collecting actuals*.

Tracking progress provides the first opportunity for the project manager to validate the estimated work effort for the planned tasks. Work is critical because costs connect to the amount of work done, not the time spent doing the work.

As a result of tracking, the project manager can continue to keep the team accountable for the quantity and quality of the project work performed. After all, if the team knows that you intend to measure their progress against their estimates, they will provide the most accurate estimates they can and be committed to them.

Some team members may not be comfortable with tracking at first. They may think it's bad enough you coerced an estimate out of them during planning, and now you're asking them on a regular basis how they're doing. The project manager has to be sensitive to concerns the team may have about the motivation for tracking.

Many organizations are not culturally prepared for the requirements posed by the project manager who wants to track. Since the project manager is often not the line manager for all of the resources, resistance to the idea of tracking may present a problem. The project manager has to consider how realistic it is to institute a tracking process in an organization that is not ready for it.

The Hawthorne Time and Motion Studies – Bell Labs (1950s)

The Hawthorne Time and Motion Studies were conducted to see what makes people productive. The environment was changed to make it bright, cheery, and comfortable. The workers were productive under these conditions. When the environment was made dark, dreary, and uncomfortable, again the workers were productive under these new conditions.

This puzzled the researchers. The unexpected conclusion was that the workers knew that the researchers were watching them, and that's what was making them productive. The theory that came out of this was if you want people to work hard, you have to watch them. This is sometimes referred to as "Theory X."

This tends to have a negative connotation, but it need not be. In reality, people do what they believe to be valued and important. If no one else cares about a plan or schedule or task accomplishment, why should the worker care? And so, tracking does not have to be intrusive or de-motivating; it can be a way of saying "What you are doing is important and matters to me and the organization."

The Seven Levels of Tracking – A Model

- ❑ **Level 0**: No actuals are tracked
- ❑ **Level 1**: Key % complete, make it up
- ❑ **Level 2**: Key % complete, collect from team
- ❑ **Level 3**: Key actual hours, make them up (weekly)
- ❑ **Level 4**: Key actual hours, collect from team (weekly)
- ❑ **Level 5**: Key actual hours, collect from team (daily)
- ❑ **Level 6**: Real-time data collection
- ❑ **Level 7**: Theory X (Big Brother, constant vigil)

Note: Anything beyond Level 4 is likely overkill.

Choosing the Right Approach

- ❑ Level 0 is a total lack of control. If there is no progress information collected, the plan is all-but dead-on-arrival.

- ❑ Level 1 is sometimes used in organizations that resist the collection of progress data. It's better than level 0 because at least something is being tracked, even though it may have only a casual connection with reality.

- ❑ Level 2 is similar to Level 1 except the project manager now collects the percent complete data from the team. Getting the information from the people doing the work gets closer to reality, but the only numbers people automatically agree on are 0 and 100%. The Level 2 approach usually leads to a large number of tasks that are *almost done*, between 90% and 99% complete.

- ❑ Level 3 is getting closer to an ideal approach. Using hours instead of % complete provides better, more objective information about how time is being used and about the costs of the project. This process is usually used by a project manager that sees the need for actuals in an organization that is not culturally prepared for it. In this case, guessing the actual work is still better than levels 0, 1, or 2, although combining this method with Level 2 may provide a good cross-check to help validate the data.

❏ Level 4 provides the project manager with a valuable amount of progress data on a regular basis. We will assume this method in our discussions of tracking with Microsoft Project.

❏ Level 5 is used on shorter projects or in environments where tight budgets or the high cost of resources warrants the use of a more frequent progress check.

❏ Level 6 is becoming more popular as personal computers permeate the work place. There are already tools that automatically log user activity. The problem, of course, is interpreting the meaning of the keystrokes; for example, does sending an e-mail contribute to project progress? Maybe.

❏ Level 7 goes beyond Level 6 to use even more of today's technologies for presence detection and other forms of real-time monitoring that can enable the tracking of project-based activities.

On most projects, a weekly tracking process that collects actual hours is a good goal (Level 4). If this cannot be achieved, something that is better than nothing should be implemented.

Of course, the frequency of tracking depends on the project duration, among other considerations. Tracking a one-week project weekly is clearly useless; it does no good to know the project is falling behind when it is already supposed to be over.

Level 1 and Level 2 tracking are often used because percent complete is fairly easy for the project manager to use with Microsoft Project, and the manager avoids having to get estimated hours or actual hours from the team. There is often latent paranoia in organizations that makes people nervous when someone starts collecting actual hours worked, which is what usually gives rise to the tracking resistance.

Unfortunately, there is at least one major drawback to percent complete tracking: it is almost impossible to measure variances in duration, as shown in the following figure:

Figure 171.

Illustration of percent complete tracking

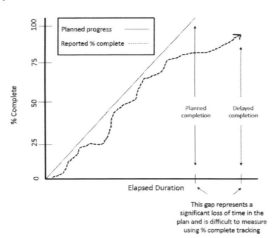

What Will You Ask For When You Track?

If you agree that Level 4 Tracking is desirable and possible in your organization, then the question becomes, "What exactly do I need to track?" The following list of project values and characteristics corresponds to the standards of a Level 4 Tracking procedure.

The project manager using Level 4 tracking needs the following information from the team each week:

❑ **Period reported (such as week-ending date)** – The tracking data has more meaning if you can tie it to a specific period of time. This will allow the project manager to ask questions like "How many hours were performed in February of last year?"

❑ **Actual task start date** – This information is important during the analysis process to gauge if the project is progressing as planned.

❑ **Actual hours worked this period** – The term *actuals* usually refers to this figure. This number is one of the keys to determining if the original (baseline) estimates are still valid. Note: Hours are not always the appropriate measure of time; smaller projects may use minutes and larger projects may use days, weeks, or even months.

❑ **Actual costs incurred this period, if any**– If team members report non-human costs, such as equipment and travel, this information should also be collected.

❑ **Estimate to complete (Remaining Work)** – This important field asks the team member to re-estimate the task based on the work performed so far. The project manager needs to be clear about how and when it's okay to modify the baseline work estimate.

❑ **Estimated or Actual Finish** – If the resource has not completed the work for the task, they should indicate if the original estimated finish date is still valid. If the task is estimated to finish later than originally expected, a new task finish date should be provided. If no work remains for the assignment, the actual finish date should be reported.

❑ **Task-related issues** – Any issues encountered while performing the task should be reported.

❑ **Reasons for exceeding estimates** – If the total actual work plus the estimated hours to complete exceed the original estimate, the reasons for the increase should be reported to help the project manager determine if these reasons will impact other tasks as well.

The real issue, of course, isn't what you should collect and track but how you can do so. Team members often resist filling out paper forms to report the needed data, and most project managers don't have the time to collect and enter actuals data manually. The latter is often the real reason actuals aren't tracked. Most project managers don't consider "data entry clerk" as part of their job description, especially if they recognize the importance of the controlling part of project execution.

In a sense, where your project *is* doesn't matter, except as an indicator of where it's going. If it's not going where you want it to (behind schedule, over budget, etc.), you have to take action to change the future direction of the project, since you can't change the past.

Fortunately, Microsoft recognizes the problems of actuals collection and inclusion, and there are a number of solutions at your disposal, depending on the support infrastructure in place.

Most users of Microsoft Project 2016 will use Project Web Application to collect actuals for tracking. Project Web App represents an automated approach to Level 4 tracking, which frees the project manager to focus on the results, rather than on entering the data into the project plan. The project manager has more time available for the human interaction and follow-up necessary to deal with unexpected results and issues. However, there will be situations where the project manager will not be able to use Project Web App and will be forced to fall back on other tools to collect the necessary information.

11.2 Tracking with Microsoft Project 2016

In this section we will focus on how you can use Microsoft Project for the successful execution of your project through good tracking techniques. Tracking is the first step toward ensuring that you're always ready to answer two questions:

❑ Is the project currently on-time and on-budget?

❑ Based on current progress, can you readily forecast that the project is still expected to finish on-time and on-budget?

Once you have built an optimized work plan, load-leveled it, and captured the baseline, you should be ready to start using your work plan to run the project.

Tracking Options in Microsoft Project 2016

In this section we will explore the options in Microsoft Project 2016 related to tracking and learn how they impact your project.

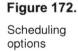 This exercise uses the file **TrackingOptions.mpp**. Be sure this project is open before beginning.

1 Click *File:Options* to access the **Project Options** dialog box, and click *Schedule* in the left sidebar. Scroll to the *Scheduling options for this project* section. Your dialog box will resemble the following:

Figure 172.

Scheduling options

The *Split in-progress tasks* option allows rescheduling of remaining duration and work when a task slips. It is selected by default, but ensure this option is selected so that you can enter the date you stopped work on a task and the date you resumed work on it when you update task-tracking information. Microsoft Project will reschedule the remaining duration and work. This is a local setting saved with the active project.

If this option is not selected, the *Reschedule Remaining Work* tool has no impact; Microsoft Project will simply not reschedule work and will give you no warning. When the option is selected, rescheduling remaining work will create a split in the task.

NOTE

> **If the checkbox is cleared, you cannot edit the** *Stop* **and** *Resume* **fields when you update task-tracking information.**

2 Scroll to *Calculation options for this project*. Your dialog box will resemble the following:

Figure 173.

Calculation options

The *Updating task status updates resource status* option allows Microsoft Project to automatically calculate the actual and remaining work and cost for resources assigned to a task as you enter percent complete information for the task in your schedule. When you select this checkbox, Microsoft Project recalculates the actual work and actual cost whenever you enter information into the *Percent Complete*, *Actual Duration*, or *Remaining Duration* fields.

If you don't select this checkbox, you must enter values in the *Actual Work* field for resources in order to have an accurate picture of the actual work and actual cost. For this reason, project managers often select (or neglect to deselect) this option, which leads to major unforeseen problems, as we'll describe later. Ensure this box is not selected! This is a local setting saved with the active project, so it's important to check any project file you receive to make sure this option is not selected.

When the *Edits to total task % complete will be spread to the status date* option is checked, changes to the *% Complete* field will affect where the status date symbols appear on the calendar bar chart. Increases in *% Complete* will move the status date symbols. When this option is cleared, changes in the *% Complete* field can cause progress bars (the black bars inside the blue and red Gantt bars) to extend through the status date.

Generally, if you choose to use status dates and progress lines, you will want to check this option so the status date and the progress bar will match. It can be misleading to have the progress bar extend past the status date, since that implies future work is completed already.

The *Actual costs are always calculated by Project* option allows Microsoft Project to calculate actual costs automatically, which means you cannot enter actual costs until the task is 100 percent complete. In practical terms, entering an actual cost value tells Microsoft Project the task is done! If you want to enter or import actual cost values, clear the checkbox to turn off all calculations of actual costs by Microsoft Project. This is a user preference option—that is, you'll have to decide if the ability to enter actual costs data during a task is important to your project.

NOTE

> **Turning this setting on will erase any user-entered or imported actual cost values.**

The *Edits to total actual cost will be spread to the status date* option becomes live when you de-select the *Actual costs are always calculated by Project* option. This functions like the total task *% Complete* option; the question is whether you want cost data to match status dates or not. If you want actual cost information to match the end of the actual duration of the task rather than the status date, clear the checkbox.

The *Default fixed costs accrual:* box is used to specify how Microsoft Project sets fixed cost when they accrue for new tasks. The options are at the start of a task, prorated through the task as resources are used, or accrued (charged to your project) at the end of a task. This only affects the spend-out curve or cash flow calculations for the project, not the overall project cost.

3 Click *OK* to close the **Project Options** dialog box.

Track Progress: Tracking Dates versus Tracking Work

There are two different ways to track progress with Microsoft Project 2016:

❑ By percent complete

❑ By using actual work and remaining work to derive the percent complete for the tasks in your project

When tracking using the *% Complete* field, Microsoft Project will calculate actual work and remaining work based on the *% Complete* you enter. Remember the scheduling option *Updating task status updates resource status*? Note: If you are entering actual work and remaining work in Microsoft Project, it is important to understand how this feature can interfere with previously updated data in your plan.

Whenever you enter actual information into Microsoft Project, the scheduling engine will automatically set the actual start and/or actual finish dates. It is important to know how to view, validate, and potentially modify the assumptions made by the scheduling engine.

In Microsoft Project 2016,

$$Work = Actual\ Work + Remaining\ Work$$

If you let Microsoft Project automatically calculate these fields for you based on *% Complete*, the *Work* field will *always* equal the Baseline Work field since a task cannot be completed at 110% or 90% of the original Work value. Consequently, when Work = Baseline Work, then Work Variance = 0.

A work variance of zero means that your actual progress always appears to match your original work estimates—perhaps a nice thought, but real life projects usually don't work out this way. In fact, using *% Complete* as the tracking tool eliminates all five types of variance calculated by Microsoft Project!

We can use Microsoft Project 2016 to tell us when our current task progress (i.e. work) is different from our original work estimate (i.e. baseline work). The key to making this happen is either enter a resource's actual work and remaining work directly in the project (and *not* use % Complete tracking) or collect a resource's actual work using Web App and use that to automatically update the project plan (as described in Section 12.3: *Tracking Progress Using Project Web App*).

11.3 Entering Actual Progress Information

When tracking information is not obtained through Project Web App, Microsoft Project 2016 allows you to enter five different types of actual task information: actual start and finish dates, % complete, actual and remaining duration, actual and remaining work, and actual and remaining costs. As we covered earlier, these are interrelated, and Microsoft Project will use whatever actual values you provide to calculate the others.

Actual task data can be entered through the **Update Tasks** dialog box—using the *Tracking* function on the ribbon—or entered directly into the Tracking Table. Using the Gantt Chart view with the *Details* option selected, actual work and actual cost can be entered in the Task Form (lower) pane. In this section, we'll look at these options and how they work.

Using the Update Tasks Dialog Box

The quickest and easiest way to track manually is to use the *Update Tasks* command. The simple rule is change whatever doesn't match the plan.

Tracking with Update Tasks

📂 This exercise uses the file **TrackingOptions.mpp**. Be sure this project is open before beginning.

1 Switch to the Tracking Gantt view.

2 Select the task *Create Statement of Work* (ID 2).

3 From *Task:Schedule* use the *Mark on Track* dropdown to select *Update Tasks*. You will be presented with the **Update Tasks** dialog box.

Figure 174.

Update Tasks dialog box

Notice that the planned (current) start, finish, and duration for the task are listed but grayed out so they cannot be changed. Only the actual values can be modified.

4 Change the *% Complete* value to 75 and click *OK*. Notice that the progress bar is displayed.

Figure 175.

Tracking Gantt bars after updating % complete

5 Double-click Task ID 3, *Obtain approval of Statement of Work*. The **Task Information** dialog box will open.

Figure 176.

Task information for Task 3

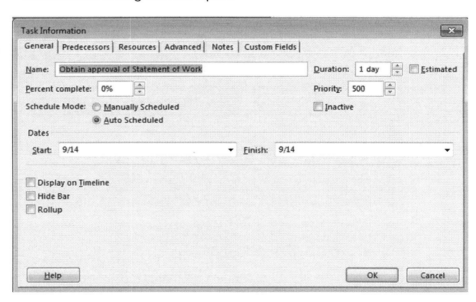

6 Set *Percent complete* in the **Task Information** dialog box to 25 and click *OK*. Notice that the completed task bar for this task once again matches the baseline bar.

Using % complete can be a simple way to track task progress.

The **Task Information** displays % complete on the *General* tab. The **Update Tasks** is a good alternative to enter % complete in **Task Information.** Other useful methods include inserting the *% Complete* field into their Gantt Chart or applying the Tracking Table in the Gannt Chart view.

.

7 Choose *Task:Table* dropdown, then *Tracking*. Notice that this includes many key tracking related fields, including %Complete.

Figure 177.

Applying the
Tracking Table

8 Update Task 5, *Review project plan with team*, to show it went according to the revised plan. You can update Task 6 if you wish, but since it is a milestone, it has no work or duration attached to it. Updating the task will flag it as complete and show the schedule variance between the baseline plan and reality.

9 Select Task 8, *Define System Environment*. To get the project back on schedule, you got the resource assigned to Task 8 to agree to complete the task in three days rather than four.

10 Open the **Update Tasks** dialog box and enter an *Actual dur:* of "3d" and a *Remaining dur:* of "0d." Click *OK*. Your screen will resemble the following: (You may want to zoom in to see the bars more clearly.)

Figure 178.

Tracking by
actual and
remaining
duration

This view was created by applying the Work Table to display the results of the Actual Work and Remaining Work fields.

11 Open **Update Tasks** for Task 8 once again. As shown in the following figure, Microsoft Project has now populated all the other fields—*Actual Start* and *Finish* and *% Complete*—based on the actual and remaining duration values you provided.

Figure 179.

Completed **Update Tasks** box

Notice that the current finish (planned finish) date is now the same as the actual finish: October 21. This illustrates an important principle familiar to every experienced project manager: reality always wins. If there is a difference, actual dates override planned dates.

This approach will accurately provide schedule variance information, but if resources have to work extra hours to get a task completed faster you will have to enter modified planned and actual work somewhere else to get work and cost variance information.

Another approach to using **Update Tasks** is to enter the actual start and actual finish dates. If a task has an actual finish date, what is its % complete?

12 Verify that you have applied the Tracking Table (*View:Table:Tracking*). Select Task 9, *Determine current architecture*. Enter an *Actual Start* date of "10/23" and an *Actual Finish* date of "10/25." Click *OK*. Your screen will resemble the following:

Figure 180.

Tracking actual dates via the Tracking Table

In general, when following the *Update Tasks* tracking method, you only have to enter two values. The exception is a task that is not complete and did not start on schedule, as in our final example:

13 Select Task 10, *Assess processes on the Server* and open **Update Tasks**. The resource working on Task 10, Julie Pawlkowski, agreed to start on October 24 to help get the project back on schedule; it's now late afternoon on October 25, and you are updating the plan for a management review Monday morning. You just called Julie and she said she did in fact start on October 24, so she has completed 2 days' work. Not only that, she thinks it will only take 9 more days to finish the task, not the 10 she originally forecasted. In the **Update Tasks** dialog box, enter an *Actual Start* date of "10/25" an *Actual dur:* of "2d", and a *Remaining dur:* of "9d." Your screen will resemble the following:

Figure 181.

Using **Update Tasks** for a task in progress

14 Click *OK* to update the task data. What does the Gantt Chart view tell you about the project schedule?

Figure 182.

Gantt Chart view of *Assess process on the Server*

Task Name	Act. Start	Act. Finish	% Comp.	ober 22 / October 29 / November 5	
7	▲ Finalize project plan and definition	10/16	NA	35%	
8	Define System Environment	10/16	10/19	100%	wski
9	Determine current architecture	10/23	10/25	100%	Mary Remington
10	Assess processes on the Server	10/25	NA	18%	

15 Save your project.

Ways to Track Other Than Using Update Tasks

Update Tasks is the quickest and easiest way to track progress if you cannot use Project Web App, but there are several other ways, many of which can be more accurate. Choose the one that works best for you, keeping in mind that **Update Tasks** has limitations when it comes to work and cost variances.

Enter an Actual Finish Date for Tasks in the Tracking Table

Microsoft Project 2016 enables you to enter task finish dates directly into your work plan. Paying attention to the finish dates of project tasks will help to:

❑ Better forecast the scheduling of future tasks

❑ Coordinate the work of resources who may have to adjust their schedules to match the changing project schedule

🗁 This exercise continues the use of **TrackingOptions.mpp**. Be sure this project is open before beginning, or open **TrackingOptions_Inst1.mpp**.

1 Make sure you are in the Tracking Gantt view.

2 From *View:Data* click the *Tables* dropdown and select *Tracking*.

3 Select the task *Assess processes on the Server* (ID 10). Notice the *Act. Start* value of 10/25 based on the update we performed.

4 In the *Act. Finish* field, select or type "11/7"

5 Select the task *Assess printer hardware* (ID 11). Enter an *Act. Finish* of "11/17." Note that Microsoft Project automatically set the actual start date by copying the value in the current planned start date and sets the task to be complete (100%). In other words, it adds another day to the task duration. Your screen will resemble the following:

Figure 183.

Tracking actual finish (Tracking Table)

6 Save your project.

Other Tracking Table Options

Scroll through the Tracking Table (or switch to the Task Sheet view and Tracking table) to see the following fields:

❑ You can enter actual and remaining durations in the Tracking Table.

If you know the amount of time that a task has been in progress, and the task is progressing as planned, you can enter the actual duration for the task in the Tracking Table as well. When you specify the actual duration for a task, Microsoft Project 2016 calculates the percentage of completion and remaining duration according to the following formulas:

Percent Complete = Actual Duration / Duration

and

Remaining Duration = Duration - Actual Duration

❑ You can enter actual work in the Tracking Table. If you want to be able to see remaining work, it's best to apply the Work Table instead, since it contains the most common work-related fields.

❑ When you specify the actual work for a task, Microsoft Project 2016 calculates the % complete and remaining work according to the following formulas:

Percent Complete = Actual Work ÷ Work

and

Remaining Work = Work - Actual Work

Entering Actual Work in a Form and Usage View

Forms enable you to enter and display detailed information about one task or resource at a time, unlike typical views where you can enter and display information on multiple tasks or resources. Seeing information in a form view can make it easier to track progress details about a task or resource.

You can use the form by itself, but it is most useful when displayed in the bottom pane of a combination view. This way, the form provides additional information about the task or resource selected in the top pane.

This exercise continues the use of **TrackingOptions.mpp**. Be sure this project is open before beginning, or open **TrackingOptions_Inst2.mpp**.

1 Confirm that you are in the Tracking Gantt view with the Tracking Table applied (if not, from *Task:View* select *Tracking Gantt* and from *View:Tables* select *Tracking*).

2 From *View:Split View* select *Details*.

3 Right-click anywhere in the Task Form (bottom pane) and select *Work*.

4 In the Tracking Gantt view, select the task *Communicate with integrator* (ID 12). Your screen will resemble the following:

Figure 184.

Task Form with Work details in a combination view

5 Mary has reported that she has performed 8 hours of work on the task so far. Enter the actual work for her assignment in the bottom pane. The recalculated values for remaining work will appear in the Rem. Work (i.e. remaining work) field. Remember to click *OK* when you make changes in the bottom pane. Your screen will resemble the following:

Figure 185.

Actual and
remaining
Work in a
form view

The Task Usage view displays project tasks with their assigned resources grouped below them, while the Resource Usage view displays project resources with their task assignments underneath them. You can use the usage views to enter actual work information.

6 Remove the split from your view (double-click the split line or uncheck the *Details* box) and switch to the Task Usage view. Adjust the screen so you can see Tasks 14 and 15 and the associated names. Right-click inside the calendar grid on the right side and add *Actual Work* to it.

7 Under the task *Conduct Session* (Task ID 14), select the resource assignment *Mike Goren*.

8 From *View:Zoom* click the *Selected Tasks* icon [Q]. Microsoft Project will take you to the week during which work on the task is scheduled to begin. Your screen will resemble the following:

Figure 186.

Task Usage
view (showing
planned work)

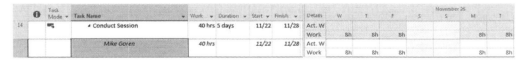

9 In the *Act. Work.* field, enter the actual work for the task. Assume Mike worked according to schedule and did 8 hours' work each day. Your screen will resemble the figure below. Note: Your timescale may look different. The look of your timeline can be adjusted by right-clicking in the top part of the calendar and changing settings with the *Timescale* command.

Figure 187.

Task Usage
view (actual
work)

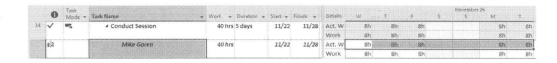

Notice that the actual hours for Mike's assignment "rollup" to the task and the summary task as well. If other resources were assigned to this task, you would expect to see the total hours worked, not just Mike's hours. Similarly, the summary task has other tasks beside this one, and you would want to see the grand total for all those tasks as well.

10 Save and close your project.

Rescheduling the Remaining Work in Your Project

Now that you have entered the actual project progress, the next step is to reschedule the remaining work. If you do not reschedule the remaining work, incomplete tasks will not show as variances.

Rescheduling is also necessary when you are faced with a situation where a resource becomes unavailable for a period of time or a crisis arises that requires a delay in your project. Splitting tasks one at a time to show a temporary stoppage is time consuming, but it is necessary to reflect these delays so that tasks and resources can be appropriately rescheduled. Microsoft Project 2016 offers techniques for rescheduling the remaining work on a project, which we will explore in this section.

📂 This exercise uses the file **RescheduleWork.mpp**. Be sure this project is open before beginning.

1 Notice that several tasks are complete and some—including *Create Statement of Work* (Task ID 2) and *Create Project Plan* (Task ID 4)—are incomplete, as indicated by the progress bars on the Gantt Chart. You have just been informed that all work on this project needs to stop for a few days to deal with a high-priority issue. Consequently, you need to have your project schedule reflect this.

2 From *Project:Properties* select *Project Information*, set the *Current Date* to "8/30", and click *OK*.

3 Let's assume that work cannot resume on your project until September 9. Select the project summary task (Task 0) *Software System Implementation*, and go to *Update Project* under *Project:Status*. You will be presented with the following dialog box:

Figure 188.

Update Project dialog box

The **Update Project** dialog allows you to reschedule the uncompleted work for selected tasks or the entire project. In this case, we will tell Microsoft Project to reschedule the remaining work for the project to start on 9/9.

Caution: While it may be convenient to trigger the Microsoft Project scheduling engine to match the actuals to the plan, in using this technique is not likely to reflect reality.

4 In the **Update Project** dialog box, click the *Reschedule uncompleted work to start after* option, and type or select from the dropdown calendar "9/9." Click the *Entire project* option and click *OK*. Notice that all incomplete tasks now have a split in the Gantt bar to reflect the stoppage of work.

Figure 189.

Gantt Chart reflecting split tasks that were re-scheduled

	Task Name	Act. Start	Act. Finish	% Comp.										
6	Finalize Project Plan and definition	NA	NA	0%										
7	⊿ Define System Environment	8/26	NA	1%										
8	Determine current architecture	8/26	NA	0%										
9	Assess processes on the Server	NA	NA	0%										
10	Assess Printer Hardware	8/26	8/28	100%										
11	Communicate with integrator	8/26	8/28	100%										
12	Complete architecture draft	8/26	8/27	100%										
13	⊿ Conduct Session	8/26	NA	1%										
14	Send out Prep packet	8/26	NA	0%										George
15	Conduct pre-interviews	8/26	8/27	100%										
16	Conduct session	8/26	8/28	100%										
17	Prepare draft document	8/26	NA	0%										George
18	Send out draft and review with key sponsors	8/26	NA	0%										George
19	⊿ Determine Additional Requirements	8/26	NA	1%										
20	Finalize Additional session Scope	8/26	8/29	100%										
21	Communicate sessions to necessary attendees	8/30	8/30	100%										
22	Conduct Requirements Sessions	9/6	NA	0%										Rebecca E

5 Because of the delay in project tasks, Task 5 (*Obtain Approval of Project Plan*) is now scheduled to begin on September 17. But Bernie Frazer has already planned a vacation for that week and will not be able to start until September 26. The other resources assigned to the task will be able to work as scheduled.

To reflect this in your project, split the window from the Gantt Chart view to display the Task Form in the bottom pane. Apply the *Schedule* details in the bottom pane (right mouse click on the Task Form), and change Bernie's scheduled start date for the task to "9/26." Did this create a split in the task? Why or why not?

Your screen will resemble the following:

Figure 190.

Split Task for re-
scheduled
resource

5 Bernie was delayed on his trip by weather. Now he will not be able to work
on the task until October 2. Change Bernie's start date to "10/2." Did this
create a split in the task? Why or why not?

Your screen will resemble the following:

Figure 191.

Split task gap
widened for re-
scheduled
resource

7 Mike Goren will not be able to work as scheduled on Task 9, *Assess
Processes on the Server*. He will not be able to start the task until October
10. Apply the Task Usage view and modify Mike's daily work in the time-
phased grid so that he now begins his work on "10/10" (leaving the number of
hours per day that he will spend on the task the same). Does this create a
split in the task in the Gantt Chart?

8 Save and close your project.

When you select *Reschedule uncompleted work to start after*, unlinked tasks without
progress are not rescheduled. This may leave the project plan in an infeasible
situation. A scheduling message will display to alert you so that you can go into your
schedule and make changes as needed. Also, you have a great deal of flexibility in
scheduling work to restart; you can select any restart date as long as it is after a
task's existing stop date (i.e. when work stopped) or actual start date.

Viewing Progress Lines

To create a visual representation of the progress of your project, you can display progress lines on your Gantt Chart. For a given progress date (or the status date of your project), Microsoft Project draws a progress line connecting in-progress tasks and tasks that should have started. This creates a graph on the Gantt Chart with peaks pointing to the left for work that is behind schedule and peaks pointing to the right for work that is ahead of schedule.

Entering a Project Status Date

When you track progress on your project, you may want to specify the date when the actuals were entered, or pick a date that meets management reporting requirements. Microsoft Project 2016 enables you to enter this date as the project status date in the **Project Information** dialog box. The default status date is the current date.

📂 The following exercise uses the file **ProgressLines.mpp**. Be sure this project is open before beginning.

1 From *Project:Status* click *Status Date*.

2 Type a project *Status date* of "8/14" or select it from the *Status date* calendar. Your dialog box will resemble the following:

Figure 192.

Status Date
dialog box

3 Click *OK*.

Setting Line Styles

The progress line connects to the actual duration of a task. It does not connect to tasks with a start date in the future. It will show progress up to, but not past, the project status date.

4 Confirm that you are in the Tracking Gantt view. From *Format:Format* use the *Gridlines* dropdown to select *Progress Lines*. You will be presented with the **Progress Lines** dialog box.

5 Click the *Line Styles* tab. Your dialog box will resemble the following:

Figure 193.

Progress Lines;
Line Styles

6 Select your preferred *Line type*, *Line color*, *Progress point shape*, and *Progress point color* for the appearance of your current progress line, which will appear at the selected status date.

7 Click the *Show date for each progress line* checkbox. Now your lines will indicate the dates on which progress reports were made.

8 Click the *Dates and Intervals* tab, and in the *Current progress lines* section, select the *Display* checkbox and the *At project status date* option button. In the *Begin at* section, accept the *Project start* default option so that your progress line will reflect the progress made as of the project status date you just entered. Your screen will resemble the following:

Figure 194.

Progress Lines
dialog with
appropriate
settings

9 Click *OK*. Your screen should look as follows:

Figure 195.

Progress Lines

Setting Time Intervals

You can designate progress lines to occur at regular intervals. For example, if you set up monthly-recurring progress lines, you will see the project progress for each passing month.

1 From *Format:Format* use the *Gridlines* dropdown to select *Progress Lines*. You will be presented with the **Progress Lines** dialog box.

2 Click the *Line Styles* tab and select a different *Line type*, *Line color*, and *Progress point shape* for *All other progress lines*.

3 Click the *Dates and Intervals* tab.

4 Accept the *At project status date* default option button selection so that your project lines reflect the progress made as of the recently entered project status date.

5 In the *Recurring intervals* section, ensure the correct options are selected to display progress lines weekly, on Fridays.

6 Accept *Project Start* as the *Begin at* default option button selection so that your project will display progress lines from the very beginning of the project.

7 Click the *OK* button. Your screen will resemble the following:

Figure 196.

Recurring
progress lines

You have the option to display progress lines in relation to the baseline. When you select this option, the progress line connects to the Baseline Start value if the task has not started and to the Actual Duration value for those that have started.

Calculation Options

Options are available that allow you to use the status date to determine when actuals are applied to a task and where the remaining work for that task is scheduled. To access these options, select *Advanced* under *File:Options*, and scroll to *Calculation options for this project*.

Figure 197.

Calculation options

The options are:

1 Move the end of completed (task) parts after status date back to status date.

1a … and move start of remaining parts back to status date.

2 Move start of remaining parts before status date forward to status date.

2a … and move end of completed parts forward to status date.

Option 1a is not available unless option 1 is selected. Likewise, option 2a is not available if option 2 has not been selected.

If *Status Date* reads "NA", the date is not set and the current date is used.

Constraints on tasks are ignored if these options are selected, as actual start always overrides a constraint.

The options are not applied when actuals are set on summary tasks.

These options only apply when making total actual value edits, such as task total actual work, task actual duration, total % complete, and % work complete. For example, if timesheet actuals are sent via Microsoft Project Server, the options do not apply; however, if % work complete is sent, then the options do apply.

End of Chapter Quiz Questions

1. Fill in the blank: _____ is the process of collecting progress information from the project team and entering it into the work plan.

2. Fill in the blank: A project manager who is actively managing the plan will always know where the project stands in relation to the _____.

3. Tracking progress provides the first opportunity for what?

   ```

   ```

4. As a result of tracking, the project manager can continue to keep the team accountable for what two things? _____ & _____

5. Why are Level 1 and Level 2 tracking often used?

6. What is at least one major drawback to % complete tracking?

7. What was the conclusion of The Hawthorne Time and Motion Studies?

   ```

   ```

8. What information does the project manager using Level 4 tracking need from the team each week?

   ```

   ```

9. Fill in the blanks: Project Web App represents a(n) _____ approach to Level 4 tracking, so that using it frees the project manager to focus on the _____, rather than on entering the data into the project plan.

10. Tracking is the first step in helping you answer two major questions:

 _____?
 _____?

11. How do you access the scheduling options for your project?

    ```

    ```

12. What does the *Updating task status updates resource status* option do?

    ```

    ```

13. What does the *Edits to total task % complete will be spread to the status date* option do when checked?

    ```

    ```

14. True or False: Turning the *Actual costs are always calculated by Project* setting on will keep any user-entered or imported actual cost values.

15. The options for *Default fixed costs accrual* are:
 a. At the start of a task
 b. Prorated through the task as resources are used
 c. Accrued (charged to your project) at the end of a task
 d. All of the above

16. What are the two different ways to track progress with Microsoft Project 2016?

 1. _____
 2. _____

17. Fill in the blank: In Microsoft Project 2016, Work = _____ + Work + _____Work.

18. What five different types of actual task information does Microsoft Project 2016 allow you to enter?

 1. _____

 2. _____

 3. _____

 4. _____

 5. _____

19. What are three different ways of entering actual task data?

 1. _____

 2. _____

 3. _____

20. What is the quickest and easiest way to track manually? _____

21. How do you access the **Update Tasks** dialog box?

22. Fill in the blank: In general, when following the update tasks tracking method, you only have to enter how many value(s)? _____

23. What is the exception to only having to enter two values when following the *Update Tasks* tracking method?

24. Fill in the blank: Update tasks has limitations when it comes to _____ and _____ variances.

25. What are the two (2) possible formulas that Microsoft Project 2016 uses to calculate the percentage of completion and remaining duration, when you specify the actual duration for a task?

_____ &

26. What are the two (2) possible formulas that Microsoft Project 2016 uses to calculate the % complete and remaining work, when you specify the actual work for a task?

_____ &

27. What is the difference between using forms and views to enter data?

28. A resource has reported that she has performed 8 hours of work on the task so far. How would you reflect this information in a Work Form in a combination view, and what happens to the remaining work value?

29. True or False: If you do not reschedule the remaining work, incomplete tasks will show as variances.

30. What are progress lines, and where can you display them?

31. What is the project status date used for, what is its default value?

chapter 12

Using Project Web Application for Tracking

- Publishing Project Assignments

- The Project Web Application Home Page

- Tracking Progress Using Project Web App

Learning Objectives for this Chapter

At the end of the chapter, the reader should be able to:

- Publish project assignments to team members
- Recognize the Project Web Application Home page
- Set up alerts
- Track published projects using Project Web App
- Display My Tasks and My Timesheets
- Make effective use of the Tasks Detail page
- Use the Project Manager's Task Time Approval

*H*istorically the single biggest weakness in project management software has been the effort required to update the project plan for tracking purposes. Versions of Microsoft Project as far back as Microsoft Project 98 had some workgroup communication tools using e-mail and, later, web-based communication. Tracking via e-mail requires that the project manager becomes or hires a data entry clerk to continually update the plan and enter actuals. Experienced project managers learn that, during project execution, their time is better spent revising and updating the project plan to keep the project on track, so actuals submitted on paper or by e-mail often don't end up being used to update the project plan.

Microsoft Project 2016 is designed to provide broad-based communication via the Internet using Microsoft Project Server 2016. Though e-mail is no longer offered as a collaboration option in Microsoft Project 2016, the *Send To* command is still available from the *File* menu. The Microsoft Project *Send To* command is similar to the *Send* command in other applications in the Microsoft Office group: it opens a new mail message window where you can compose a message and attach a picture of the active project window.

For effective project collaboration, team members use Microsoft Project Web App to view project plans and report actuals through Internet Explorer. Project Web App communication provides tools at the program and enterprise levels as well, as covered in the preceding chapter. These tools provide executives with information about project status and resource utilization without having to use Microsoft Project.

This chapter will focus on the tracking tools available through Project Web App, and the next chapter will describe the additional features and tools available through Web App.

12.1 Publishing Project Assignments to Team Members

Microsoft Project 2016 uses Project Web App to exchange project information with team members who do not have Microsoft Project themselves. Project managers know that early involvement and participation in detailed planning builds commitment to project tasks and goals; unfortunately, they are often forced into a position of either scheduling face-to-face meetings with busy team members or just telling them what has been decided. The tools in Microsoft Project 2016 support true two-way communication with team members.

The tracking process begins with the project manager publishing assignments to Project Server. We will review how the plan is created and published, and then describe how team members view and respond to the assignments. Finally, we will discuss how the project manager incorporates the information into the original Microsoft Project 2016 plan.

The creation of project assignments consists of four steps:

❑ **Develop the plan** – Put together a list of tasks that need to be performed and create a schedule.

❑ **Add necessary resources** – Assemble the team needed to perform the tasks using the enterprise resource pool.

❑ **Make assignments** – Create a connection between each task and the necessary resource(s) using the Assign Resources command in Microsoft Project.

❑ **Publish the project** – Export the task and assignment information to Project Server.

Once the project is published, team members will access Project Server so that they can use Project Web App to respond.

12.2 The Project Web App Home Page

Project Web App (PWA) is a browser-based SharePoint application that provides access to information on Microsoft Project Server. Project Web App is used primarily by people who do not need the full power and requisite knowledge required by the Microsoft Project scheduling engine. PWA users typically include team members, resource managers, project stakeholders, and other such roles

Team members who do not have, or know how to use, Microsoft Project may need access to the information that will help them do their part in the project. Project Web App was developed to make project information available to team members and to enable them to contribute information to the project using only their web browser. These days, most people know how to browse the web, and the features and uses of Project Web App are easily mastered.

The project manager uses Project Web App as a message center and to collect information about project progress. They can even simultaneously use it in their role as a team member on someone else's project!

Microsoft Project Web App requires each user to have Internet Explorer and appropriate permissions from the Project Server administrator. Project managers and team members automatically have accounts created for them when they are added to the enterprise resource pool.

Viewing Your Home Page:

1 Launch Internet Explorer, enter the Project Server URL in the address bar, and click *Go*. You may also receive the URL in an e-mail, or Project Web App may be added to your list of browser favorites.

Note to users accessing Project Online from Office 365: Refer to the following sub-section, *Accessing Project Online from Office 365*.

Your Home page will resemble the following:

Figure 198.

Sample
Microsoft
Project Web
App Home
page

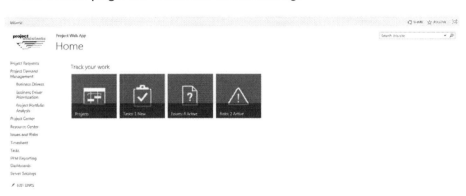

Each person's Home page is unique and has their name in the upper right hand corner. The exact content of the Home page is determined by the role each person plays—e.g. team member, project manager, resource manager, administrator—and the appearance can be modified by the Project Server administrator. By default, all home pages contain a Quick Launch sidepane to the left, which lists the pages and tools you can access.

"Tiles" that help you perform tasks and find options quickly are new as of Microsoft Project 2013. The arrangement of these tiles on your Home page is called the *carousel.* As you can see in the preceding figure, an un-customized PWA site provides two rows of these tiles, with options to *Get Started* and *Track your work*.

Project Server 2016 continues the use of the ribbon presentation for function selection. Note that the Home page includes a search tool in the upper-right corner.

Accessing Project Online from Office 365

Note: This section applies only to Project Online users (not Microsoft Project Server on-premise implementations).

1 Go to portal.microsoftonline.com to access your Office 365 login screen.

Figure 199.

Office 365 login screen

2 Enter your login information (email and password) and click *Sign in* to log in to Office 365. The toolbar at the top-right of your screen will resemble the following:

Figure 200.

Office 365 application tiles icon

3 Click the Application Tiles icon on the upper-left corner of the Office 365 page and click on *Project*.

Figure 201.

Office 365
applications list of
licensed
applications

You should now see your Project Online Home page:

Figure 202.

Project Web App

The Project Center

A frequently used link is the *Project Center*. You can access the Project Center either by clicking the *Project Center* link in the sidebar or by clicking the *Projects* tile in the carousel.

Note: The sample projects in this section have been published to the Microsoft Project Server environment that was used to write this training material. If you want your screens to look exactly as they appear in this book, you first need to publish the appropriate exercise files to a Microsoft Project Server or Office 365 Project Online environment to which you have access.

Figure 203.

Two links to the Project Center

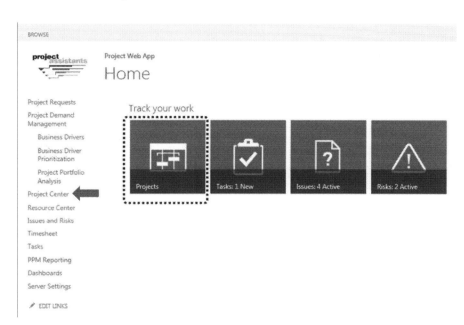

In the *Project Center*, you will see a list of the projects you have permission to view. Notice the fluent ribbon interface has a *Browse* tab and a *Projects* tab (with function buttons collapsed).

Figure 204.

The Project Center view

1 Click the *Projects* tab to display the ribbon options, which are visible in the following figure.

Figure 205.

Project Center
with *Projects*
displayed

2 In the list of projects in the Project Center, click on the project name
 Commercial Product Launch Phase 2 link to navigate to the Project Details
 page for that project.

Figure 206.

Project Details
page

3 Click *Projects* in the ribbon to activate the function icons. From *Project:Navigate* click the *Project Site* icon [] to access the SharePoint workspace for the selected project. The Project Site will open in a new window, as in the following figure:

Figure 207.

Sample Project Site stored in SharePoint

4 Click on *Projects* on the left-side list of functions to close the Project Site to and return to your primary Project Center view.

Adding an Alert

There are several features on the Project Center page that you can personalize. If you are not already there, navigate to your Project Center (to see how, refer to the opening of the preceding sub-section, *Project Center*).

1 In the upper-right corner of your screen, click the settings sprocket and select *PWA Settings*.

Figure 208.

PWA Settings option

You will see a view that resembles the following:

Figure 209.

People and
Groups –
User
Information
view

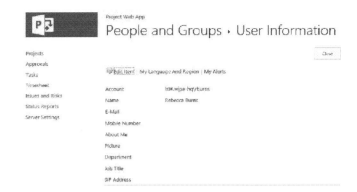

2 Click *My Alerts* to navigate to the My Alerts on this Site page.

3 Click *Add Alert*. Your screen will resemble the following:

Figure 210.

New Alert
submenu

4 Select the *Project Detail Pages* option, and click *Next* at the bottom of the
 page. You will see the New Alert page.

Figure 211.

New Alert page

5 Complete this page as follows:

❑ *Alert Title*: Project Detail Pages (default)

❑ *Delivery Method*: Email (default)

❑ *Change Type*: All changes (default)

 ❑ *Send Alerts for These Changes*: Someone else changes a document

 ❑ *When to Send Alerts*: Send notification immediately (default)

6 Click *OK* to establish your alert. You will now be notified by email every time someone other than you changes a document on a Project Details page for one of the projects to which you are assigned.

My Queued Jobs

As requests for action reach Project Server, they take their place in a queue (like the spooler function in a printer). Project Server maintains two separate queues: one for information related to saving, publishing, reporting and OLAP cube building, and another for timesheet information. If you select this option and receive notification that a job in your queue has failed, you can click on *error details* for more information. Be warned, however, that what you will usually get is the actual coding associated with the failed action, which may be more detail than you want.

1 Click the *Server Settings* link in the sidebar to see the PWA Settings page, similar to the following:

Figure 212.

PWA Settings page

2 Under *Personal Settings* click see the *My Queued Jobs* link. You will see a list of jobs currently in the Project Server queue.

Figure 213.

List of jobs in the Project Server queue

3 Use the *View* dropdown list to select the job category you prefer (available options are displayed in the preceding figure). Project Server will provide a list of all jobs of the selected type that are currently in the queue.

12.3 Tracking Progress Using Project Web App

Tracking progress has different implications for different roles and groups within an organization. Additionally, different organizations require different levels of detail. Consider the following roles:

- ❏ **Project Manager** – Project managers are typically interested in the progress on tasks for a particular project. They will be concerned with knowing that past tasks were finished on time, that the expected level of work (and cost) is being applied to present ones, that the total work (and cost) is in line with the original estimate, and that they will finish on time.

 It is quite possible that the team member doing the work is also working on other projects. The project manager will have little interest in work on someone else's project, provided that work does not interfere with progress on his or her own project.

- ❏ **Resource Manager** – The manager of a department is typically interested in the utilization of his or her department members. Are they fully utilized (on project work or otherwise)? Are they not working because of leave, etc.? If they are working overtime, how is that to be approved and funded? The resource manager may not be interested in the exact project tasks but is likely to be concerned with the amount of each type of work. This will probably have to be reconciled with the original estimates for the number of staff required to meet the department's different obligations.

- ❏ **Team Member** – The person actually doing the work may be concerned with showing that they are carrying out a full day's work or that they are legitimately off work. They would also like reassurance that their managers are aware of their workload and are taking care to balance it out.

Also, senior management is interested in high-level performance statistics, such as the balance of workload between departments or cost-effective use of skilled resources across the organization.

As a result of these different motivations, the people filling these roles often make different choices about what should be reported, making it generally a governance decision to determine how actual time spent by team members should be reported.

The method for reporting time spent on assignments is decided centrally and configured by the Project Server administrator. There are two basic approaches:

- ❏ Enter time against *task updates* only. The task update option is aimed at providing nothing but task update information from the team member to the project manager(s).

- ❏ Enter time in a *timesheet* against tasks and non-project (or administrative) time. The timesheet option is aimed at providing use of time information from the team member to the resource manager. This is for a managed reporting period (e.g. a week) and includes non-project work.

Assignments are listed on the Tasks page, which you can access from either the *Tasks* link in the sidepane or the *Tasks* tile in the Carousel.

The task update entries and timesheet entries can be entered separately and synchronized using the import method. The Project Server administrator can set the Single Entry Mode option on the server, which combines timesheet and task update information into a single entry view.

After the project manager publishes the assignment information, each team member receives an e-mail message with a link to Project Web App (unless this notification is turned off).

In addition to the task assignments from the projects, task updates and timesheets will also display administrative time categories that have been set up by the Project Server administrator.

The following figure shows an example of how the Project Server administrator sets administrative time:

Figure 214.

Configuring
Administrative
Time pane

Displaying My Tasks and My Timesheets

Team members can view individual task assignments on their personal *Tasks* page, which is accessed either by an e-mail link or from the Home page.

1 From your Project Web App Home page, click *Tasks* in the sidebar or click the *Tasks* tile in the carousel.

Figure 215.

Links to the
Tasks page
(note the *Tasks*
tile is
configured to
alert you to
newly assigned
tasks)

A grid view similar to the following figure appears by default, listing basic data about each task, grouped (by default) by project. As is generally the case with PWA views, sections of the view can be collapsed or expanded. You can select a field for sorting by clicking on the column heading.

Figure 216.

My Tasks
page with
New
and Updated
tags

	ⓘ	Task Name	Start	Finish	Work	Actual Work ↑
		‹Planning Window: Completed	1/5/2015	7/29/2016	438h	438h
		‹Project Name: Company Web Site (Agile)	1/5/2015	12/2/2015	125h	125h
☐		Concept Creation	1/5/2015	9/24/2015	12h	12h
☐		System in Use	12/1/2015	12/2/2015	22h	22h
☐		Acceptance Test	6/30/2015	8/4/2015	32h	32h
☐		Requirements Specification	1/15/2015	10/29/2015	59h	59h
		‹Project Name: Company Web Site 2	1/5/2015	7/29/2016	169h	169h
☐		System in Use	7/29/2016	7/29/2016	0h	0h
☐		Acceptance Test ⊡ NEW	6/29/2015	8/20/2015	40h	40h
☐		Concept Creation	1/5/2015	10/8/2015	57h	57h
☐		Requirements Specification	1/15/2015	2/18/2016	72h	72h
		‹Project Name: Router Benchmark System ‹	8/3/2015	9/24/2015	144h	144h
☐		Distribute lessons learned	8/3/2015	9/24/2015	144h	144h

2 Click on the *Tasks* in the ribbon to reveal the function buttons. From *Tasks:Period* click the *Select Period* icon [⊞] to access the **Select Period** dialog box, where you can specify the timesheet period you would like to see.

Note: The Project Server administrator can control which time periods are available for display. For example, time periods in the past may be closed and therefore cannot be updated. The same may be true for time periods beyond the active current accounting period.

Your view will resemble the following:

Figure 217.

Select Period
dialog box

3 Click *OK* or *Cancel* to close this dialog box and return to your *Tasks* page.

4 From *Tasks:Display* click the *Layout* button [▣], and then select *Gantt Chart* as follows:

Figure 218.

Selecting the
Gantt Chart
view

Notice the commands on the ribbon include *Zoom In*, *Zoom Out*, and *Scroll to Task*, each of which is familiar to Microsoft Project users. Other team members, however, might need an explanation of the meaning of a Gantt Chart and the use of these tools.

5 From *Tasks:Display* click *Layout* and then select *Timephased Data* to return to your original (default) view.

The ribbon includes selections for filtering and grouping displayed tasks, as in the following figure:

Figure 219.

View options

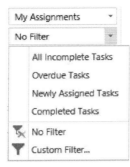

Depending on the level of the reporting detail for the organization, some fields will be grayed out where data cannot be changed. You can enter the appropriate Actual Work values for the selected task as in the following figure:

Figure 220.

Entering actual work

You may also change the Remaining Work value if appropriate. This is sometimes necessary, since the Remaining Work value is automatically recalculated after entering your actual hours, so you may notice that the newly calculated value is too low (you estimate the task will take longer) or too high (the task will take less time to complete). For example, if the timesheet still shows there are remaining hours after entering your actual hours for an already completed task, you can manually change the remaining hours to "0."

Remember to click *Save* after entering or changing information in this view.

Figure 221.

Remaining work ("ETC")

6 Click on a task name to see a detail page for the selected task. Here, a team member can enter additional task information and comments. Again, remember to click *Save* after entering or changing information on this page. The Tasks Detail page will resemble the following:

Figure 222.

Tasks Detail page for *Requirements Specification*

Functions and information on the Tasks Detail page for a specific task include:

❑ **General Details** – View and update basic task information such as total work, percent complete, start, finish, and remaining work

❑ **Recent Task Changes** – View the history of task changes, updates, and approvals

❑ **Attachments** – View, add, or edit related information such as documents, issues, or risks

❑ **Contact** – Contact your project manager, others assigned to this task, or project team members

❑ **Related Assignments** – View related assignments with enterprise resources assigned. To view contact options, click on the resource name

❑ **Notes** – Free-form text area where you can add, enter, and view notes related to the task

7 Once task information is updated on the Tasks Detail form for a specific task, users can submit the updated information to the project manager by clicking *Save* and then *Send*.

To submit updated information, from the Tasks main page select *Send Task Status*. To do so, from *Tasks:Submit* click the *Send Status* icon [🗎] and select either *All Tasks* or *Selected Tasks*.

Figure 223.

Send Status
dropdown

Timesheet Page

Project Web App includes a separate timesheet function that can be connected to an organization's accounting system. Many organizations also like to have a timesheet approval process in place, potentially delaying updates the project manager needs, so these functions are now separated. Users can update information on the Tasks or Timesheet pages first and import the data from one location to the other.

1 From the Project Center, select a project by clicking in the empty white box to the far left of the Project Name.

Figure 224.

The Project
Center

2 From the Quick Launch sidebar, click the *Timesheet* link. Your screen will resemble the following:

Figure 225.

Timesheet

3 Click the *Timesheet* tab to view all Timesheet ribbon options.

Figure 226.

Timesheet ribbon options

4 From *Timesheet:Period* click the *Select Period* icon where you can select one of the predefined options.

Figure 227.

Select Period options

5 Alternatively, click *Select Period* to view the **Select Period** dialog box.

Figure 228.

Select Period dialog

6 In the **Select Period** dialog box, select a date in the period for which you want to report. Click *OK*. A table of your tasks will appear, similar to the following, pre-populated with your assignments for the selected period and with administrative tasks pre-defined for the organization.

Figure 229.

Table of tasks

7 Use the options in *Timesheet:Tasks:Add Row* to select additional tasks not displayed or, if permitted, to specify a new Personal Task.

Figure 230.

Add Row

8 If your organization does not use Single Entry mode for task updates and timesheets, you can import the values from the timesheet to the task updates view using the *Import Task* functionality. To do so, select *Tasks* in the sidebar, and from *Tasks:Tasks* click the *Import* icon [🖼️] to see the Import Timesheet page.

Figure 231.

Import Timesheet page, top portion

9 Use the *Timesheet* dropdown arrow to select the timesheet period you want to import. Then, preview the current task status as well as the number of hours that will be imported from the timesheet. Next, click the *Submit* checkbox if you want to submit the previewed tasks to your manager. Finally, add any desired comments, and click *Import*.

Another important function accessed through the Timesheet page includes the following:

❑ **Replace Actual with Planned** – This is used when the time to be reported closely matches the planned work. The planned values are duplicated in the Actual Work fields, and the user can edit them to the correct values. This function is accessed via *Options:Tasks:Import*.

When all Timesheet entries are complete, and you are at the end of the reporting period, click *Timesheet:Submit:Send* and then click the *Turn In Final Timesheet* option to forward the timesheet to your resource manager. This action closes the timesheet to new entries.

Task Time Approval

Once a team member submits actuals, the project manager reviews and accepts or rejects the data and updates the project plan.

1 Project managers are notified of pending approvals via the Project Web App home page. By default, the *Approvals* tile in the carousel notes the number of approvals that are pending:

Figure 232.

One update requires the project manager's approval

2 To approve or reject timesheet updates, click the *Approvals* tile or the *Approvals* link in the Quick Launch sidebar. You will see a list of items awaiting your approval, similar to the following:

Figure 233.

Task Updates page

3 On this page, you have the option to select one or more of the entries in the table, as well as *Accept*, *Reject*, or *Preview Updates*. *Preview Updates* shows what the impact on the project would be if the selected updates were accepted, as in the following example:

Figure 234.

Previewing updates

4 You will notice the Approval Preview page opens in a new window. You can switch between the Approvals window and the Preview window, making changes in the former and refreshing the latter to see the effect of different approval scenarios.

5 Actuals represent reality, so the project manager will generally accept this data. The exception, of course, would be obvious errors, like 40 hours' work reported on Monday. To accept (or reject) some or all of the updates, click the *Accept* (or *Reject*) icon under *Approvals:Actions* for the selected entries in the *Approval* table.

Figure 235.

Approval: Actions

6 You will see a **Confirm Approval** dialog box, similar to the following, where you can enter comments for your team members if you wish.

Figure 236.

Confirm Approval dialog box

7 Click *OK* to confirm the update approval.

8 Any entries that are still waiting for approval or rejection will remain. If there are none, you will see the following message: "There are no new approvals to review at this time. If you have published your plan and still do not see approvals, have your resources submit updates from 'Tasks' or 'Timesheet.'"

As in Project Server 2010, task updates are applied to the project through processing on the server.

If you have the project checked out in Microsoft Project Professional at the time you are accepting updates to it, the updates will not be applied until the project is checked in. You can, however, see the *Update* job queued in Project Web App (*Server Settings:My Queued Jobs*).

Once the project is checked in, you will see the updated actuals when you next open Microsoft Project Professional or Project Web App.

End of Chapter Quiz Questions

1. True or False: Microsoft Project 2016 cannot use Project Web App to exchange project information with team members unless they have Microsoft Project themselves.

2. What four steps does the creation of project assignments consist of?

 1. _____
 2. _____
 3. _____
 4. _____

3. – 6. Match the step listed in the left column of the table below, to the correct description from the right column, by entering the letter that the step corresponds to in the blank line.

3. Develop the plan ____	A. Assemble the team needed to perform the tasks using the enterprise resource pool.
4. Add necessary resources ____	B. Create a connection between each task and the necessary resource(s) using the Assign Resources command in Microsoft Project.
5. Make assignments ____	C. Export the task and assignment information to Project Server.
6. Publish the project ____	D. Put together a list of tasks that need to be performed and create a schedule.

7. What are the most common features of Project Web Application used by project managers?

8. Fill in the blank: Project managers and team members automatically have accounts created for them when they are added to the _____ _____ _____.

9. What will you see in the Project Center?

10. How do you access the SharePoint workspace for a selected project?

11. How do you access the My Settings options?

12. How do you add an alert in PWA?

```
┌─────────────────────────────────────────────────────────────┐
│                                                               │
│                                                               │
│                                                               │
│                                                               │
│                                                               │
└─────────────────────────────────────────────────────────────┘
```

13. Fill in the blank: As requests for action reach Project Server, they take their place in the _____ _____.

14. What are the two basic approaches for reporting time spent on assignments?

 1. _____

 2. _____

15. What does the task update approach provide?

```
┌─────────────────────────────────────────────────────────────┐
│                                                               │
│                                                               │
│                                                               │
└─────────────────────────────────────────────────────────────┘
```

16. What does the timesheet approach provide?

```
┌─────────────────────────────────────────────────────────────┐
│                                                               │
│                                                               │
│                                                               │
└─────────────────────────────────────────────────────────────┘
```

17. Which page lists assignments, and how can you access it in PWA?

```
┌─────────────────────────────────────────────────────────────┐
│                                                               │
│                                                               │
│                                                               │
└─────────────────────────────────────────────────────────────┘
```

18. What does Single Entry Mode do and who can set it as an option?

```
┌─────────────────────────────────────────────────────────────┐
│                                                               │
│                                                               │
│                                                               │
└─────────────────────────────────────────────────────────────┘
```

19. Why would you want to change the Remaining Work value in the My Tasks view?

```
[                                                                    ]
```

20. What are some of the things that you can view and update in the General Details section of the Tasks Detail page for a specific task in PWA?

21. How do you submit updated information, from the Tasks main page?

```
[                                                                    ]
```

22. What are some of the benefits of the timesheet function of PWA?

```
[                                                                    ]
```

23. What function on the timesheet page should you use if the time to be reported closely matches the planned work, and how can you access it?

```
[                                                                    ]
```

24. What is the final step when all timesheet entries are complete when?

```
[                                                                    ]
```

25. How can the project manager review and accept or reject the data and update the project plan?

```
[                                                                    ]
```

26. How do you see what the impact on the project would be prior to accepting?

```
[                                                                    ]
```

chapter 13

Other Features in Project Web Application

- Organizing and Viewing Information in Project Web App

- Web-based Projects

- Team Builder

- Resource Engagements

- Risks, Issues, Deliverables, and Documents

- Project Details

- Publishing a Task List in SharePoint

- Reporting

- The Business Intelligence Center

- Project Web App Review Exercise

Learning Objectives for this Chapter

At the end of the chapter, the reader should be able to:

- Understand basic Project Server security
- Create an enterprise project from Project Web App, including the use of SharePoint tasks lists
- Organize and view information in Project Web App
- Use Team Builder from Project Web App
- Request resource engagements from the project manager's end
- Manage resource engagement requests from the resource manager's end
- Manage non-project time
- Use the Resource Center to display availability vs. capacity and manage resource allocations across projects
- Use the project sites (workspace) to access, edit, manage, and report on risks, issues, and documents
- View and update Project Details

*T*he tracking features of Project Web App 2016 are extremely valuable, since they help overcome one of the great frustrations in using older project management software. There are a number of new and improved features in Project Web App that will appeal to everyone in the organization. As a specific configuration of SharePoint for Project Management functions, Project Web App includes many standard SharePoint features that have been designed and set up for project management use.

One of the most versatile aspects of SharePoint is its list management capability. This chapter describes some of the more common uses of this functionality.

13.1 Organizing and Viewing Information in Project Web Application

In the previous chapter and this one, we are discussing the exchange of assignment and progress information between the project manager and team members using Microsoft Project Web Application. Projects are managed in organizations and use organizational resources, which means executives and resource managers need information about project activities and resource utilization.

The primary sources of such information are the Project Center and Resource Center pages in Project Web App. The information you see in the Project Center and Resource Center is based on the security setting established by the Project Server administrator(s).

Overview of Project Server Security

Microsoft Project Web Application ships with eight pre-defined groups: Team Members, Team Leads, Resource Managers, Proposal Reviewers, Project Managers, Portfolio Managers, Executives, and Administrators; additional groups can be created by an administrator. Individuals are assigned to one or more groups. Each group has predefined permissions which govern what they can and can't do in the application.

Note to users accessing Project Online through Office 365: Your instance of Project Server is usually hosted in an arrangement known as a tenant. A tenant is a separate instance of Project Server that is co-hosted with other tenants (typically users from other organizations that are separated from your instance). Office 365 is designed with additional layers of security that protect access to your organization's information from users in other organizations. As a result, your default groups may be set up differently. Refer any questions about this to your organization's Project Online administrator.

Groups are given access to categories, which contain objects such as projects and views. The combination of groups and categories defines the security for information in Project Server. For example, resources in the Team Member group given access to the My Tasks category (the default for team members) will see only the Project Center views given to the My Tasks category by the Project Server administrator; they will not see the *Resources* link at all on their individual Home pages.

Resources in the Project Manager group will see their own projects (those they have published or are assigned to) in the Project Center page and can view assignment information in the Resource Center.

Project Web Application Views

The content and format of views in Project Web App is defined by a Project Server administrator and cannot be changed by users, just as enterprise views in Microsoft Project cannot be changed by project managers. The significant difference is only data appearing in a Project Web App view can be used for filtering and grouping, whereas all data in Microsoft Project is available, whether visible or not. For example, you can filter the data in the Entry Table in the Gantt Chart by cost, even though cost data is not visible.

This means that, especially in the early stages of a Microsoft Project 2016 implementation, solid communication between administrators and users is critical. Administrators of course work to provide the information and organizational tools needed, but often this effort requires estimation on their part. If required information isn't available, contact your administrator.

13.2 Web-based Projects

As we learned in the previous chapter, clicking the *Projects* link in the Quick Launch sidebar, or the *Projects* tile in the carousel, takes you to a list of the enterprise projects you are authorized to view. The Project Center page provides links to a multitude of functions and activities. In this chapter we will attempt to group these functions logically and to provide a complete description for each.

In addition to web-based projects, this chapter will describe reporting, status reports, risks, issues, deliverables, and document management in Project Web App.

Note: Your sidebar options and the overall look and feel of your Project Web App views may differ slightly from those in this section. This is dependent on the permissions your Project Server administrator has granted to you.

Project Center

🗁 For this exercise, you will need to launch Internet Explorer and connect to Project Web App.

1 From your Project Web App home page, click the *Projects* tile in the carousel or select the *Projects* link in the sidebar. Your screen will resemble the following:

Figure 237.

Project Center

2 Click the *Projects* tab to see all *Projects* ribbon options, including the following groups: *Project, Navigate, Zoom, Data, Timeline, Share,* and *Project Type.*

Figure 238.

Project Center
ribbon options

Following is a summary of the available editing options in the *Projects:Project* group:

Figure 239.

Projects:Project group options, with *New* options expanded

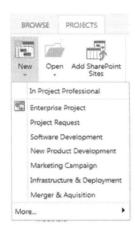

Clicking the *New* icon found in *Projects:Project* provides you some options:

- ❑ *In Project Professional* – Launches Microsoft Project 2016 so you can build a new project plan

- ❑ *Enterprise Project* – Takes you to the **Basic Info** dialog box where you enter summary project information; once you click *Save*, this information is saved as a new Enterprise Project

Figure 240.

Creating a new enterprise project (web page 1: what kind of project?)

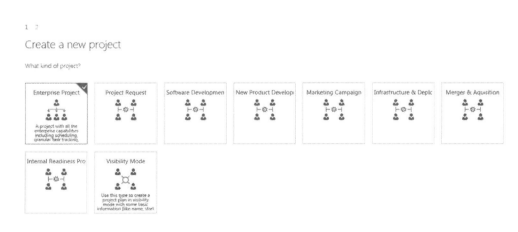

Figure 241.

Creating a new
enterprise project
(web page 2)

1 2

Create a new project

Project Request Information

Name *

Description

Business Owner

Project Scope

Business Need Description
Describes the key business
benefits expected from the
project.

Clicking the *Open* icon found in *Projects:Project* provides you, by default,
four options for opening an existing project:

Figure 242.

Projects:Project
group options,
with *Open* options
expanded

BROWSE PROJECTS

New Open Add SharePoint Build Re
 Sites Team

 In Browser

 In Browser for Editing

Proje In Microsoft Project

Appr In Microsoft Project for Editing

❏ *In Browser* – Opens the project in Project Web App for viewing or for
editing if the project is already checked out to you; this is the same
as if you just clicked on the project name in the Project Center view

❏ *In Browser for Editing* – Opens the project in Project Web App for
editing

❏ *In Microsoft Project* – If you have the Microsoft Project Professional
client on your personal computer, opens the project for viewing
(Read-Only)

❏ *In Microsoft Project for Editing* – If you have the Microsoft Project
Professional client on your personal computer, opens the project for
editing

The edit functions noted above include the ability to access the project as read-only or to update in either Project Web App or Microsoft Project Professional.

Note: Update functions are dependent on having permission to update this project. You will also be unable to edit a project if it is checked out to someone else.

Add SharePoint Site is the final option in the *Projects:Project* group. This option allows you to create a new project in Project Web App from an existing tasks list. Your project will show up in features such as reporting and resource availability.

In the *Projects:Navigate* group you will find:

Figure 243.

*Projects:
Navigate*
group options

- ❑ *Build Team* – Allows resource managers, or other users with appropriate permissions, to create a team for a project; they cannot assign resources to project tasks but can add them to the team

- ❑ *Resource Plan* – Takes you to the resource plan associated with a selected project; the resource plan allows you to plan for resource allocation without requiring you to have specific assignments (NOT AVAILABLE in Microsoft Project 2016)

- ❑ *Project Permissions* – Takes you to the Project Permissions page, where you can set permissions for a selected project; you can give users permission to view or edit the project

- ❑ *Check in My Projects* – Takes you to a page where you can check in stranded enterprise projects; note that this is not project specific: all your checked out projects will be listed

The *Projects:Zoom* group options help you define the timescale displayed on your screen.

Figure 244.

*Projects:
Zoom* group
options

- ❑ *Zoom In* and *Zoom Out* – Allow you to show a smaller/larger time increment on the timescale

- ❑ *Scroll to Project* –Move the timescale to the area on the Gantt Chart containing the bar for the selected project

The options shown in the *Projects:Data* group dropdown menus provide tools to help you isolate the data you need.

Figure 245.

Projects:Data
group options

❑ *Outline* – Provides options for adjusting the level of detail you wish to display in the projects listed in the Project Center

❑ *View* – Allows you to customize the appearance of the Project Center list

❑ *Filter* – Allows you to select built-in filters, create a custom filter, or turn on Auto-filter

❑ *Group By* – Groups projects by any field in the selected view, to three grouping levels; *Clear All* returns you to the default no group.

Other Project Center features of note include:

Figure 246.

Additional
Projects ribbon
options

❑ *Add Project* and *Add Tasks* – Adds projects and tasks to the timeline, just as in Microsoft Project Professional

❑ *Export to Excel* – Exports the data displayed in the grid to Microsoft Excel

❑ *Print* – Prints the data as it is displayed in the grid

❑ *Show/Hide Subprojects* – Displays subprojects in the Project Center; if you have a master project, this will display its associated subprojects

❑ *Show/Hide Time with Date* – Changes the display for all dates to also include time, as in the following figure:

Figure 247.

*Show Time
with Date*

ⓘ	Project Name		Health Trend	Start ↓	Finish	Overall Health	Schedule Health	Budget Health
🖹	Apparel ERP Upgrade	•••	◆	5/24/2017 8:00 AM	4/26/2019 4:40 PM	○	●	○
🖹	Construction safety equipment	•••	◆◆	5/24/2017 8:00 AM	9/15/2021 10:40 AM	○	●	●
🖹	Content Filtering Design and Implementatic•••		◆◆	5/24/2017 8:00 AM	3/20/2018 5:00 PM	○	●	○
🖹	Commercial Product Launch Phase 2	•••	◆	2/18/2017 8:00 AM	3/1/2017 12:00 PM	○	○	●
🖹 ▦	ABC Integration	•••	◆	2/12/2017 8:00 AM	6/7/2019 4:00 PM	○	●	○

❑ *Change:Project Type* – Allows you to update the enterprise project type associated with the project, including the workflow, pages, and custom fields

❑ Clicking a column name sorts the projects by the entries in that field in ascending or descending order.

❑ Clicking a project name opens a Project Details page where the user can see a series of predefined views of data for that single project. The commands in the toolbar are similar to those in the Project Center.

Figure 248.

Commercial Product Launch Phase 2 Project Details page

❑ To exit the Project Details, click on *Project Center* in the left navigation links.

❑ Clicking the empty box to the far left of the Project Name column allows you to select that row's project. This is necessary when you're performing functions on a specific project.

Figure 249.

Selecting a project

	ⓘ	Project Name		Health Trend	Overall Health	Schedule Health	Budget Health
	🖻	Voice Recognition Product	•••	↔	●	●	●
	🖻	Resource Assignment (Cloud)	•••	↔	◐	◐	◐
	🖻	Dynamics CRM Deployment EMEA	•••	↔	●	●	○
	🖻	Squash and Racquet Ball Eye Wear	•••	↑	●	●	●
	🖻	General Ledger (GL) currency update	•••	↔	○	●	○
	🖻📊	Biothermal ear heating system for helmets	•••	↔	●	●	●
	🖻	Expand raw material acquisition vendor list	•••	↔	○	○	●
	🖻📊	Health Assessment Reporting Tool	•••	↔	○	●	●

❑ Clicking the *Browse* tab displays a *Search this site* field, as
displayed in the following figure. This functionality allows you to
search for content across the site.

Figure 250.

Project Center
Search tool

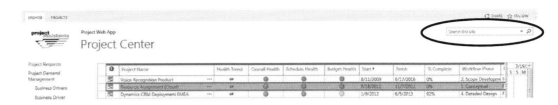

13.3 Team Builder

In many organizations, the process for determining the team that should work on
a project is separate from the process that defines the tasks in the work
breakdown structure. There are team building functions in both Microsoft
Project Professional and Project Web App.

📂 For this exercise, you will need to launch Internet Explorer and connect to
Project Web App.

1 Click the *Projects* link in the sidebar to navigate to the Project Center
page.

2 From the Project Center page, click a *Project Name* to open the
Project Details page for that project.

3 Click the *Project* tab to display the *Project* tab options.

Figure 251.

Project tab
options

4 From *Project:Navigate* click the *Build Team* icon [🖳]. The resulting
view (similar to the following) will display the current project team (if
any) for the selected project and the resource pool.

Figure 252.

Build Team page

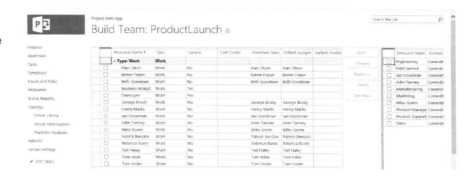

From this view, you have the following options:

❑ *Add* – Adds selected name(s) from the resource pool to the project team; the selected names will become grayed out in the resource pool

❑ *Remove* – Removes selected name(s) from the project team

❑ *Replace* – Replaces the selected name from the project team with the name from the resource pool; if the team member is assigned to any tasks, using *Replace* assigns the replacement resource to those tasks

❑ *Match* – Filters the displayed list of resource pool names to show only those with the same selection attributes as the selected project team name

❑ *Clear Match* – Clears the filter from *Match* to display the entire resource pool

Figure 253.

Select the names from the Resource Pool to be added, from the Project Team to be removed, or one from each to replace the Team member.

5 Once you have built the appropriate team using the functions noted above, click the *Save & Close* option that is under *Team:Team.*

13.4 Resource Engagements

A project's initiation and planning stages may include an evaluation or approval step before a project is ready for execution. Resource planning is a helpful technique when developing a rough estimate of the resource load and cost of a project. These estimates provide high-level resource demand information at the project level.

Resource engagements, a new feature in Microsoft Project Online and Project Server 2016, is the way project managers and resource managers come to agreement on resource allocations. The resource engagement feature substitutes the resource plan feature you might know from the previous version of Project Online or Project Server.

Checking Assignment Attributes

Before using resource engagements, resource managers have to assign resources that require approval to projects.

You can use the Resource Center to see if a resource requires approval. (We will cover the Resource Center in much greater detail in the sub-section titled *Resource Center.*)

1 To access the Resource Center, click the *Resources* link in the Quick Launch sidebar of the Project Web App Home page.

Figure 254.

The Resource Center

2 Under the *Editing* tab, click *Edit Resource*. This will bring up the Edit Resource page.

3 Under Assignment Attributes, you will find the *Resource requires approval for all project assignments toggle*, as show in the following figure:

Figure 255.

Property to define
if resource
requires approval

Assignment Attributes

Note: The Resource Engagement option will also need to be activated by your Microsoft Project Online administrator under *Server Settings*.

Resource engagements look and operate differently depending on the user's role. The following exercises will show how to request, assign, and manage resource engagements from both ends.

Resource Engagements from the Project Manager's End

Creating Requests Using the Task and Engagement Inspectors

📂 This exercise uses the file **ResourceEngagement.mpp**. Be sure this project is open before beginning.

1 From *Task:View*, click on the arrow next to *Gantt Chart* and select the *Resouce Plan* view. If you have, for the selected project, existing resource engagements or migrated resource plans, you can see their status.

Figure 256.

Viewing resource
engagements
and their status

When in Project Professional, the *Engagements* tab is available, as shown in the next figure.

Note: Resource engagements are only available on Microsoft Project Professional 2016 or Microsoft Project Professional for Office 365, connected to Project online or Project Server 2016. Project Standard 2016 does not support resource engagements.

Figure 257.

Engagements tab

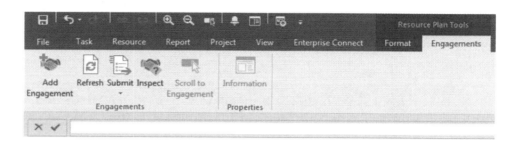

2 Now it's time for the project manager to do the planning and assign resources to tasks. The project contains one engagement for user *Elea Bailey* and two simple tasks. You build your team from the enterprise resource pool. On the *Resource* tab, click on *Add resources:Build Team from Enterprise...*

Or add the resources to your Resource Sheet view as displayed in the Project resources list below

Figure 258.

Build Team from Enterprise...

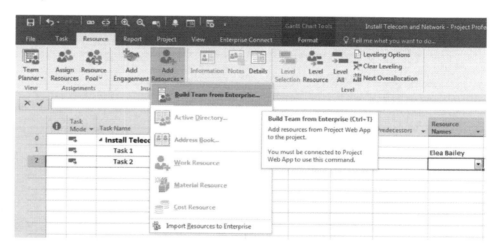

3 Select two more resources, both requiring approval.

Figure 259.

Build Team
dialog for a given
project

4 Assign *Elea Bailey* to the first task. Since she is already committed
via a resource engagement, there is no specific action to perform.

Now assign *Leo Cullen* to the second task. Notice the warning
message on the indicators column: An engagement is required for this
resource.

Figure 260.

Engagement
error indicator

5 To resolve this problem, right-click on the icon and select *Fix in*
Engagement Inspector.

Figure 261.

Opening
engagement
inspector

6 The engagement inspector opens in a pane on the left side of your
 screen. Click on *View engagement conflict in Task Usage*.

Figure 262.

Engagement
inspector pane
with mouse over
*View
engagement
conflicts in
Task Usage*

7 The Task Usage screen will display with *Leo Cullen* highlighted and a
 message in the Inspector pane that says "This task assignment is
 outside of the boundaries of an engagement. This means the
 assignment of *Leo Cullen* on *Task 2* is not covered by a committed
 resource engagement.

Figure 263.

Task Usage screen with engagement conflict highlighted

Note: The indicator for "This task assignment is outside of the boundaries of an engagement" [] displayed above on the Gantt Chart view, is not displayed on the Resource Plan view.

8 To create a new engagement, you can right-click on the icon and select *Create New Engagement*. Alternatively, you can click on the button *Create and save new engagement for this assignment's resource* on the inspector pane.

Figure 264.

Creating a new engagement using right-click method

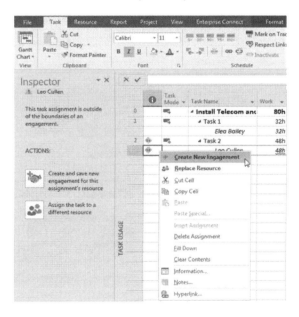

9 Set the engagement information following the example in the below figure. Enter the comment "Need Leo on this project to perform Task 2" for the resource manager who will review the request. Click *OK*.

Figure 265.

Engagement Information dialog with adjusted information

10 The request is created as draft and needs to be submitted. Click on *Submit my engagement for review*.

Figure 266.

Submitting engagement

11 After the request is sent, assignment status is updated to "Proposed."

Figure 267.

Proposed engagement

Note: If you check on the *Resource Plan* view, you can see the "Proposed" status. The note (icon on the indicators column) contains the comment you set on the engagement request.

Note 2: There is no need to publish or check the project in for the request to be sent.

Manually Creating Requests

In addition to the Task Inspector tool, a project manager can manually create a request for a resource engagement.

1 Go back to the Resource Plan view, and click on *Engagements:Add Engagement*.

2 The **Engagement Information** dialog box pops up. Fill in your request with the resource name, a description if required (this will be displayed into the Name field on the input table), start and finish dates, and finally the requested units (percentage) or work. You may put a comment for the resource manager who will review the request.

3 Click *OK*. The resource engagement is created with a status "Draft."

Figure 268.

Resource engagement created with status "Draft"

		Name	Proposed Start	Proposed Finish	Proposed Max Units	Engageme Status
3		▲ Nieve Fraser	Mon 06.03.17	Fri 10.03.17	50%	
	✽		*Mon 06.03.17*	*Fri 10.03.17*	*50%*	*Draft*

4 Select the newly created resource engagment, and click on *Engagements:Submit:Submit Selected Engagements* (in this case, you can also choose to *Submit All Engagements*).

Figure 269.

Submitting resource engagement

5 The resource engagement status is updated to "Proposed."

Creating the resource engagement from the Task Inspector or manually does facilitate the request creation, but the amount of work requested is spread evenly across date ranges. You can decide to split the work differently by manually creating the resource engagement.

Before submitting this resource engagement, you can edit the proposed work or proposed max units by using the Timephased Data view.

Figure 270.

Resource engagement: Original split of work

Figure 271.

Resource engagement: Updated split of work

Note: An indicator [🗲] appears for that says "This engagement work contour has been edited…"

You then have to submit the resource engagement request as usual.

The Resource Manager's End

The request is sent from the project manager to the resource manager, who will accept or reject the request using Project Online. Note that there is no individual resource "owner"; all resource managers are able to review any resource engagement, no matter who the resource is.

☞ This exercise continues use of the file **ResourceEngagement.mpp**. Be sure this project is open before beginning.

1 As a resource manager, go on the Resource Center. Let's say you want to see resource requests for *Leo Cullen*. Click in his cell, then click on *Resource Requests* under *Resources:Navigate*.

Figure 272.

Resource Requests

2 The list of requests and their status is displayed, which you can view in either the Sheet or Timephased Data view. The previous request for *Leo Cullen* for the *Install telecom and network* project is pending approval with a "Proposed" state.

Figure 273.

Resource engagement requests (Sheet view)

Figure 274.

Resource engagement requests (Timephased Data view)

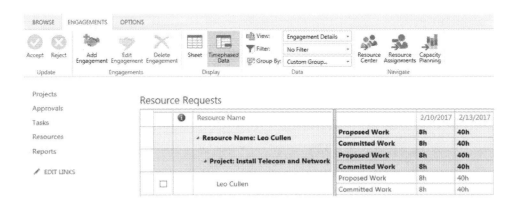

3 You can see request comments by ticking the checkbox for the proposed resource and clicking *Engagements:Edit Engagement*. This will bring up the **Edit Engagement** dialog box with comments at the bottom, as in the following figure:

Figure 275.

Edit Engagement dialog

You can also update resource names, start and finish dates, and allocation information. Note: the pick-list for resource names contains only resources you have selected on the Resource Center before clicking on resource requests.

4 The Capacity and Engagements Heatmap is another new feature of Microsoft Project 2016. It allows you to see the discrepancies between resource capacity and committed engagements.

Figure 276.

Capacity and Engagements Heatmap

In this example, we see that Nieve Fraser is not available to work on the project *Laptop Deployment for Employees*, but Ulrike Alvena, who has the same role, has some availability in this period.

5 You can swap the two resources, either by editing the engagement or rejecting this one and creating a new one. (From Project Online, resource managers can create new engagements by clicking on *Add Engagement* under the *Engagements* section of the *Engagements* tab.)

Figure 277.

Add Engagement

The screen to create a new engagement has all of the same fields as the one to screen for editing existing engagements, as you can see in the following figure:

Figure 278.

New Engagement

When you select a proposed engagement, *Accept* and *Reject* actions become available on the ribbon under *Engagements:Update*.

Figure 279.

Accept or *Reject* engagements

6 Click *Reject*. You will be prompted with the **Confirm Reject** dialog, which offers an opportunity to add a comment for the project manager who made the request.

Figure 280.

Confirm Reject
dialog with
comment box

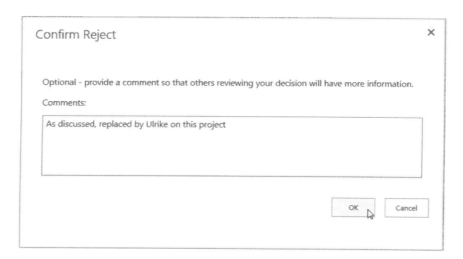

Resource engagements can have any of the following states:

❑ Committed (i.e. Approved)

❑ Proposed

❑ Draft (this only occurs when there is an engagement that hasn't been submitted yet)

❑ Rejected

Note: You should be careful not to confuse the state "Committed" with regards to a resource engagement and the resource's booking type "Committed." A "Committed" resource engagement is an approved engagement. A "Committed" resource booking type (default booking type), is used for a resource you are 100% sure is availability.

On the other hand, a "Proposed" resource's booking type, is used when you need to remove the planned workload from various calculations like portfolio optimization. This booking type is also used to remove the tasks from the resources' My Tasks page (a best practice for closed projects) and to prevent the system from sending automated emails when the project is published.

Returning to the Project Manager's View

1 Return to the Resource screen on Project Professional 2016. Note that you can see the rejected engagement for *Nieve Fraser* and the new one for *Ulrike Alvena*, which is already committed.

Figure 281.

What the project
manager sees
after resource
manager replies
to requests

From a Portfolio Analysis Perspective

There are no big changes related to an assessment of resource capacity for the sake of portfolio analysis. When setting your portfolio analysis, you must be careful on how calculating resource utilization is defined.

Note: In Project 2016, resource utilization is defined from Project Professional, on the *Project:Project Information* form. This is a change from previous versions of Project, where resource utilization was set when defining the resource plans.

Figure 282.

*Calculate
Resource
Utilization
from:*

The options are you can *Calculate Resource Utilization from:*

❑ *Project Plan* – Resource workload is defined from tasks assigned to the resource in the project schedule.

❑ *Resource Engagements* – Resource workload is defined from resource engagements (committed or proposed).

❑ *Project Plan until* – This is used for rolling estimates. You will use resource workload defined from tasks assigned to the resource in the project schedule until the specified date (e.g. end of first phase) and resource workload defined from resource engagements for other parts (e.g. phase 2).

Note: By default, resource utilization is calculated from *Project Plan*. Hence, if you have set resource engagements, you must manually select *Calculate Resource Utilization from Resource Engagements* in order to use it. Otherwise, the resource utilization from Project Plan is used.

Request Reminders

Another feature in Project 2016 is request reminders. This gives you the option to receive reminders via email upon every resource engagement request for selected resources.

1 In the Resource Center, select any resource. Under *Resources:Share and Track*, click *Request Reminders:Subscribe to selected resources*. A pop up will confirm your subscription has been updated.

Figure 283.

Request Reminders

2 Now you need to enable the email alert and the frequency. Navigate to *PWA Settings:Manage My Resources' Alerts and Reminders:My Resource Requests*.

My Resource Requests

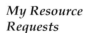

3 Set the frequency of email alerts

Figure 284.

Setting reminder frequency

My Resource Requests

Create resource request reminders to help keep your team running smoothly. Your team consists of all resources you have resource engagement permissions for. Choose which resources you are subscribed to from Resource Center.

Resource Requests

☑ Send a reminder about pending resource requests: Every [Day ▾] [Week] [Month]

Note: In order to use the request reminders feature, notifications should be turned on, on the *Additional Server Settings* page.

Figure 285.

Notification email settings

Notification Email Settings

Determine whether users can subscribe to alerts and reminders.

☑ Turn on notifications

Managing Non-project Time

Non-project time refers to activities that have an impact on the resource capacity but are not related to a specific project—e.g. vacations, operational duties, sales, training, sickness.

There are three main options in order to manage non-project activities:

❑ *Creating a separate project* – You can create a stand-in project, then create a new task assigned to a specific resource to depict this non-project activity.

Figure 286.

Managing non-project time into a project schedule

Task Mode ▾	Task Name ▾	Duration ▾	Start ▾	Finish ▾	Predecessors ▾	Resource Names ▾
🔧	⊿ Non-project Time 2017	85 d?	Mon 02.01.17	Fri 28.04.17		
🔧	⊿ Vacations	55 d	Mon 13.02.17	Fri 28.04.17		
🔧	Leo Winter break	5 d	Mon 13.02.17	Fri 17.02.17		Leo Cullen
🔧	Elea Easter vacations	10 d	Mon 17.04.17	Fri 28.04.17		Elea Bailey
🔧	⊿ Training	1 d?	Mon 02.01.17	Mon 02.01.17		
🔧	Ulrike: PM using MS Project 2016	1 d?	Mon 02.01.17	Mon 02.01.17		Ulrike Alvena

❑ *Creating resource engagements* – The resource manager can create a new engagement for his/her resource to depict this non-project activity. This is a good way to manage recurring tasks, such as operational duties (e.g. application support, help desk). The exercise below will demonstrate this option.

❑ *Using Administrative Time in timesheets* – A resource can set time in the future when filling in their timesheet. This can be found a category defined as Administrative Time. Note: This category work type must be set as "Working" if you want the time reported here to have an impact on the resource's capacity.

❑ *Manually updating individual calendars* – You can also update individual resource's calendars for non-work time, such as vacations. This is our least recommended option, as it is not ideal for big companies with a lot of resources to manage.

Creating Resource Engagements to Manage Non-project Time

In this exercise, we will use the second option outlined above (creating resource engagements) in order to manage non-project time.

1 Create a new engagement by clicking *Add Engagement* under *Engagements:Engagements*.

Figure 287.

Creating new resource engagement from

2 In the **New Engagement** dialog box that pops up, put "Leo Cullen" under *Resource Name*, and fill in the remaining fields as you wish. Click *OK*.

3 Navigate to *Availability:Views* and click on *Resource Utilization* to see the following screen:

Figure 288.

New resource engagement, as displayed in the Resource Utilization report

4 Similar to what we did as on the project manager end, we can edit the resource engagement request's work distribution manually. First, select the *Timephased Data* view in the *Engagement:Display* section.

Figure 289.

Switching to
Timephased Data
view

5 Input new values for your resource engagement request.

Figure 290.

Updated
Resource
Engagement
work request

		Project: Non-project Time 2017	Proposed Work	6h	6h	6h	6h
			Committed Work	8h	8h	4h	4h
☐		Leo Cullen	Proposed Work				
			Committed Work				
☑		Leo Cullen	Proposed Work	6h	6h	6h	6h
			Committed Work	4h	8h	8h	4h

6 Repeat step 3 to see your changes reflected in Resource Utilization.

Figure 291.

Resource
engagement
updated in the
Resource
Utilization report

Now, *Leo Cullen* is assigned to tasks in the *Laptop Deployment for Employees* project and has a resource engagement for his operational duties linked to the *Non-project time 2017* project.

Resource Center

The Resource Center lists all enterprise resources you are authorized to see, as configured by the Project Server administrator.

This information can be presented in a variety of ways using the *View* options found on the *Resources* tab. This view menu contains the views prepared by the Project Server administrator, including the default All Resources, Cost Resources, Material Resources, and Work Resources views.

1 As we covered at the beginning of this section, you can access the Resource Center by clicking the *Resources* link in the Quick Launch sidebar of the Project Web App Home page.

2 Click the *Resources* tab at the top of the screen to display all *Resources* tab options.

Figure 292.

Resources tab options

3 From *Resources:Data* click the *View* dropdown list to view all pre-defined resource views.

Figure 293.

Default resource view options

Note: The *All Resources* default is another way of describing a view without a filter applied.

4 From the *View* dropdown list, click *All Resources*.

5 From *Resources:Data* click the *Group By* dropdown list and select *Generic* (to separate generic resources from named ones). Your screen will resemble the following:

Figure 294.

All Resources view with generic resources grouped separately

Resource Name ↑		ID	Checked Out	Email Address	Generic	Timesheet Man	Type
▲ Generic: No			**No**		**No**		**Work**
☐	Averill Mariano	186	No		No	Averill Mariano	Work
☐	Eduard Marley	191	No		No	Eduard Marley	Work
☐	Elea Bailey	174	No		No	Elea Bailey	Work
☐	Fernand Stewart	187	No		No	Fernand Stewart	Work
☐	Jeremy Cottino	170	No		No	Jeremy Cottino	Work
☐	Jessi Marjolein	188	No		No	Jessi Marjolein	Work
☐	Leo Cullen	172	No		No	Leo Cullen	Work
☐	Leon Grayson	189	No		No	Leon Grayson	Work
☐	Nieve Fraser	175	No		No	Nieve Fraser	Work
☐	Ollie Fernie	190	No		No	Ollie Fernie	Work
☐	Tammara Lewis	185	No		No	Tammara Lewis	Work
☐	Ulrike Alvena	173	No		No	Ulrike Alvena	Work
▲ Generic: Yes			**No**		**Yes**		**Work**
☐	Business Analyst	192	No		Yes		Work
☐	IT Manager	194	No		Yes		Work
☐	Program Manager	193	No		Yes		Work

6 In the *All Resources* view, check several boxes in the column to the left of the Resource Name column to select the associated resources, as in the previous figure.

Notice that the ribbon contains similar commands as those available in the Project Center, as well as the commands *Resource Assignments* and *Resource Availability*.

Resource Assignments takes the user to the Resource Assignments page. You can view the assignments of one resource or a group of resources. The default summary view presents the resource assignment(s) in a Gantt Chart format, although you can also select a Timephased view.

Figure 295.

Resource Assignments page with Gantt Chart

Resource Assignments

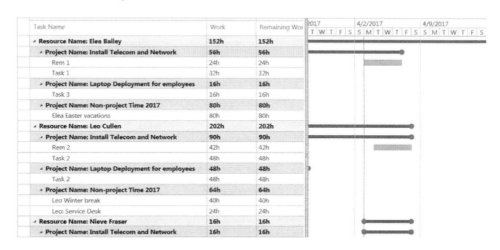

Capacity Planning allows you to examine availability of one or more resources by selecting one of the five standard views: Capacity and Engagements Heatmap, Resource utilization, Resource Utilization by project, Remaining Availability, and Work by Resource.

To access these view settings, click the *View* dropdown arrow found in *Availability:Views*.

Figure 296.

Capacity planning view options

The timescale can be adjusted using the *View Options* selections in the lower-right corner of the view. The Assignment Work by Resource view shown in the following figure presents the data in both a histogram and a grid format. If multiple resources are selected, the view is color coded.

Figure 297.

Capacity
planning:
Capacity and
Engagements
Heatmap

The following figures provide examples of additional Capacity Planning view options:

Figure 298.

Capacity
planning:
Resource
utilization

Figure 299.

Capacity planning: Resource utilization by project

Figure 300.

Capacity planning: Remaining Availability

Figure 301.

Capacity
planning: Work
by resource

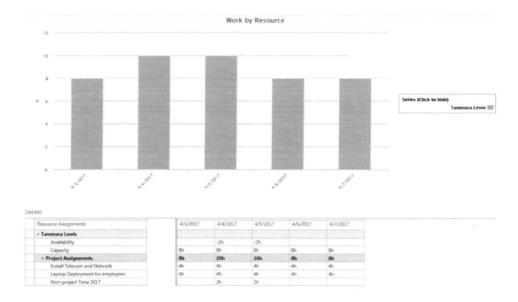

Conclusion on Resource Engagements

To recap the process of working with resource engagements, here are the four steps you'll follow:

1 The resource manager sets resources requiring approval to be assigned to projects on the Resource Center (Edit resource page).

2 A project manager can request a resource.

3 The time-phased request is done in Project Professional 2016 or Project Professional for Office 365.

4 It can contain a percentage of resource work required or a set of hours for the period.

The resource manager reviews the request and accepts or rejects it. Note that engagements aren't fully editable. Depending on the change required, the request should be resent by the project manager. The resource can start working and the "contract" is signed.

Here are some additional takeaways regarding resource engagements:

❏ Project managers manage resource engagement in Project Professional, while resource managers use only Project Online.

❏ As was the case with resource plans, engagements don't impact project schedule.

❏ Generic or named resources can be requested using resource engagement.

❑ Resource managers can also create resource engagements without a previous request from a project manager.

Note: *Resource engagements* feature is activated by default on all new Project Online tenants. If you have an existing tenant, you can decide when to activate the new features (activation is done on *Server Settings:Additional Server Settings*). For an on-premises installation, options will be available when migrating to Project Server 2016. When activated, published resource plans will be converted into engagements, and the old resource plan view will be removed.

Resource engagements and resource plans cannot cohabitate in a single tenant.

Figure 302.

Resource engagement activated, (*Resource Plan* button has disappeared)

13.5 Risks, Issues, Deliverables, and Documents

Project Web Application 2013 includes other tools that extend the usefulness of project plans throughout the organization. Teamwork is critical in most projects, and the ability to view and work with project plans can be very helpful in building team involvement and commitment.

Project managers quickly learn that agreement is easy to get but commitment can be hard. It's especially difficult in matrix organizations where the importance of a project manager's good will to a person's career isn't as clear as their line manager's. If you could only keep one of them happy, whom would you pick?

When a project is published, a project workspace is also created, along with tools to manage risks, issues, deliverables, and documents. These will be described in this lesson.

Project Sites

SharePoint can automatically create a project site when a project is published. The project site provides a focus for project-related functions as well as a cyberspace warroom, which allows for the project team to work together. This is especially useful when true co-location is not possible.

📁 For this exercise, launch Internet Explorer and connect to Project Web App.

1 Navigate to the *Project Center*. Click a Project Name from the list to go to the Project Details page for that project. From *Project:Navigate* click the *Project Site* icon. Your screen will resemble the following.

Figure 303.

Project Site home page

Just as your Project Web App Home page contains items specific to you, the project home page contains items specific to the project, which can be shared with all members of the project team. When a new project is first published, the project manager is prompted to create a project workspace for the project. This workspace is created from a template setup as part of enterprise configuration, so all workspaces initially look very similar.

Project sites enhance project team collaboration on projects. Project managers can quickly update themselves on what's going on in a project, and team members can see how their work fits into the overall context. Through project work sites, team members and project managers can access and share data, documents, and communication. By default, the main project workspace page provide access to the following functions:

❑ Visual timeline of the project's tasks

❑ Complete task schedule for a project

❑ Library for storing relevant project documents

❑ Notebook for quickly capturing and organizing information about the project

❑ Shared calendar for team events

❑ Ability to connect to the Project 2016 client application

❑ Ability to connect to Project Web App

As you can see in the preceding figure, the main window provides sidebar options, as well as typically including tiles that provide access to pages that allow you to customize, share, and brand the site. This page by default also allows you to add documents and other information to the site, including links to other webpages of interest.

Functions accessible from the Project Site main page include the following:

❑ **Documents** – Allows you to add, edit, view, track, group, and share project-related documents, workflows, notes, and other electronic artifacts

❑ **Tasks** – Allows you to add, edit, view, track, and annotate project task-related information. Provides a space for team "action items" that are important but not shown in the project plan itself

❑ **Calendar** – Shows the current month (by default), day, or week with project-related meetings, events, deadlines, etc. that have been added to the project

❑ **Project Details** – Links to the Project Details page, which provides a summary of basic project information (e.g. project name, description, start, finish, owner); also links to the Project Site, Build Team, and other resource-related functionality, and project-related documents, issues, and risks

❑ **Deliverables**, **Risks**, and **Issues** – Provides access to sites where you can add, edit, view, and track project-related Deliverables, Issues, and Risks.

❑ **Site Contents** – Provides access to all documents, site assets, calendars, issues, tasks, risks, deliverables, and other information related to the project; the *add an app* tile also provides the capability to create new items to this page.

Figure 304.

Site Contents page

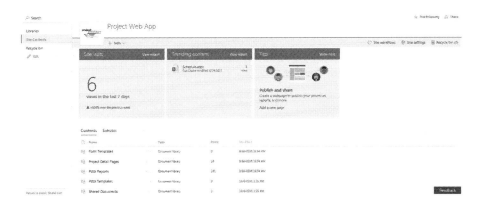

Risks, issues, deliverables, and documents can be managed from the project SharePoint workspace or from Project Web App. In the following exercises, we will work with them from the appropriate location in Project Web App.

13.6 Project Details Page

You can use different routes to get to the same point or access the same data. This occurs frequently in SharePoint, which is useful because you may need to access the same information while doing a variety of project management activities. The trick is to recognize that the information itself is the same, though you've accessed it through different paths.

1 Navigate to the *Project Center* and click on a project in the table; for this example we clicked *ProductLaunch*. You will see the Project Details page for this project:

Figure 305.

Project Details page for ProductLaunch, with high-level details

2 From *File:Navigate* click the *Project Site* icon to navigate to the Project Site for your selected project, where you can access links that include *Documents*, *Tasks*, *Calendar*, *Project Details*, *Issues*, *Risks*, *Documents*, and *Deliverables*.

Figure 306.

Project Site options for ProductLaunch project

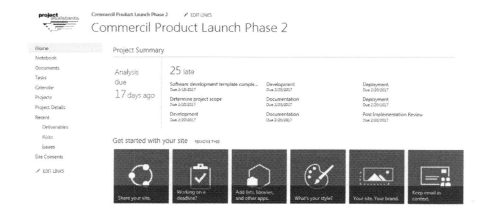

Issues

Issues are events, often outside of the project, that might have an impact on the project. Circumstances such as contractor bankruptcy, new legislation, or changes in management could affect a project, even though they are external to it and are usually not considered as part of issue management. These often appear by surprise during the lifespan of the project and must be managed in some way. Previously, issues were often (and sometimes still are) tracked and managed using Excel spreadsheets attached to or stored with the project file. Now, SharePoint provides a convenient location for issues management as a seamless part of the project database.

1 Navigate to the Project Site for a project—*Biothermal ear heating system for helmet* in this case (see Steps 1 and 2 immediately preceding this section).

2 From the Project Site for this project, click the *Issues* link in the sidebar to see the project's Issues page.

Figure 307.

Issues page for *Biothermal ear heating system for helmets*

3 Click the plus sign by *new item* to add an issue to the list. Your screen will resemble the following:

Figure 308.

New issue entry screen

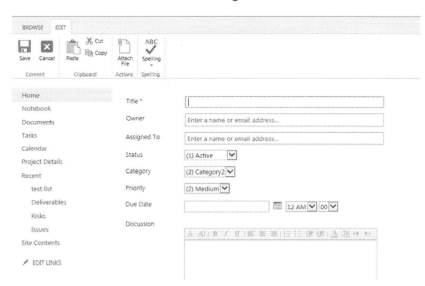

4 Enter data into this screen as follows:

- ❏ *Title* (the only required field): "Does not have experience with this product"

- ❏ *Owner*: "QA Hub"

- ❏ *Assigned To*: "QA Hub"

- ❏ *Status*: "Active"

- ❏ *Category*: "Category1"

- ❏ *Priority*: "High"

- ❏ *Due Date*: "8/1"

Note: Your training environment may be configured differently. Select options that are appropriate in your environment. Your Project Server administrator can configure many of these values to reflect your organization, such as Status, Category, and Priority.

5 From *Edit:Commit* click *Save*. Your new issue will appear on the Issues page for your project.

Figure 309.

New issue

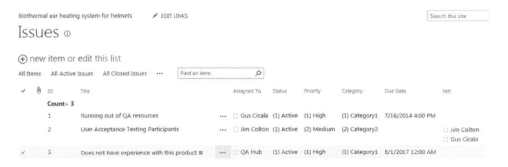

6 Click the *Projects* link in the sidebar to return to your Project Center page. An icon will notify you that there are issues associated with this project:

Figure 310.

Issue(s) indicator in the Project Center

Now that there are issues associated with your project, you may want to link the issues with a specific task that each impacts. The method for linking list items—such as issues, risks, or deliverables—to a task in a SharePoint task list or enterprise project plan in Project Server 2016 has changed from the method used in earlier versions. This is due to changes in both SharePoint Server 2016 and Project Server 2016 architecture.

To link an issue to a task in your project plan:

1 Again, navigate to the Project Center and click the *ProductLaunch* link to see the Project Details screen for your project.

2 Toward the top of the left sidebar, click the *Schedule* link. You will
see the Schedule page for *ABC Integration*.

Figure 311.

*ABC
Integration
Schedule
page*

3 Select Task 10, *Design*, by clicking on the Task Name.

4 Click the *Options* tab, and from *Options:Link To* click the *Related
Items* icon, as in the following figure. You will see the Task Detail
screen for *Design and order final packaging*.

Figure 312.

*Options:Link
to:Related
Items*

Figure 313.

Task Detail
screen for
Design

5 In the Task Detail screen shown in the preceding figure, click *ADD RELATED ITEM*. It is in the resulting Select an Asset page that you can link issues (and other list items) to tasks in your project.

Figure 314.

Select an Asset page

6 On the Select an Asset page, scroll down the left navigation list and find your project name. Click the *Issues* link under *ABC Integration* to see the Issues associated with that project.

Figure 315.

List of associated issues

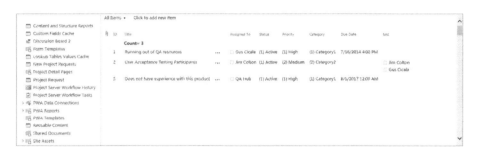

7 Click the link for the issue you would like to attach to the task. You will be sent back to the Task Details page for the linked task, where you will see that issue is now linked to this task.

Figure 316.

Issue successfully linked to task

8 You will be returned to the selected task and will see the issue linked with the *Design* task.

Figure 317.

Issues linked to *Design* task

This project can only be edited through Project Web App. Edit project.

Task Name	Design
Start Date	2/13/2017
Due Date	3/8/2017
Assigned To	☐ Mark Forsythe
% Complete	0 %
Related Items	☐ User Acceptance Testing Participants

ADD RELATED ITEM

See also

📄 Design ...
📄 Vendor X late with d... ...

SHOW MORE

Content Type: Task
Created at 3/12/2017 9:07 AM by ☐ System Account
Last modified at 3/12/2017 9:18 AM by ☐ System Account

Close

Risks

Risks are usually inherent to projects themselves. They may involve unavailability of a critical material or skill, lack of experience on the part of the project manager or team, the use of new or untested technology—the list is almost endless.

The Risks page interface resembles that of the issues page, which we just reviewed. The major difference is that *Probability* and *Impact* are new fields relating to Risks, and each is a required field.

Also, instead of *Discussion* and *Resolution* threaded discussion boxes, Risk fields include *Description*, *Mitigation Plan* (how will we decrease the probability or impact or both?), *Contingency Plan*, and *Trigger* (what will tell us that it's time to activate the contingency plan?) fields. Items can be linked to the mitigation or contingency plan, or they can be flagged as affected by the risk or as triggers. Documents can also be attached to a Risk entry.

As with issues, if a risk is assigned to you, you will see a reference to it on your Project Web App issues and risks page, accessed from the *Issues and Risks* link on your home page sidebar.

Figure 318.

Project Web App issues and risks page (risk circled)

You will also see a link to it on the Project Center page:

Figure 319.

Project Center
page with risk
assignment
highlighted

1 Navigate to the Project Details page for *ABC Integration*, and from
 Project:Navigate click the *Risks* [⬛] icon. You will see the Risks
 page for this project.

Figure 320.

Risks page for
ABC Integration

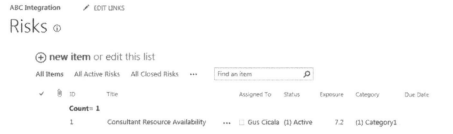

2 Click the plus sign by *new item* to add a new risk to your project.
 Your screen will resemble the following:

Figure 321.

New risk entry
screen

3 Enter data into this screen as follows:

 ❏ *Title* (required field): "New risk"

 ❏ *Owner*: "John Tierney"

 ❏ *Assigned To*: "John Tierney"

 ❏ *Status*: "Active"

 ❏ *Category*: "Category1"

 ❏ *Due Date*: "8/1"

 ❏ *Probability* (required field): "50%"

 □ *Impact* (required field): "2"

Note: Your training environment may be configured differently. Select options that are appropriate in your environment. Your Project Server administrator can configure many of these values to reflect your organization, such as Status, Category, Probability, and Impact.

 4 From *Edit:Commit* click *Save*. Your new risk will appear on the Risks page for your project.

Figure 322.

New Risk

ProductLaunch ✎ EDIT LINKS

Risks ①

⊕ new item or edit this list

| All Items | All Active Risks | All Closed Risks | ••• | | Find an item | 🔍 |

✓	📎	ID	Title	Assigned To	Status	Exposure	Category	Due Date
			Count= 1					
		1	New risk ✿ •••	☐ John Tierney	(1) Active	1	(1) Category1	8/1/2013 12:00

 5 Click the *Projects* link in the sidebar to return to your Project Center page. An icon will notify you that there are risks associated with this project.

Figure 323.

Risks
notification

Editing Issues and Risks

The value of managing issues and risks in a project site is that team members collaborate in their recognition, assessment, tracking, and resolution. Maintaining the status of each open issue and risk is part of the work of the people to whom they are assigned. Team members review and update their issue and risk entries via the project workspace. Reviewing their statuses is a regular part of project management.

Team members view their issues and risks by clicking the *Issues and Risks* link in the sidebar of their Project Web App Home page:

Figure 324.

Project Web App Home page sidebar with *Issues and Risks* highlighted

The Issues and Risks page resembles the following:

Figure 325.

Issues and Risks page

Clicking the project link takes you to the Issues page or Risks page for that project, where you can edit the issues or risks lists. You can edit any of your issues or risks by clicking *edit this list*.

Figure 326.

Issues page with *edit this list* message bubble

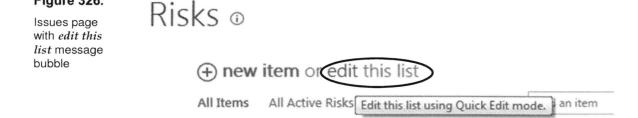

You will see your list (in the case of the preceding example, the list of issues assigned to you) in editable table form, similar to the following figure. Edit the list options as appropriate, and then click *Stop editing this list* to save your changes and return to the original (issues or risks) list.

Figure 327.

Stop editing this list

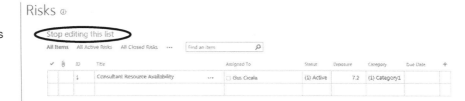

List Management

As a project manager, you are responsible for the effective operation of the project team. An essential part of this is the simple and regular communication of information between team members. As well as your normal leadership functions, you may also choose to adjust the configuration of the tools used for communication, particularly SharePoint. The organization will typically set default methods that are deployed through project workspace templates, but you may have the ability to adjust these templates to make team operation smoother and more efficient. Examples of common adjustments include defining list columns and views.

1 Navigate to the Project Site for *ProductLaunch*.

2 Click the *Issues* link to view the list of issues associated with the project.

Figure 328.

Issues selected

3 Click the *List* ribbon to reveal the function icons. From *List:Settings* click the *List Settings* icon [⚙] to navigate to the Settings page for this issues list.

Figure 329.

List Settings
page

Selecting Versioning

One of the options for lists and documents is versioning. This means that previous copies of entries or documents are stored, though only the most recent version is generally displayed. Versioning is useful if there are multiple people making entries against a particular item, and you need to refer back to an earlier draft. You should only select Versioning when you are certain it will be needed. There is a danger that the SharePoint storage demands will expand rapidly if this function is used indiscriminately.

1 To work with versioning, go to the list Settings page (shown in the previous figure) and click the *Versioning settings* link (in the *General Settings* section).

You will see the Versioning Settings page, where you can select the appropriate level of version retention.

Figure 330.

Versioning
Settings

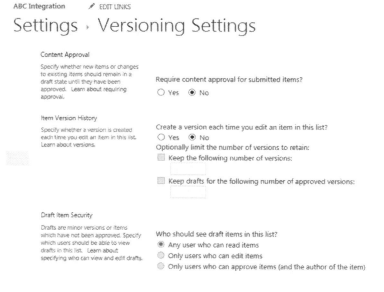

2 Click *OK* to save your changes, and return to the List Settings page.

Defining a List Column

1 In the *Columns* section of the list Settings page, you can click a column to be redefined or select the *Create column* option to make a new one.

Figure 331.

Columns section

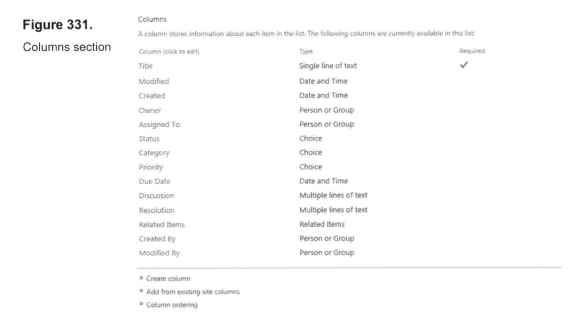

Columns

A column stores information about each item in the list. The following columns are currently available in this list:

Column (click to edit)	Type	Required
Title	Single line of text	✓
Modified	Date and Time	
Created	Date and Time	
Owner	Person or Group	
Assigned To	Person or Group	
Status	Choice	
Category	Choice	
Priority	Choice	
Due Date	Date and Time	
Discussion	Multiple lines of text	
Resolution	Multiple lines of text	
Related Items	Related Items	
Created By	Person or Group	
Modified By	Person or Group	

□ Create column
□ Add from existing site columns
□ Column ordering

2 Clicking any attribute in the *Columns* list will take you to the Edit Column page, where you will be presented with a list of field attributes (appropriate to the field type, which cannot be changed) for the column you selected. Edit these attributes as appropriate.

In the following example, we are changing the *Title* field to have a maximum of 100 characters.

Figure 332.

Edit Column
page for *Title*
field

3 Scroll to the bottom of the screen and click *OK* to save the changes. Return to the list Settings page.

Defining a List View

Lists can be displayed in different layouts and with different parameters. They typically have one or two default views, depending on the type of data being displayed. For instance, one of the standard views for a calendar list is a monthly table, while a group discussion list has a threaded discussion view. You can create your own view to display relevant information.

To define or edit a list view:

1 From the List Settings page for ProductLaunch, click the *Create view* link located at the very bottom of the page. You will see the View Type page:

Figure 333.

View Type page

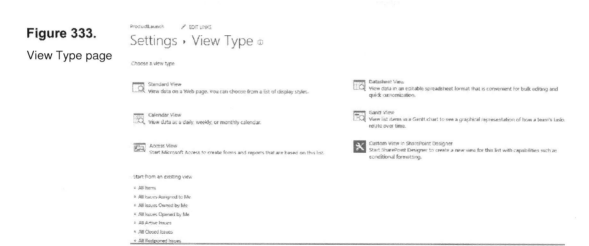

2 On the View Type page, click the view style that best suits your needs. For this exercise, we clicked the *Standard View* link, which took us to the Create View page for this type of view.

Figure 334.

Create View
page (for
Standard View)

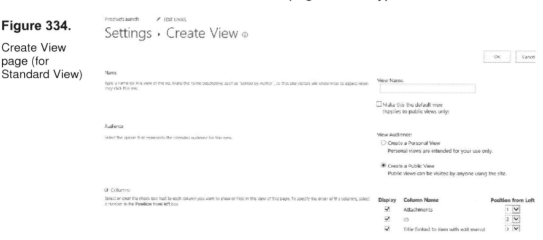

3 The Standard View presents data in a traditional table format. On the data entry page in the preceding figure, enter the following information:

❑ *View Name*: "New ProductLaunch List View"

❑ *View Audience*: Select *Create a Public View* so that anyone using the site can access the view.

❑ *Columns*: Select the default Column Names for this view (*Attachments*, *ID*, *Title*, *Assigned To*, *Status*, *Priority*, *Category*, and *Due Date*).

4 Toward the bottom of this View Definition page, you will see sections for additional view parameters, such as *Sort*, *Filter*, and *Group*. Accept all of the default values in these sections.

Figure 335.

Sections on
bottom of view
definition page

5 At the bottom of the view definition page, click *OK* to save this view.

6 Click the *Issues* link in the sidebar to navigate again to the Issues
 page for your project. From *List:Manage Views* click the *Current
 View* dropdown list to select the view you just defined, as in the
 following figure:

Figure 336.

Newly created
issues list view

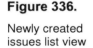

Documents

Document libraries are used to store, organize, and share documents with
people. By keeping documents in a central location, everyone who needs one
has access at any time. You can also sync documents to your local computer so
you have offline access to them.

Projects usually include documents, such as a project charter, statements of
work, and closeout reports. Project Web App 2016 uses SharePoint to manage
project documents.

Document libraries can either be shared by all who use your Project Web App
site or can be specific to a project. In this section we will discuss how to view,
edit, and add both types of libraries.

Shared Document Libraries

1 At the top-right corner of all Project Web App, you will see a *Settings* [
 ⚙] icon. Click this icon to see the following options:

Figure 337.

Settings options

Office 365 settings

SharePoint settings
Shared with...

Add an app

Site contents

Change the look

Site settings

Getting started

Send Feedback

PWA Settings

Note: The options you see may differ slightly from the list in the preceding
figure as well for following Project Web App settings, according to the
permissions the Project Server administrator has granted to you.

2 In the *Settings* options list, click *Site Settings* to see the Site Settings
 page for your Project Web App site, similar to the following:

Figure 338.

PWA Site Settings
page

Project Web App

Site Settings

Users and Permissions
People and groups
Site permissions
Access requests and invitations
Site collection administrators
Site app permissions

Web Designer Galleries
Site columns
Site content types
Web parts
List templates
Master pages
Themes
Solutions
Composed looks

Site Administration
Regional settings
Language settings
Site libraries and lists
User alerts

Look and Feel
Design Manager
Title, description, and logo
Device Channels
Navigation Elements
Change the look
Import Design Package
Navigation

Site Actions
Manage site features
Enable search configuration export
Reset to site definition
Delete this site

Site Collection Administration
Recycle bin
Search Result Sources
Search Result Types
Search Query Rules
Search Schema
Search Settings

The Site Contents page provides a series of tiles that identify and provide links to all lists, libraries and other apps associated with your Project Web App site.

3 Suppose you'd like to change the look of your Project Web App pages. To do so, click *Change the Look* under *Look and Feel*.

You will see a page that offers a variety of options.

Figure 339.

Change the Look of Project Web App under *Look and Feel*

4 You can also select *Title, Description, and Logo* to customize your page for your organization.

Figure 340.

Title, Description, and Logo page

5 You can enter your company name or department in the *Title* to change the display on all Project Web App pages

Figure 341.

Change Project
Web App title

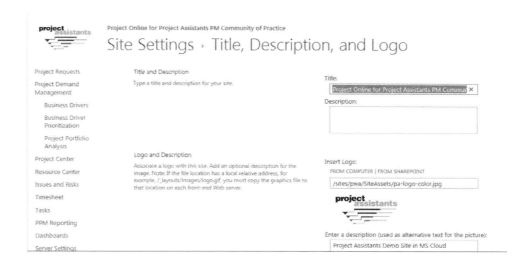

6 Click the *OK* to apply the changes

Project-Related Document Libraries

The project owner has the ability to create and manage the document library for each specific project.

1 From your Project Web App Home page, click the *Projects* link in the sidebar to navigate to the Project Center.

2 Click on the project *ABC Integration* to navigate to the Project Details page for the project. From *Project:Navigate* click the *Project Site* icon. Note the *Documents* section toward the bottom of the screen.

Currently there are no documents in the default documents library associated with *ABC Integration*.

Figure 342.

Documents for
ABC Integration

Adding Documents to a Document Library

1 To view the documents in a document library, you can either click the sidebar link to the library or the appropriate tile on the project's Site Contents page. For the purposes of this exercise, from a project's Project Site (in this case *ABC Integration*), click the *Documents* link in the sidebar.

Figure 343.

Default
document library
for *ABC
Integration*

2 Click the *Upload* icon to add a new document to the document the library.

Figure 344.

Upload file to
document library

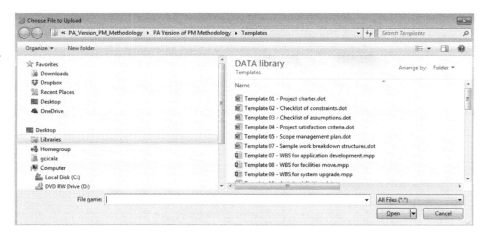

To create a folder in your library, from *Files:New* click the *New Folder* icon to see the **Create a new folder** dialog box.

Figure 345.

**Create a new
folder** dialog
box

8 Name your new folder and click *Save*. The newly created folder will appear in the library.

Figure 346.

New folder in
the library

ProductLaunch ✎ EDIT LINKS

Documents

⊕ new document or drag files here

All Documents ⋯ | Find a file 🔎 |

✓	▯	Name		Modified
		NewFolder	⋯	A few seconds ago
	🗋	NewLibraryDocument ✳	⋯	18 minutes ago

10 You can view and upload files to a folder in the same manner as you
 view and upload folders to a library.

End of Chapter Quiz Questions

1. What is the difference between opening the project using the *In Microsoft Project* function and the *In Microsoft Project for Editing* function and for both of these to work, what do you need to have?

2. What option takes you to a page where you can view and check in all of your checked out projects?

3. The options in which groups, help you define the timescale displayed on your Project Center screen?

4 – 7: Match the group option listed in the left column of the table below, to the correct description from the right column by entering the letter that the step corresponds to in the blank line.

4. Outline _____	A. Categorizes projects by any field in the selected view, to three category levels
5. View _____	B. Allows you to select built-in filters, create a custom filter, or turn on Auto-filter
6. Filter _____	C. Provides options for adjusting the level of detail you wish to display in the projects listed in the Project Center
7. Group By _____	D. Allows you to customize the appearance of the Project Center list

8. How can you sort projects by the entries in a particular field?

9. How can you open the Project Details page from the Project Center, and what can the user see after it's open?

10. What does clicking the empty box to the far left of the Project Name, in the Project Center, allow you to do, and why would it be necessary?

11. What do you need to do in the Project Center if you want to search for content across the site?

12. Which of the following has team building functions?
 a. Microsoft Project Professional
 b. Project Web App
 c. Both a and b
 d. None of the above

13. What are the options available from the Build Team view of PWA?

14. What does the *Match* option in Team Builder do?

15. What can the default summary of the Resource Assignments view be used for?

16. What are the four standard Resource Availability views?

17. True or False: A "Committed" engagement means the resource's booking type is committed.

chapter 14

Variance Analysis, Plan Revision, and Project Communication

- Variance Analysis

- Plan Revision and Scope Management

- Project Communication Principles

Learning Objectives for this Chapter

At the end of the chapter, the reader should be able to:

- Understand variance analysis and apply these concepts in Microsoft Project
- Perform root cause analysis for unfavorable variances
- Comprehend the project management principles of plan revision and scope management
- Understand how to plan, manage, and apply change control principles for project scope changes
- Identify project communication principles
- Define the elements of a meaningful status report, communications planning considerations, and the concept of the communications management plan
- Close a project

14.1 Variance Analysis

Variance analysis is the process of identifying and understanding differences between current progress and the initial baseline estimates for a project work plan. Variance analysis is an important aspect of project control because the process highlights potential trouble spots in an evolving project.

Overview of Variance

Here's a quote that can help conceptualize the importance of tracking variances.

"Question: How does a large software project get to be one year late?

"Answer: One day at a time!"

--*The Mythical Man-Month: Essays on Software Engineering* by Fred Brooks

Types of Variances

Favorable versus Unfavorable Variances

In project management terms, a variance is the difference between the anticipated state of the project and the actual state at a given point in time. At the beginning of the project, when the planned schedule, budget, scope, etc. have just been calculated, the actual state and the predicted state are exactly the same—i.e. there are no variances. This is the point at which the project should be baselined.

As time progresses, the execution of the project may not follow the plan exactly. For example, if a task starts later than it was scheduled to start, there is a difference between the baseline start date and the actual start date for the task. The actual start date is later (a larger number) than the baseline start, so the difference between these two dates is a positive number—i.e. there is a positive variance. As this example illustrates, a positive variance is unfavorable. In this case, where a task is late to start, subsequent tasks may also be delayed, and the recalculated schedule may show a finish delay.

All values captured as part of the project baseline information can be compared with the current schedule's value. You may have variances for work, start, finish, duration, and cost. In each case, a positive variance is unfavorable and means that the current schedule is greater than the baseline value. On the other hand, if tasks are completed earlier than scheduled, or with less effort or less money, the corresponding variance would be a negative number and would be regarded as favorable.

The most common work plan variances (work, cost, start, and finish) measure the difference between the current estimate and the original baseline estimate. If tasks are being completed late or in excess of their original work estimates, the project manager should look for trouble signs regularly to be sure that the plan is revised to adjust to the day-to-day realities of the project. If progress is not as expected, the project manager has to figure out how to revise the plan to extend the scheduled finish date, adjust resource assignments, or reduce scope.

The values in the current work, cost, start, finish, and duration fields are usually modified through the tracking process. As team members report unexpected changes in the plan, the current values will diverge from the original baseline values, causing variances.

Summary of Variance Types (using Microsoft Project field names)

Variance Name	Calculated as:	Task field?	Phase field?	Resource field?
		Available In:		
Work Variance	(Current Work – Baseline Work)	Yes	Yes	Yes
Cost Variance	(Current Cost – Baseline Cost)	Yes	Yes	Yes
Duration Variance	(Current Duration – Baseline Duration)	Yes	Yes	No
Start Variance	(Current Start – Baseline Start)	Yes	Yes	No
Finish Variance	(Current Finish – Baseline Finish)	Yes	Yes	No

It's important to note that variance calculations in Microsoft Project require baseline data. If there is no baseline, there will be no variance.

The two tables that follow illustrate how Microsoft Project automatically generates variances to the baseline based on the application of actual progress information.

Figure 347.

Before applying actual progress

Current Estimate	Field Content	Baseline (original estimate)	Field Content	Variance (Current-original)	Field Content
Work	40h	B. Work	40h	Work var.	0h
Actual work	0h	NA	NA	NA	NA
Rem. work	40h	NA	NA	NA	NA
Cost	$4,000	B. Cost	$4,000	Cost var.	$0
Start	11/5	B. Start	11/5	Start var.	0d
Finish	11/9	B. Finish	11/9	Finish var.	0d
Duration	5d	B. Duration	5d	Duration var.	0d

Figure 348.

After applying actual progress

Current Estimate	Field Content	Baseline (original estimate)	Field Content	Variance (Current-original)	Field Content
Work	56	B. Work	40h	Work var.	16h (unfav.)
Actual work	24h	NA	NA	NA	NA
Rem. work	32h	NA	NA	NA	NA
Cost	$5,600	B. Cost	$4,000	Cost var.	$1,600
Start	11/6	B. Start	11/5	Start var.	1d
Finish	11/14	B. Finish	11/9	Finish var.	2d
Duration	7d	B. Duration	5d	Duration var.	2d

Interpreting Variances

"Those who say they can perform project control without comparing project performance to a baseline do not fully understand the meaning of project control."

-Harvey Levine,
Project Management Using Microcomputers

Finding Trouble Spots in the Plan with Variance Analysis

Variance analysis is key to addressing critical questions for the project manager, including:

❑ Can the remaining work be performed by the end date?

❑ Do estimates need to be adjusted based on current variance trends?

❑ Are resources arriving as scheduled?

❑ Are schedule bottlenecks preventing tasks from starting and completing as planned?

❑ Which tasks or resources require additional attention to get back on course?

Looking for trouble

One of the key questions resulting from variance analysis is, "Will the project still finish on time?" One of the key indicators is the total remaining work for the entire project.

Consider this example: There are 10 months left on the project, 10 people assigned full-time, and 18,000 hours of remaining work; will the project complete on time? One person can comfortably perform about 130 hours in a month, so 10 people can perform 1,300 hours in a month and 13,000 hours in 10 months. In this example, it looks like the 18,000 remaining hours will not be completed by the target end date.

What if you look at the work variances each week and they keep getting worse? Consider this example:

Date	Project Work Variance
10/8	50 hours
10/15	100 hours
10/22	200 hours

If the variances are worsening each week, your estimates may need to be adjusted. What happens if resources arrive late? Your work variances may be acceptable, but what will the date variances look like?

Other Considerations

Note the way that start and finish variances are calculated: they use the current estimated date, not the actual date. This means a task that has not started yet can create a variance, but how?

There are two primary ways to make sure your plan remains dynamic and up-to-date: rescheduling unstarted, late tasks and rescheduling remaining work on in-progress tasks. These rescheduling processes help you avoid stagnant work plans, a common problem for late and overbudget projects.

An Example

Field	Value
Baseline	1000 hours
Actual Work	500 hours
Remaining Work	500 hours

- ❏ This project was estimated to be 10 months in duration. It is now 8 months into the project.

- ❏ What is the estimated vs. actual burn rate?

- ❏ How many hours of actual work should have been consumed?

- ❏ How many hours have been consumed?

- ❏ Based on the current burn rate, what is the estimated total duration of this project at completion?

- ❏ What would we see if we looked at the start variances for this plan?

The current estimated work for this project is 1,000 hours (500 actual plus 500 remaining). The baseline is 1,000 hours, so this project is in good shape, right? But the project was supposed to be 10 months in duration and 8 months have already passed. There's obviously some kind of problem, but we don't see it by looking at the work variance (which is zero hours).

What's the Problem?

- ❏ Assume a constant resource load on this project. If the total baseline work is 1,000 hours, how many hours should be used per month on a 10-month project? (100 hours)

- ❏ How many hours have been consumed to this point? (500 actual hours)

- ❏ How many hours should have been consumed to this point? (8 months times 100 hours per month is 800 hours)

- ❏ How many hours are really being consumed per month? (500 hours ÷ 8 months = 62.5 hours per month)

- ❏ At this rate, how long will this project take to complete? (16 months)

Another Example

- ❏ The current date is 2/15. Five tasks were scheduled to start on 2/1, but have not.

- ❏ What is the start variance for these tasks?

What's the Problem?

If a task does not start when it's supposed to, it will not create a variance unless it is re-scheduled. The task in this example's baseline start is 2/1, and its current start date is 2/1, therefore its variance is 0 days.

The task has to be re-scheduled before there is a variance. What if the task is re-scheduled to 2/20? Now its baseline is 2/1, but its current start date is 2/20. A variance of 19 days will be calculated (assuming all days are working days).

> 2/1 Baseline Start

> ──────────────► 2/20 Current Start

It might be tempting to wait until actuals start arriving for the task, since an actual start date will override the start date (reality always wins), creating a start variance. The problem is, by the time actuals begin to arrive, it may be too late to do anything about the variance. Remember, the sooner you can identify and analyze an unfavorable variance, the greater chance you have to mobilize effort to recover and the more options you have.

14.2 Plan Revision and Scope Management

"I come from an environment where if you see a snake, you kill it. At General Motors, if you see a snake, the first thing you do is hire a consultant on snakes."

- H. Ross Perot

Preserving the Integrity of the Plan

Creating and publishing a project plan is only part of a project manager's duties. Another key function is maintaining the state of a project plan so that it continues to show an accurate picture of the project as time passes. This is where maintenance of the project plan is important. It must reflect not only that time has passed, but also that some work has been done on tasks. It must also account for the fact that there may have been changes in how reality actually turned out compared with what was anticipated when the plan was originally created.

If a project is in trouble, it's important to remember to use the plan to manage the project—don't deviate from the plan, change it! Depending on the type of problem you are having, there are different strategies you'll need to employ to get your plan back on track. The bottom line is that something needs to change *in the future* if you are required to deliver on-time and on-budget with high quality and all expectations met.

Tools can help the project manager revise the schedule, but first you have to know what will work for you on this project in your particular situation. Changing the work plan is not as easy as simply changing scope, schedule, or resources. There are usually some pretty limited options; for example, your sponsors don't want to cut scope, the schedule is not negotiable, and resources (people, machines, and money) are limited. Some project managers fail to recognize the need to adjust one of these factors and end up compromising quality.

Getting Concurrence

Before the project manager can revise the plan, there are often project sponsors that must approve your revision strategy. This is a situation where a project manager is often forced to make trade-offs. Some examples of trade-offs include:

❑ A cheaper resource can help the project stay within budget, but the work estimates may increase due to lack of experience of the cheaper resource.

❑ A scope reduction may help, but you are probably sacrificing some of your objectives to stay within schedule and budget.

❑ Adding lead (overlapping tasks) may appear to shorten the schedule but often increases the risk of missing the schedule because of the possible need for rework.

The unfortunate reality is that serious oversights in the SOW or plan will significantly reduce the chances of completing the plan according to all of its original expectations.

Why Plans Should Be Revised

"**Management must have a purpose and dedication that must have an emotional commitment. It must be built in as a vital part of the personality of anyone who truly is a manager.**"

- Harold Geneen, IT&T

When can a plan be changed? Minor plan revisions can turn into major revisions that require the project manager to ask for more funding, to redefine the project scope, or to re-baseline the plan.

Stage-limited commitment provides for re-planning at the end of each phase. If this expectation is set properly, the project manager may have the opportunity to make major plan revisions at every major milestone.

Sometimes the project manager has to accept the reality that unfavorable variances are continuing to mount and the trends cannot be reversed. This situation should force a major re-think of the overall project SOW and a new plan to deal with the problems before the project fails completely. Communication is critical at a time like this. The project manager must let management and the sponsors know what's going on and why.

Variance analysis records should be maintained to provide good documentation for why the plan must be modified.

Aggressive Revision

How can the project manager avoid these problems?

Project plans must be regularly and aggressively revised to keep them in line with current activities. Drastic changes to the plan are often the result of too much time passing between the project control cycles of tracking, analysis, and revision.

Strategies for Plan Recovery

Plan Recovery Using a Tool

The advantages of using software for this process include:

- ❑ Project management tools can help with "what-if" analysis.
- ❑ Multiple options can be rapidly generated.
- ❑ Output can be summarized for management presentation.
- ❑ Data can be extracted to answer very specific questions.

Crashing the Schedule

When the project manager is presented with the need to make drastic changes to achieve the original schedule, project management tools can help investigate strategies quickly.

Some ways a tool can help you visualize the effects of plan revision include:

- ❑ Changing the critical path
 - ○ Adding or breaking links
 - ○ Adding more tasks to the critical path by including tasks with small amounts of slack
- ❑ The possibility of displaying multiple critical paths
- ❑ Adding lead or lag time to tasks
- ❑ Decreasing the task duration
 - ○ Adding resource(s) to effort-driven tasks
- ❑ Decreasing a resource's work on a task
- ❑ Reducing scope
- ❑ Deleting tasks
- ❑ Using Risk contingencies

- o Drawing upon "buckets" or a management contingency line
- o Assigning overtime work

All these strategies are simply ways to visualize what could be done; actual solutions require stakeholder support and agreement.

The Foundations of Change Control

Effective scope management makes two important assumptions:

❑ **The project manager has made it clear what the scope is.**

A sound approach to change control highlights the importance of the definition document, specifically completion criteria.

Strict scope management also requires adherence to the deliverables acceptance procedure.

❑ **Change requestors acknowledge that their request is out of scope.**

This second crucial assumption relies on the communication and acceptance of the change control procedure at the start of the project.

Even when these two assumptions are valid, scope management requires a tenacious attitude from the project manager.

Project managers sometimes become overly concerned with client satisfaction when they are asked to make "free" scope changes. Effective project managers manage scope well by knowing how to say "no" with a smile; perhaps more importantly, effective project managers know how to say "Here's what it will cost, is that OK?" with a smile.

Planning for Change

A project manager can avoid the worst effects of project change by being prepared. Some strategies include:

❑ Anticipate probable changes on the next project. This may mean being more rigorous when developing the work package descriptions or including additional risks in the list.

❑ Have an explicit change management process. This may include process documents such as:

- o Project Change Request (PCR)
- o Change Order
- o Change Authorization
- o Contract Amendment

❑ Define, plan for, and track project and management reserves with management. These may be represented as a "bucket of hours" or a contingency budget.

With a change management process, it should be clear that a change request is not the only step. There needs to be an impact assessment; approval for any change in schedule, budget, scope, or quality; and a formal update to the plan.

Impact Analysis

When project managers are presented with requests for change, they are usually asked to estimate the impact of making the change. A common set of questions might be: how much will it cost and when can I have it?

Since the project manager can anticipate that changes are inevitable, s/he can also anticipate that requests for impact analysis are inevitable. As a result, the project manager needs to load a task in the plan and allocate hours for "analyzing the impact of change." For a plan with 2,000 hours of project management time, the impact analysis might be allocated 10%, or 200 hours of time.

Each time a request for change is submitted, there will be a budget of hours to perform the impact analysis without adding to the overall cost of the project.

If your project sponsor resists a line item for impact analysis, you might need to inform your sponsor that even impact analyses are out of scope. Yes, you do charge for estimates!

Summary Change Control Procedure

Following is a sample change control procedure:

- ❏ Change request is completed by team member or user and submitted to project manager for evaluation

- ❏ Project manager and primary client contact approve change for impact analysis.

- ❏ Project manager records time spent on analysis and reports impact (price, schedule, scope) and recommendation for approval or disapproval to client.

- ❏ Out-of-scope changes are recorded and deferred, if possible.

- ❏ In-scope changes may have to be added to work plan immediately.

- ❏ In- or out-of-scope changes may be disputed and sent for arbitration in extreme cases.

- ❏ Approved changes are recorded and signed by project manager and client to indicate approval.

Crossing the Line

This procedure should be adopted early in the definition stages of the project. The expectation that scope will be tightly managed must be set from the beginning.

A good project manager will quickly condition the project team and project sponsors to the idea that scope changes will be tightly managed and will not be implemented without a formal, written procedure.

There are a variety of ways to keep change control in the front-and-center of attention:

❑ Introduce it in the SOW

❑ Review it at the project kick-off

❑ Devote a section to it on the status report, such as in the following figure:

Figure 349.

Example status report with a section on change control.

14.3 Project Communication Principles

The Elements of a Meaningful Status Report

The project status report is a regular project management deliverable. Therefore, its structure should be communicated in the deliverables guideline of the SOW, as follows:

❑ Summary

❑ Planned accomplishments for this period

❑ Actual accomplishments for this period

❑ Explanation of differences

❑ Major tasks planned for next period

❑ Issues / Concerns / Recommendations

❑ Project work plan trend analysis (often displayed graphically)

 ❑ Cumulative task summary

 ❑ Work variances (see Section 14.1: *Variance Analysis* for a refresher on variances)

 ❑ Start variances

 ❑ Finish variances

 ❑ Week-to-week trends (gaining or losing ground)

❑ Change control summary

❑ Financial summary / cost variances

Project Communication Planning

There are several important questions about communication that a project manager must consider as part of the project planning process:

❑ What information does each stakeholder or group of stakeholders need?

❑ When will they need it?

❑ What's the best way to communicate it to them and what tools are available?

❑ How and how often should we review the communication plan for effectiveness?

Most project communications planning is done as part of the early project planning phase, since that's when communication begins to become necessary. It is tempting but dangerous to assume that decisions made in the very early days of the project will remain true and useful as the project matures.

Communications Planning Considerations

Communications requirements – Communications requirements include the type and the format of information required by all stakeholders. The project manager should also consider the value of the information needed. Since communication requires resources, those resources should only be spent to communicate information when doing so bolsters project success (or poor communication prevents it). Other issues that might be necessary to consider include:

❑ Project organization and stakeholder positions

❑ Technical disciplines and departments included in the project

❑ How many people will be involved and where they will be located

❑ External communication (e.g. likelihood of public interest)

Communications technology – The available communications technologies can range from hallway conversations to formal meetings, from simple written items to online project plans and data. Some factors the project should consider include:

❑ Does project success require having frequently updated information constantly available, or would regular written reports do?

❑ Are necessary communication systems already in place, or should implementing those systems be part of the project?

❑ Will project participants require training?

❑ Is the available communication technology in the organization likely to change during the project; how might that affect the project?

Constraints – Constraints in this context are factors that limit the project manager's options. Are there information security needs or contract provisions that might limit the team's choices?

Assumptions – Assumptions are factors that must be considered real for planning purposes. Assumptions involve risk, but unrecognized or unstated assumptions greatly increase that risk.

Communications Management Plan

A communications management plan is a part of the overall project plan that includes:

❑ The methods which will be used to collect and store needed information; these should also cover updates and corrections

❑ A description of what information (status reports, schedule, technical documents, etc.) will flow to whom and what methods (written reports, meetings, etc.) will be used to distribute the information

❑ A description of each item of information to be distributed, including the format, content, level of detail, and conventions or definitions to be used

❑ A schedule showing when each type of communication will be produced

❑ A description of the procedures to be followed to get information between scheduled communications

❑ A plan for reviewing and updating the communications plan as the project progresses

As with many of the plans we've covered to this point, a communications management plan may be formal or informal, highly detailed or broadly framed, depending on the needs of the project.

Administrative Closure

The Guide to the Project Management Body of Knowledge includes *administrative closure* as part of the project communication process. Administrative closure consists of documenting project results for formal acceptance by the sponsor, client, or customer. It includes collecting project records, ensuring that products meet final specifications, analyzing project success and effectiveness, and archiving such information for future use.

Administrative closure activities should not be delayed until project completion. Each phase of the project should be properly closed to ensure that important and useful information is not lost.

The overall purpose of administrative closure is two-fold. One critical issue, of course, is formal acceptance of the project (or phase of the project) by the project client. Some form of documentation that the client or sponsor has accepted the product of the project should be prepared and distributed to management and team members.

The second purpose is to support continuous improvement of the project process within the organization. Being good at what we do is always easier than getting better at what we do. A major way to do that is to have some form of "lessons learned" process, beyond the usual terminal project report. The most effective approach is a face-to-face meeting among the project team where team members focus on what they have gotten from the project experience that is worth keeping for their own use and sharing with other members of the organization. This helps overcome the natural resistance to the "report card" approach, which is far more common in organizations.

The real issue isn't how did I do on the project (because I can't change that); it's how will I use this experience on my next project?

End of Chapter Quiz Questions

1. What is variance analysis?

 ┌───┐
 │ │
 │ │
 │ │
 └───┘

2. Fill in the blank: In project management terms, a variance is the difference between the _____ state of the project and the _____ state at a particular point in time.

3. In project management, what are the most common work plan variances and what do they measure?

 ┌───┐
 │ │
 │ │
 │ │
 └───┘

4. What are the two primary ways to make sure your plan remains dynamic and up to-date?

 ┌───┐
 │ │
 │ │
 │ │
 └───┘

5. True or False: If a task does not start when it is supposed to, it will create a variance when it is not re-scheduled.

6. Fill in the blank: The project plan must reflect not only that time has passed, but also that some _____ has been done on tasks.

7. Who usually must approve the revision strategy before the project manager can revise the plan? _____

8. What are some examples of trade-offs that project managers may be forced to make?

 ┌───┐
 │ │
 │ │
 │ │
 └───┘

9. What are some of the ways that project management tools can be used as part of the plan recovery strategy?

10. What are some ways a tool can help you visualize the effects of plan revision?

11. What two important assumptions does effective scope management make?

12. Effective project managers manage scope well by knowing how to say what word? Explain.

13. What are some strategies that a project manager can implement to avoid the worst effects of project change and be prepared?

14. What are some ways to manage stakeholder expectations about scope change?

15. How should the project status report be structured?

```

```

16. What is the overall purpose of administrative closure?

```

```

chapter 15

Presenting Project Information with Microsoft Project 2016

- Communication Options

- Using Tables, Filters, and Views

- Defining and Using Custom Fields

- Communicating Project Information

- Exporting Project Information

Learning Objectives for this Chapter

At the end of the chapter, the reader should be able to:

- Describe the communication options in Microsoft Project, especially as it pertains to options available to format the Gantt Chart
- Effectively create, utilize, and modify the tables, filters, groups, and views features available to display meaningful project information
- Sort information in views
- Define and use custom fields
- Communicate project information as it pertains to the dashboard and visual reports available in Microsoft Project
- Know how to set up and manipulate the information in dashboard and visual reports
- Export project information

*I*n earlier chapters we've discussed the importance of updating project plan information with actuals and updating the plan itself to reflect the results of work done and changes in scope. For this information to be useful, you must be able to easily display the information you need and be able to present it to project stakeholders, often in the form of status reports and progress reports. These presentations require organized data and graphics, so this chapter will discuss the presentation options available to users of Microsoft Project 2016.

15.1 Communication Options

One presents information with Microsoft Project 2016 using one or more of the following options:

❑ Capture what is on the screen in a format that allows the user to paste the image directly into a Microsoft Word or PowerPoint document or as an image that can be sent as a picture to stakeholders. Recall the *Copy Picture* tool discussed in Section 9.5: *Taking a Picture of Your Gantt Chart.* This approach is a major avenue for reporting graphics.

❑ Display a view containing the information you need.

❑ Print the information, or a selected set of information, on the screen to prepare hard copy reports.

❑ Export the data to another application for manipulation or to prepare electronic reports.

Options with the Gantt Chart View

The Gantt Chart is a relatively simple picture of your project. Since it is a calendar bar chart, it is easily explained, even to someone who is unfamiliar with the format. Microsoft Project 2016 has made the Gantt Chart even more visually appealing by adding three-dimensional texturing and enhanced colors to the calendar bars, as well as cell background formatting to the table portion of the view.

The standard Gantt Chart presentation can be modified in several ways:

❑ The **Bar Styles** dialog box is the quickest way to make extensive changes to the Gantt Chart.

❑ The *Format Bar...* button allows users to change one bar at a time.

❑ Drawing on the Gantt Chart allows users to add notes and explanations to the calendar field.

We'll examine these three approaches in the following exercises.

Using Bar Styles to Change the Appearance of the Gantt Chart

The **Bar Styles** dialog box (which can be accessed from the *Format* tab on the ribbon or by right-clicking the Gantt Chart itself) provides a great deal of flexibility in formatting the Gantt bars and the attached text on a Gantt Chart display.

As mentioned earlier in this book, you can display interim plans on your Gantt Chart. The following lesson explores how this can be done using the **Bar Styles** dialog box.

Displaying Current, Interim, and Baseline Plans on Your Gantt Chart

By comparing a task's baseline to its plan in the Tracking Gantt view, you can see how a task's actual schedule compares to its original estimate. If the project is only one week old, then this comparison might be sufficient. But suppose we are three months into the project and would like to be able to see the current situation, as well as the baseline and forecast for the remainder of the project.

Microsoft Project 2016 gives you the capability to save interim plans as well as baseline plans. An interim plan is a snapshot of your project's scheduled start and finish dates at a specific point in time. You can save up to ten interim plans. By presenting the baseline, a dated interim plan, and the current updated plan, you can show the evolution of the project plan since project execution began.

📁 This exercise uses the file **InterimPlan.mpp**. Open this project before beginning and ensure you are in the Gantt Chart view.

1 From *Project:Properties* click *Project Information*, and in the **Project Information** dialog box, set the *Current date* to "6/26."

2 Switch to the Tracking Gantt view.

3 You would like to save a snapshot of the plan as of today (June 25 [of the current year]) and display it on your Tracking Gantt Chart for a future management presentation. From *Project:Schedule* use the **Set Baseline** dropdown to select *Set Baseline...*. You will be presented with the **Set Baseline** dialog box.

4 Select the *Set baseline* option button. Your screen will resemble the following:

Figure 350.

Set Baseline
dialog box

5 Click *OK* to close the dialog box.

6 Apply the Baseline Table: *View:Date:Table* dropdown and choose *More Tables*.

Figure 351.

Applying the
Baseline Table,
part 1

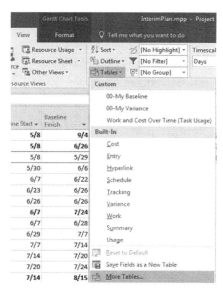

7 Click on *Baseline* table then *Apply*.

Figure 352.

Applying the
Baseline Table,
part 2

11 Now apply the Tracking Table (*View:Data:Tracking*).

Enter following Actual start dates:

 i. Task 3: 5/12

 ii. Task 4: 6/3

 iii. Task 5: 6/12

Figure 353.

The Tracking
Table

	Task Name	Act. Start	Act. Finish
1	⊿ Software System Implementation	5/12	NA
2	⊿ Build Project Plan	5/12	NA
3	Create Statement of Work	5/12	5/29
4	Obtain approval of Statement of Work	6/3	6/12
5	Create project plan	6/12	6/27

12 Now apply the Variance Table (*View:Data* then choose *Variance*).
Note the difference network the start date and baseline start. Also,
note the difference between the finish date and the baseline finish.

Figure 354.

The Variance
Table

13 Apply the Tracking Gannt view. Then, choose *View:Zoom*, and from
the *Timescale* dropdown, choose *Weeks*. Note that each task has two
Gantt bars. Also, note that the bars are separated for each task.
What does this mean?

Figure 355.

The Tracking
Gantt view

12 Now investigate how the Bar Styles are configured on the Tracking Gantt view. Right-click in the Gantt Chart (in the white area) and select *Bar Styles* from the menu that appears. (Alternatively, from *Format:Bar Styles* click the *Format* dropdown to select *Bar Styles*). Your screen will resemble the following:

Figure 356.

Bar Styles
dialog box

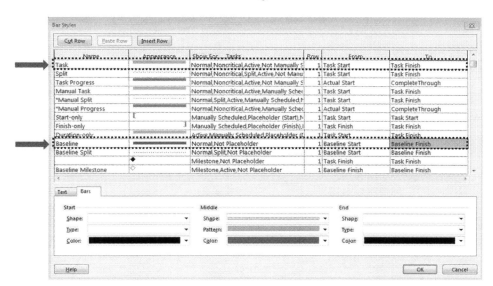

13 Save your project.

Viewing the Gantt Chart Bars without Resource Names

Microsoft Project allows you to customize and control almost all aspects of information presentation, including views, formats, and layouts. By default, the Gantt Chart shows resource names next to task bars, but you can change the names to initials or remove them completely as you desire.

📂 In this exercise, we continue the use of the file **InterimPlan.mpp** from the previous exercise. If you did not perform that exercise, you can use **InterimPlan_Inst1.mpp** from your exercise directory.

1 Apply the Gantt Chart view, and from *Format:Bar Styles* click the *Format* dropdown and select *Bar Styles*. You will see the **Bar Styles** dialog box as before.

2 Select *Task* in the *Name* column, and the *Text* tab in the bottom half of the dialog box.

3 Select *Resource Initials* from the *Right* dropdown list. Make this
 change for both the Critical row and the Task (non-critical) row. Your
 screen will resemble the following:

Figure 357.

Bar styles
(Text)

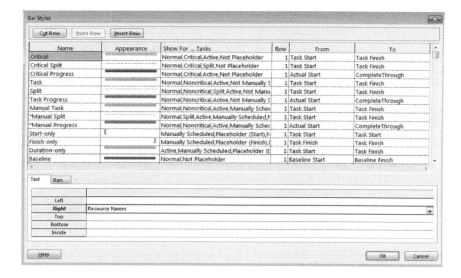

4 Click *OK*. Your screen will resemble the following:

Figure 358.

Task bars
with initials

5 Save and close your project.

Changing Bar Style or Color

Along with the drawing tools, changing the bar style or color can be used to
communicate information. Let's say that the assessment task involves an
outside contractor, so you would like to highlight it for the next management
review.

📁 In this exercise, we continue the use of the file **Reports.mpp** from the
 previous exercise. Alternatively, you can open **Reports_Inst1.mpp** from
 your exercise directory.

1 Right-click the bar for Task 11, *Assess printer hardware*. From the
 dropdown list, select *Format Bar...* to see the **Format Bar** dialog box:

Figure 359.

Format Bar
dialog box

2 Select a new *Color* for the task bar and click *OK* to save your change. Notice the new color for the bar for Task 11.

The *Format Bar...* option allows you to change one bar. You can also change several at-a-time, just as the *Bar Styles...* option changes all similar bars (task bars, summary bars, etc.).

3 Save and close your project.

Analyzing Variances in Your Project with Microsoft Project 2016

Keeping your project under control requires that you periodically look for tasks that are not progressing as originally planned. Once you have begun capturing your project's progress, you're ready to analyze plan variances.

Microsoft Project 2016 *automatically* calculates the difference between current progress and original estimates. Microsoft Project places the result into five different variance fields, as follows:

❑ Work Variance = Work - Baseline Work

❑ Cost Variance = Cost - Baseline Cost

❑ Start Variance = Start - Baseline Start

❑ Finish Variance = Finish - Baseline Finish

❑ Duration Variance = Duration - Baseline Duration

You may find it easier to remember these by thinking of the Work field as current estimated work and the Baseline Work as original estimated work. The Work Variance is then the *difference* between the current estimated work and the original estimated work.

The same holds true for the four other variance fields listed above.

When using Project Web App to collect actual hours of work, Microsoft Project assumes the first day actuals were entered on the actual start date. This is one reason % complete can be so misleading; Microsoft Project assumes the task started when it was supposed to and took the originally calculated or planned number of hours to complete. The only way to get accurate variance data when using % complete tracking is to manually populate the actual start and actual finish fields, or the actual work fields.

Any time the current estimated values are higher than the baseline values, the resulting variance will be a positive number. As we covered in Section 14.1: *Types of Variances*, this means it is unfavorable.

There are several ways to locate unfavorable variances in Microsoft Project. If none of these are suitable, we can always build new tables and other tools to help isolate trouble spots, as described later in this chapter.

Comparing the Baseline to Actual Data

Project baselines and actual data can be displayed graphically in charts or numerically in tables.

Displaying Project Statistics

The Project Statistics summary gives you a high-level overview of how you are progressing against the baseline. You can see a comparison of the current (or scheduled), baseline, and actual values for each of the five main value fields (i.e. start, finish, work, cost, and duration). You will also be able to see variance for the start and finish dates.

📁 This exercise uses the file **VarianceAnalysis.mpp**. Be sure this project is open before beginning.

 1 From *Project:Properties* click the *Project Information* button to see the **Project Information** dialog box for your project.

Figure 360.

Project Information dialog

 2 Click *Statistics...* at the bottom-left of your screen to see the **Project Statistics** summary for your project, similar to the following:

Figure 361.

Project Statistics summary

Notice this project summary data includes % duration complete and % work complete.

3 Click *Close.*

As vital as presenting project information is, we first have to locate it and organize it in a way that the receiver can use. Microsoft Project 2016 offers so many ways to organize information that some users are overwhelmed and have difficulty using Microsoft Project effectively as a presentation tool. The remainder of this chapter will examine how to organize and present project information useful to project stakeholders.

15.2 Using Tables, Filters, Views, and Groups in Microsoft Project 2016

Most project views include a table. A table is a set of formatting instructions that tells Microsoft Project which data fields (columns) you want displayed on the screen. The default Entry Table, for example, contains the ID, Indicators, Name (always Task Name), Duration, Start, Finish, Predecessors, and Resource Names fields. The default Cost Table contains the ID, Name, Fixed Cost, Fixed Cost Accrual, Cost (always total cost), Baseline, Variance, Actual, and Remaining (cost) fields.

Microsoft Project 2016 provides seventeen predefined task tables and ten predefined resource tables. If none of the standard tables meet your needs, you can create a new table or modify an existing one (be sure to give it a different name). When you save your project, your new or modified table is saved with the project.

If the new table would be useful to other project managers, the Project Server administrator can import it into the Enterprise Global and make it available for all enterprise projects.

Selecting the Right View

NOTE

> **In order to clearly understand the concepts presented in this chapter, it is critical that you understand the guidance offered in Section 3.3:** *Navigating in Microsoft Project 2016 Views.*

As we covered in Section 3.5: *Finding the Right Information*, a view is simply a set of formatting instructions that tell Microsoft Project what you want to see on the screen. Selecting the default Gantt Chart view, for example, tells Microsoft Project you want to see a calendar bar chart on the right, a matching table (by default the Entry Table) on the left, and a list that includes All Tasks (the default filter).

Microsoft Project 2016 contains a variety of views, including sheet views, chart and graph views, and form views. Examining them will provide ideas for different presentations of project information.

The six most commonly used ones are shown in the decision tree in 3.5. For tasks, the Gantt Chart and split Gantt Chart are very useful; for resources, the Resource Sheet and split Resource Sheet; and for assignments, the Task Usage and Resource Usage views. Microsoft Project 2016 automatically opens other views for you (for example, custom tracking views when you set up the tracking method to be used for the project), but remembering these six views will save you valuable time.

During project execution, the Tracking Gantt Chart becomes another useful view you should remember.

These seven views, along with several new dashboard views (discussed later in this chapter), will meet most of your information presentation needs.

NOTE

> **If your organization wants to use equivalent views to those above for all enterprise projects, they should be created by the Project Server administrator and named "Enterprise [name of the corresponding default view]." If Project Server contains views, tables, and so on with the same names as the ones used locally, you will constantly be asked to rename or replace your local items to avoid conflict.**

What Type of Information Are You Looking For?

Each view in Microsoft Project displays a unique combination of project information. The trick to using Microsoft Project effectively is first to know what type of information you are looking for, and then to know which view you can use to find this information. Once you are in the correct view, you can adjust the display to see the exact information you require.

If no view exists that comes close, you can create your own. Again, please see Section 3.3: *Navigating in Microsoft Project 2016 Views* for a detailed overview of this subject. The following exercises will explore how these views work with enterprise (published) projects.

Standard Views

📁 For this exercise, launch Microsoft Project 2016 and connect to Project Server. Open **Task+ResourceWorkload.mpp** and publish it to Project Server.

1 From *Task:View* use the dropdown arrow to select *Task Usage*. Choose *View: Zoom, Timescale* dropdown: *Weeks*. Your screen will resemble the following:

Figure 362.

Task Usage view

The Task Usage view presents the task list just as in the Gantt Chart view, but it also shows resource assignments for each task. The right side of the view is a timephased grid, which lists the planned work for the project by default. Other fields may be added or substituted in the timephased grid, and the timescale can be changed just as in the Gantt Chart view.

2 If you are looking for resource information but aren't interested in task assignments, from *View:Resource Views* click *Resource Sheet*. Your screen will resemble the following:

Figure 363.

Resource Sheet view

The Resource Sheet view presents both generic and specific information about enterprise and local resources. Although task assignments are not shown, over-allocated resources are flagged in red boldface with an alert in the *Indicator* field.

3 If you require a more detailed resource view but would like a static (rather than timephased) view, from *View:Split View* select the *Details* checkbox. You will see the Resource Form view in the lower frame with the Resource Sheet in the upper frame, as follows:

Figure 364.

Resource
Sheet over
Resource
Form

This view provides the "big picture" about resources in the upper window and details about an individual's tasks in the project in the lower window. For enterprise projects, the Resource Form includes the total work, costs, and schedule for all activities on Project Server under the category *Other projects and commitments*.

NOTE

Remember, when you are in a split-window (combination) view, only half of the window is active. To make any changes, click the pane that you want to edit before typing. Clicking the appropriate pane confirms that your keystrokes and mouse clicks affect the pane you wish to modify.

Notice that changes made to enterprise resources, other than changes in the open project, will be lost when the project is saved and re-opened. Enterprise-level resource information must be changed in the checked-out Enterprise Resource Pool by an administrator.

Also, it is best to <u>remove the split view before applying a new view</u> unless you wish to maintain a split window view of your schedule.

4 If the resource-based information you are looking for requires task assignments with details over time, remove the window split (double-click the line between the two panes), and from *View:Resource Views* click *Resource Usage.* Choose *View: Zoom, Timescale* dropdown: *Weeks.*

Figure 365.

Resource Usage view

Just like the Task Usage view, the Resource Usage view lists a resource's assignment to all other projects in total hours, along with the planned work for the tasks in the open project. Another advantage of the Resource Usage view is that it always begins with the local resource *Unassigned*—a handy listing of tasks in the project that have not yet been distributed to the team.

5 From *View:Task Views*, use the *Gantt Chart* dropdown to select *Tracking Gantt.* This shows you the critical and non-critical tasks, as well as progress against those tasks. This view is truly comprehensive; it shows estimates, actuals, and baselines all on the same Gantt Chart.

As shown in the following figure, the top half of each bar represents the current estimate, with actual progress represented in a solid color and the remaining estimate shaded. Also, the bottom half of each bar represents the baseline. Finally, critical path tasks are represented in red, and non-critical tasks are blue.

Figure 366.

Tracking Gantt view

Customizing Tables

In the following set of exercises, you will modify an existing table, create a new table based on an existing table, modify its layout, and apply it to your project.

Modify an Existing Table

 This exercise uses the file **TablesandViews.mpp**. Be sure this project is open before beginning.

1 You should be in the Gantt Chart view with the Entry Table applied. Suppose that you would like to see start variance information along with the defaults for a progress report. Move the divider to the right until you can see the Finish column.

2 To add the Baseline Start column between the Start and Finish columns, right-click the Finish column header. Your screen will resemble the following:

Figure 367.

Column commands menu

3 Click *Insert Column* to see the Column Name dropdown list.

Figure 368.

Column Definition dropdown list

4 From the Column Name dropdown list, select *Baseline Start*. Your screen will resemble the following:

Figure 369.

Table with
new column

	ⓘ	Task Mode	Task Name	Duration	Start	Baseline Start	Finish
1		⬛	⬛ Software System Implementation	98 days	2/27	2/26/2013	7/12
2		⬛	⬛ Build Project Plan	23 days	2/27	2/26/2013	3/29
3		⬛	Create Statement of Work	13 days	2/27	2/26	3/15
4		⬛	Obtain approval of Statement of Work	1 day	3/16	3/15	3/16
5		⬛	Create project plan	8 days	3/17	3/18	3/28
6		⬛	Review project plan with team	1 day	3/29	3/28	3/29
7		⬛	Obtain approval of project plan	0 days	3/29	3/28	3/29
8		⬛	⬛ Finalize project plan and definition	24 days	3/30	3/29	5/2
9	⬥	⬛	Define System Environment	12 days	3/30	3/29	4/14
10		⬛	Determine current architecture	5 days	4/17	4/16	4/21
11		⬛	Assess processes on the Server	3 days	4/24	4/23	4/26
12		⬛	Assess printer hardware	3 days	4/27	4/26	5/1
13		⬛	Communicate with Integrator	1 day	5/2	5/1	5/2
14		⬛	⬛ Complete architecture draft	22 days	5/3	5/2	6/1
15	⬥	⬛	Conduct Session	6 days	5/3	5/2	5/10
16	⬥	⬛	Send out prep packet	1 day	5/11	5/10	5/11
17	⬥	⬛	Conduct pre-interviews	3 days	5/12	5/13	5/16

5 Save your project.

Inserting a column works well as a temporary way to view data, but you may not want to make extensive changes or re-use the "temporary" table for every upcoming progress report. A more effective approach is to start with an existing table that is close to what you want. The following technique could also be used to start with a "blank sheet of paper" to create a table.

Copy and Customize an Existing Table

📂 In this exercise, we continue the use of the file **TablesAndViews.mpp** from the previous exercise. Alternatively, you can open **TablesAndViews_Inst1.mpp** from your exercise directory.

Since there is no table that shows all five types of variance, you have decided you want to create one. The Variance Table comes closest, since it has start and finish variance, so that seems like a good place to start.

1 From *View:Data* select the *Table* dropdown and click *More Tables…*. You will be presented with the **More Tables** dialog box:

Figure 370.

More Tables
dialog box

2 With the *Task* option selected, select the *Variance* table and click the *Copy...* button. You will see a **Table Definition** dialog box similar to the following:

Figure 371.

Table Definition
dialog

3 In the *Name* field, overwrite the existing text with "Complete Variance."

4 Select Baseline Start and click the *Delete Row* button. The Baseline Start row will disappear from the **Table Definition** dialog box.

5 Delete the Baseline Finish row as well.

6 Select Finish and click the *Insert Row* button. A blank row will appear above the Finish row.

7 Use the *Cut Row* and *Paste Row* buttons to move Start Variance between Start and Finish.

8 Click in the blank cell below Finish Variance and select *Duration Variance* from the *Field* dropdown list.

9 In the *Title* field for Duration Variance, enter *Duration Var*.

10 Repeat step 9 for Cost Variance and Work Variance. Your screen should resemble the following:

Figure 372.

Completed **Table Definition** dialog box

11 Click *OK*. The *Complete Variance* table will appear in the **More Tables** dialog box. If you would like to see it in the short list of commonly-used tables, click the *Edit* button and, in the **Table Definition** dialog box, select *Show in menu*.

Figure 373.

Complete Variance table in **More Tables** dialog box

NOTE

You can specify how date fields are displayed in the table. If you keep the default option under the date format, it will use the format as defined under *File:Options:General.*

12 Confirm that the *Complete Variance* table is selected in the **More Tables** dialog box and click *Apply*. Your new table will be applied to the Gantt Chart view. Save and close your project.

Viewing Variance Data in Tables

The following exercise uses the file **VarianceAnalysis-2.mpp**. Ensure this file is open before beginning.

The following set of exercises steps you through the process of viewing cost, work, and schedule variances.

1 To view cost variances in your project, use the *Gantt Chart* dropdown under *Task:View* to apply the *Task Sheet* view to your project.

2 From *View:Data* use the *Tables* dropdown to select the *Cost Table*.
 Notice the Cost Table includes the Cost Variance field and other cost-
 related fields that show how the Cost Variance was calculated (i.e.
 Baseline Cost - Cost = Cost Variance).

Figure 374.

Cost Table
applied

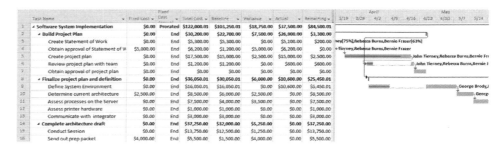

3 To view work variances, from *View:Data* use the *Tables* dropdown to
 select the *Work* table. Notice the Work Table includes the Work
 Variance field and other work-related fields that show how the Work
 Variance was calculated (i.e. Baseline Work - Work = Work Variance).

Figure 375.

Work Table
applied

4 To view schedule variances, go to *View:Data* and use the *Tables*
 dropdown to select the *Variance* table. Notice the *Variance* table
 includes the Start and Finish Variance fields and other schedule-
 related fields that show how the Start and Finish variances were
 calculated (i.e. Baseline Start - Start = Start Variance and Baseline
 Finish - Finish = Finish Variance).

Figure 376.

Variance Table
applied

5 Close your project.

Filtering Project Information

A filter is a set of formatting instructions that tells Microsoft Project which rows to display on the screen, in the same way that the table determined which columns are on the screen. If your project is especially complex with many tasks and resources, filters can help you organize your information and display a specific range of information at any time. For example, you may want to see only the tasks on your critical path, project milestones, or tasks that have not started yet.

Microsoft Project 2016 provides pre-configured filters for viewing specific task and resource details. If these filters do not match your needs exactly, you can modify an existing filter or create a brand new one.

In addition to standard filters, Microsoft Project 2016 offers AutoFilters which are visible in most sheet views.

AutoFilters

AutoFilters enable you to locate a specific type of project data quickly and efficiently. By default the AutoFilter tool is activated for each column that appears in your project table. When a particular criterion has been selected from an AutoFilter dropdown list, the dropdown arrow and column title will have a filter symbol to the right. Each type of column has a different set of AutoFilter options.

👉 This exercise uses the file **Filters.mpp**. Be sure this project is open before beginning.

1 Apply the Task Sheet view to the project.

2 From *View:Data* click *Tables*, and from the dropdown list select *Cost*. Your screen will resemble the following:

Figure 377.

Task Sheet with Cost Table

	Task Name	Fixed Cost	Fixed Cost	Total Cost	Baseline	Variance	Actual	Remainin
1	⁴ Software System Implementation	$0.00	Prorated	122,000.01	$103,250.01	$18,750.00	$37,500.00	$84,500.01
2	⁴ Build Project Plan	$0.00	End	$30,200.00	$22,700.00	$7,500.00	$26,900.00	$3,300.00
3	Create Statement of Work	$0.00	End	$5,300.00	$5,300.00	$0.00	$5,100.00	$200.00
4	Obtain approval of Statement of Work	$5,000.00	End	$6,200.00	$1,200.00	$5,000.00	$6,200.00	$0.00
5	Create project plan	$0.00	End	$17,500.00	$15,000.00	$2,500.00	$15,000.00	$2,500.00
6	Review project plan with team	$0.00	End	$1,200.00	$1,200.00	$0.00	$600.00	$600.00
7	Obtain approval of project plan	$0.00	End	$0.00	$0.00	$0.00	$0.00	$0.00
8	⁴ Finalize project plan and definition	$0.00	End	$36,050.01	$30,050.01	$6,000.00	$10,600.00	$25,450.01
9	Define System Environment	$0.00	End	$16,050.01	$16,050.01	$0.00	$10,600.00	$5,450.01
10	Determine current architecture	$2,500.00	End	$8,500.00	$6,000.00	$2,500.00	$0.00	$8,500.00
11	Assess processes on the Server	$0.00	End	$7,500.00	$4,000.00	$3,500.00	$0.00	$7,500.00
12	Assess printer hardware	$0.00	End	$1,000.00	$1,000.00	$0.00	$0.00	$1,000.00
13	Communicate with integrator	$0.00	End	$3,000.00	$3,000.00	$0.00	$0.00	$3,000.00
14	⁴ Complete architecture draft	$0.00	End	$37,250.00	$32,000.00	$5,250.00	$0.00	$37,250.00
15	Conduct Session	$0.00	End	$13,750.00	$12,500.00	$1,250.00	$0.00	$13,750.00
16	Send out prep packet	$4,000.00	End	$5,500.00	$1,500.00	$4,000.00	$0.00	$5,500.00
17	Conduct pre-interviews	$0.00	End	$3,000.00	$3,000.00	$0.00	$0.00	$3,000.00

3 From *View:Data* use the *Filter* dropdown to select *Display AutoFilter*. Note: this option is applied by default.

4 Click the AutoFilter dropdown arrow in the Baseline Variance cost
 column, select *$1,500.00*, and click *OK*. The Baseline Variance cost
 column will filter your project data for all tasks that have an estimated
 cost equal to $1,500. Note that the Baseline Variance column header
 has a filter symbol next to it. Your screen will resemble the following:

Figure 378.

Baseline cost
AutoFilter
($1,500)

NOTE

An AutoFilter includes both the tasks that meet the criteria <u>and the</u>
<u>summary tasks</u> associated with them—the outline structure is
maintained.

4 Again, select the Baseline AutoFilter dropdown, click *Select All*, then
 OK. The column's original data will reappear.

NOTE

A caution when using AutoFilter: it is possible for an AutoFilter selection to
be active, yet the field on which the AutoFilter applies may not be displayed
on the screen. In this case, it is not obvious why some tasks are not being
displayed. A good practice when working with AutoFilter is to periodically
deselect and reselect the AutoFilter option. This has the effect of removing
any forgotten, residual AutoFilter selections.

Creating a Custom Filter

This exercise continues use of the file **Filters.mpp**. If it is not already
open, please open it now.

From time to time, the predefined filters in Microsoft Project 2016 will not
meet your specific needs. In these cases you can customize filters to select
the information you want to display.

1 Ensure your project is open in the Gantt Chart view with the Entry Table applied.

2 From *View:Data* select *New Filter* from the *Filter* dropdown list. You will see the **Filter Definition** dialog box:

Figure 379.

New **Filter Definition** dialog

3 In the *Name* field, replace the existing text with "Starts on or after 6/11."

4 From the *Field Name* dropdown list, select *Start*.

5 From the *Test* dropdown list, select *is greater than or equal to*.

6 In the *Value(s)* field, enter "6/11" and click *Apply*. Your new filter will appear in the **Filters** menu dropdown.

Figure 380.

New filter in *Filters* dropdown menu

7 Select this filter on the **Filters** dropdown menu. All tasks that are
 scheduled to start on or after 6/11 are displayed. Note: Only
 summary tasks that independently meet the filter criteria are displayed
 (in this case no summary tasks are displayed).

Figure 381.

Filter applied

8 Save your project.

Creating a New Filter by Copying an Existing Filter

This exercise continues use of the file **Filters.mpp** from the previous
exercise. Alternatively, you can open **Filters_Inst1.mpp**.

One easy way to create a new filter is to use a similar or related filter as a
foundation for the new one.

1 From the *Filter* dropdown, select *[No Filter]* to clear your filter.

2 From the *Filter* dropdown, select *More Filters...* .

3 In the **More Filters** dialog box, select *Starts on or after 6/11* and click
 Copy... .

4 In the *Name* field of the **Filter Definition** dialog box, replace the
 existing text with "Starts on or after 6/11 and finishes before 7/31"

A filter can contain more than one condition; the *And/Or* field determines the
relationship of the various criteria. If you select the value *And*, then both
conditions must be true in order for the task or resource to be displayed. If
you select the value *Or,* either condition can be true and the task or resource
will be displayed.

5 In the second row of the *And/Or* column, select *And*.

6 In the same row, select *Finish* from the *Field Name* dropdown list.

7 In the same row, use the *Test* dropdown list to select *is less than.*

8 In the same row, enter into the *Value* field "7/31." The **Filter Definition** dialog box will resemble the following:

Figure 382.

Existing filter copied and modified

9 Click *Save*.

10 Select this filter on the *Filters* dropdown menu. Your screen will resemble the following:

Figure 383.

Combined filter results

11 From the *Filter* dropdown, again select *[No Filter]* and save your project.

Value Lists in Filters

When you created a filter with earlier versions of Microsoft Project, the *Value(s)* field did not allow you to choose values from a pick-list. For example, if you had defined the Text 1 field to include a pick-list with the values of A, B, and C and wanted to create a filter that found all tasks with the letter A in the Text 1 field, you would have had to remember what value you want to filter for and typed it into the *Value(s)* field.

This wasn't too hard to manage if your value pick-lists were simple. However, with hierarchical fields, remembering exactly what value to enter into your filter could be difficult. In Microsoft Project 2016 you can use a pick-list to select the value(s) for your filters by entering the custom field in the *Value(s)* area.

Filters can be specific or interactive. Interactive filters prompt you for information during the process, so you can specify criteria for each search.

Creating a Custom Interactive Filter

The predefined interactive filters that ask for information in Microsoft Project may not always meet your requirements, so you may want to create a custom interactive filter.

 This exercise continues use of the file **Filters.mpp** from the previous exercise. Alternatively, you can open **Filters_Inst2.mpp**.

1 Confirm you are in the Gantt Chart view with the Entry Table applied.

2 The date range filter you wrote earlier was useful, but you have decided it would make more sense to be able to re-use it by entering the "Starts after" and "Finishes on or before" dates. From the *Filter* dropdown list, select *More Filters...*. You will be presented with the **More Filters** dialog box.

3 Select the *Starts on or after 6/11 and finishes before 7/31* filter and click *Edit...*. The **Filter Definition** dialog box will appear.

4 In the **Filter Definition** dialog box, change the *Name* field to "Starts on or after and finishes before".

5 In the *Value(s)* field for the *Start* line, type *"Enter the start date"? (include the quotation and question mark after the double quotes)* and in the *Value(s)* field for the *Finish* line, type *"Enter the finish date"?* The text contained within the quotes is what you will be prompted for when the filter is applied, and the question mark tells Microsoft Project this is an interactive filter. Your screen will resemble the following:

Figure 384.

Interactive filter definition

6 Click *Save*. In the **More Filters** dialog box, ensure the new filter is selected and click *Apply*. You will be prompted to enter a start date; enter "6/11" and click *OK*. Notice that there is a dropdown calendar you can use to select the date, if you prefer.

7 You will be prompted to enter a finish date; enter "7/7" and click *OK*.

8 You will again see only those tasks that meet the selected parameters. Your screen will resemble the following:

Figure 385.

New filter applied

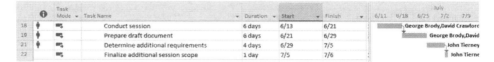

9 Save your project.

Applying a Highlighting Filter

By default, whenever you apply a filter to your project, the tasks or resources that do not fit the filter criteria are hidden. However, if you want to view all of the tasks in your project and simply distinguish which tasks do and don't fit the filter, Microsoft Project 2016 enables you to apply a highlight filter to your tasks.

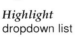 This exercise continues use of the file **Filters.mpp** from the previous exercise. Alternatively, you can open **Filters_Inst3.mpp**.

1 Ensure you are in the Gantt Chart view with the Entry Table applied. From the *Filter* dropdown list, again select *[No Filter]* to provide an unfiltered view of your project.

2 In *View:Data* click the *Highlight* dropdown list. You will see the following options:

Figure 386.

Highlight dropdown list

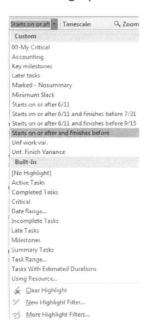

3 Click the *Starts on or after and finishes before* filter.

4 When prompted, provide a *Start date* of "6/2" and *Finish date* "6/30."

5 Tasks that meet the established criteria will now be highlighted, as
 shown in the following figure:

Figure 387.

Highlighted
tasks

6 From the *Filter* dropdown list, again select *[No Filter]* to restore the
 original appearance.

7 Save your project.

Microsoft Project 2016 has additional uses for the filtering function. For
example, the **Assign Resources** dialog box includes a *Resource list options*
feature that includes a filtering capability. Resources can be filtered by their
availability to work a certain number of hours, or they you can use a number
of built-in resource filters.

Project Web App views offer many of the same filtering options, with the
exception of interactive and highlight filters.

Sorting Project Information

By default, Microsoft Project 2016 displays the tasks and resources in your
project from lowest to highest ID number. You can sort tasks or resources by
other criteria such as task name, deadline, and resource name. Sorting can add
value when you need to see tasks in a particular sequence.

Sort the Task List

 This exercise continues use of the file **Filters.mpp** from the previous
 exercise. Alternatively, you can open **Filters_Inst4.mpp**.

1 Apply the Task Sheet view to your project and then apply the Cost
 Table.

2 From *View:Data* use the *Sort* dropdown to select *by Cost*. The
 summary tasks in your project will be sorted by descending cost and
 the tasks within each summary will be sorted by descending cost.

Sort by Multiple Fields

3 From *View:Data* use the *Sort* dropdown to select *Sort By.....* You will
 see the **Sort** dialog box.

4 Choose *Cost* in the *Sort by* dropdown.

5 Next to the *Sort by* field, select the *Ascending* button.

6 From the *Then by* dropdown list, choose *Duration* and select the
 Descending button.

Figure 388.

Sort dialog
box

6 Click *Sort*. Your screen will resemble the following (insert the
 Duration field next to the Total Cost column to see how the dual sort
 works):

Figure 389.

Sorted by
ascending cost
and descending
duration

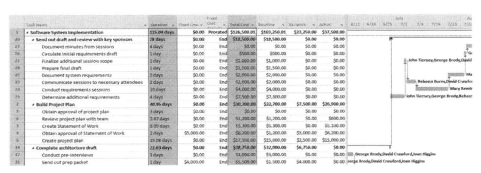

Note: You may wish to insert the Duration filed to validate your results.

7 From the *Sort* dropdown, select *by ID* to restore the original task
 order to your project.

8 Save your project.

Grouping Project Information

Grouping allows a project manager to view tasks or resources in pre-defined or customized "sets." Grouping creates new summary tasks to show rolled-up totals. Microsoft Project 2016 allows you to group based on assignment fields as well as tasks or resources in Usage views. The dialog box has a checkbox option for *Group assignments, not Tasks* (in a Task Usage view) or *Group assignments, not Resources* (in a Resource Usage view). All assignment timephased fields are rolled-up to summary tasks except for Cumulative Percent Complete, Over-allocation, Peak Units, and Percent Allocation.

📁 This exercise continues use of the file **Filters.mpp** from the previous exercise. Alternatively, you can open **Filters_Inst5.mpp**.

 1 Apply the Task Sheet view with the Entry Table selected.

 2 From *View:Data* use the *Group by* dropdown list to select *Duration*. Your screen should resemble the following figure:

Figure 390.

Project grouped by duration

 3 From *View:Data* use the *Group by* dropdown list to select *[No Group]* to restore the original view.

 4 Apply the Resource Usage view.

 5 From *View:Data* use the *Group by* dropdown list to select *Resource Group*. Collapse the assignment information for each resource so that all assignment are hidden (Hint: Click the black triangle next to each resource's assignments). Your screen will resemble the following figure:

Figure 391.

Resource Usage view grouped by resource group

	ⓘ	Resource Name	Work	Details	1st Quarter			2nd Quarter			3rd Quarter		
					Jan	Feb	Mar	Apr	May	Jun	Jul	Aug	
		▷ Group: No Value	1 hr	Work								1h	
		◢ Group: IT	1,083 hrs	Work		19.25h	234.28h	354.47h	176.52h	207.52h	80.75h	10.22h	
1		▷ John Tierney	211.67 hrs	Work		6.22h	86.97h	83.48h		14.68h	20.32h		
2		▷ Rebecca Burns	202.67 hrs	Work		8h	61.18h	83.48h		14.68h	35.32h		
3		▷ Bernie Frazer	242.17 hrs	Work		5.05h	86.13h	83.48h	67.5h				
7	✦	▷ Joan Higgins	317 hrs	Work					52h	51.52h	178.17h	25.1h	10.22h
8		▷ Mike Goren	109.5 hrs	Work					52h	57.5h			
		◢ Group: Management	1,127 hrs	Work				176.47h	321.62h	423.28h	185.43h	20.22h	
4	✦	▷ George Brody	393 hrs	Work					67.47h	112.07h	178.17h	25.1h	10.22h
5	✦	▷ Julie Pawlkowski	174.5 hrs	Work					52h	89.02h	33.48h		
6	✦	▷ David Crawford	337 hrs	Work					57h	51.52h	178.17h	40.32h	10h
9	✦	▷ Ted Haley	102.5 hrs	Work						69.02h	33.48h		
10		▷ Mary Remington	120 hrs	Work							120h		

6 Grouping can be customized just like filtering and sorting.

7 Apply the *Gantt Chart* view. From the *Group* dropdown, select *New Group By...* to see the **Group Definition** dialog box:

Figure 392.

Group Definition dialog box

9 Click in the *Field Name* column in the *Group By* row, and select *Start* from the dropdown list. Click *Apply*. Your screen should resemble the following figure:

Figure 393.

Tasks grouped by start date

10 From the *Group* dropdown, select *[No Group]* to return to the original view and save your project.

Microsoft Project Server/Project Online Grouping Styles

Project Web App views also offer grouping as a tool to clarify and evaluate the information contained. The Microsoft Project Server administrator can set colors for different grouping levels in the views as well as set the color and font style of the text displayed inside the cells.

Defining Custom Views

If none of the views included with Microsoft Project meet your needs, you can create a new view or modify an existing one. When you save your project, your new or modified view is saved with the project. In the following exercises, you will create a new single view and a new combination view, a split-screen combination of two single views.

Creating a New View

📁 This exercise continues use of the file **Filters.mpp** from the previous exercise. Alternatively, you can open **Filters_Inst6.mpp**.

1 From *View:Task Views*, click *Other Views* and then *More Views...*. You will be presented with the **More Views** dialog box.

2 In the **More Views** dialog box, click *New...* to see the **Define New View** dialog box.

Figure 394.

Define New View dialog

3 Ensure the *Single view* default option is selected, click *OK* to see the **View Definition** dialog box.

Figure 395.

View Definition dialog

4 In the *Name* field, replace the existing text with "Cost Variance."

5 From the *Screen* dropdown list, select *Task Usage*.

6 From the *Table* dropdown list, select *Variance*.

7 From the *Group* dropdown list, select *No Group*.

8 From the *Filter* dropdown list, select *Cost Greater Than...*.

9 Select the *Highlight Filter* checkbox so that Microsoft Project distinguishes your filtered data from the rest of the data in the view.

10 Select the *Show in menu* checkbox so that your new view will be easy to access from the *View* ribbon.

11 Click *OK*. Confirm that *Variance* is selected in the **More Views** dialog box.

12 In the **More Views** dialog box, click *Apply*. Enter "5000" in the interactive filter box (**Cost greater than**) that appears, and click *OK*. Your screen will resemble the following:

Figure 396.

Variance custom single view

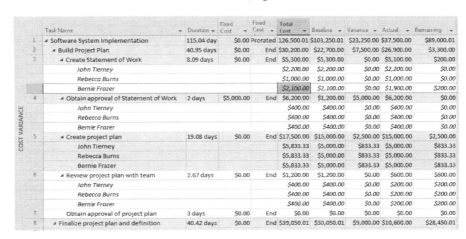

13 Save your project.

Creating a Combination View

This exercise continues use of the file **Filters.mpp** from the previous exercise. Alternatively, you can open **Filters_Inst7.mpp**.

1 From *View:Task Views* click the *Other Views...* dropdown and select *More Views...*.

2 In the **More Views** dialog box, click *New*.

3 In the **Define New View** dialog box, select the *Combination* view option button and click *OK*.

4 In the **View Definition** dialog box, replace the existing text in the *Name* field with "Resource Allocation Diagram"

5 From the *Primary View* dropdown list, select *Resource Usage*.

6 From the *Details Pane* dropdown list, select *Resource Graph*. Your screen will resemble the following:

Figure 397.

View Definition (Combination view)

7 Click *OK*, confirm that *Variance Diagram* is selected in the **More Views** dialog box, and click *Apply*. Your screen will resemble the following:

Figure 398.

Resource Allocation Diagram (Custom combination view)

8 Save and close your project.

15.3 Defining and Using Custom Fields

There are two major categories of custom fields:

❑ **Local custom fields** – These are fields that can be set up by the project manager within a project plan and shared across other project plans using the Organizer and the Global.mpt. We will cover the Organizer and Global.mpt in greater depth later in this chapter.

❑ **Enterprise custom fields** – These are fields set up by the Project Server administrator that can be used across all projects that are saved and published on Project Server.

This chapter focuses on the use of local custom fields.

🗁 For this exercise, launch Microsoft Project 2016 and connect to a valid Project Server account. Open the **ABCIntegration.mpp**. Check out the project.

1 From *Format:Columns* click the *Custom Fields* icon [⊞]. You will see the **Custom Fields** dialog box:

Figure 399.

Custom Fields dialog box

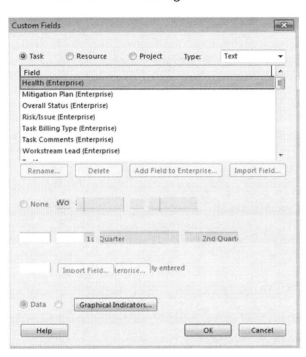

Notice that *Task*, *Resource*, and *Project* fields are available. A custom Task field will be assigned to every task in a project; a custom Resource field will be assigned to every resource; and a custom Project field will be assigned only to the project summary task (title). Project fields are applicable only as enterprise tools.

2 Click the dropdown arrow by the *Type* field to see the related options, per the following figure:

Figure 400.

Type dropdown list

Most of the field types are self-explanatory: *Cost* fields contain costs, *Date* fields contain dates (including the Start and Finish fields), and so on. Two fields, however, may not be self-explanatory:

❑ *Flag* fields are yes/no fields used to mark any kind of status. They are *No* by default and can be changed to *Yes* to mark the task, resource, or project.

❑ *Outline Code* fields are hierarchical fields used to describe something like the location of a task or resource. The outline format allows you to specify information such as country, state, and city in a geographical or location description.

Notice that the commands below the window allow you to rename a field (which then displays the field both by its generic name and by the new name in field lists) or to define the contents and presentation of information. We will explore these options later.

3 In the **Custom Fields** dialog box, ensure the *Task* option is selected and select *Number* from the *Type* dropdown list. Note that all Enterprise fields of this type (Number) are listed, as well as the local fields (*Number 1*, *Number 2*, etc.). You cannot change the details of these enterprise fields here, but you are able to see their parameters.

4 Next, from the *Field* list, select *Number 1* and click *Rename*. You will see the **Rename Field** dialog box.

Figure 401.

Rename Field
dialog box

5 We want to use this field to assign a hazard level to tasks involving flammable or toxic materials, so in the **Rename Field** dialog box, rename *Number 1* as *Hazard*, and click *OK*.

6 Note that *Hazard (Number 1)* now appears in the list of available fields in the **Custom Fields** dialog box. The Hazard level will be assigned as follows: 0 indicates no known hazard, while 3 indicates a hazard requiring the highest level of safety precautions. To allow users to properly assign a Hazard level, ensure the *Hazard (Number 1)* field is selected, and then click *Lookup* to see the **Edit Lookup Table for Hazard** dialog box.

Figure 402.

Edit Lookup Table for Hazard dialog box

7 In this dialog, enter *0, 1, 2,* and *3* in the *Value* column, using *Enter* to move from one row to the next. You can also add descriptive information about each of the values noted. This additional information is not saved with a project but may be useful at the time the selection is being made. Because we want the default value for the *Hazard* field to be *0,* click *Use a value from the table as the default entry for the field*, select *0*, and click *Set Default*. Now click *Close*, and then click *OK* to accept the changes made in the **Custom Fields** dialog box.

8 In the Gantt Chart view for your sample project, right-click the column header Duration and select *Insert Column*. From the list of fields, select the new *Hazard* field as indicated in the following figure:

Figure 403.

Selecting the Hazard field

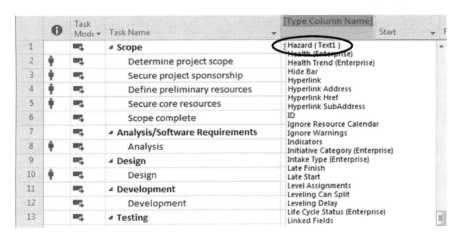

Notice that if you scroll through the field names, you will also see your new field listed as *Number 1 (Hazard)*, a result of renaming the field.

If you insert a new column in this manner while in an Enterprise view (such as the Enterprise Gantt Chart view) that has been defined in the Enterprise Global, Microsoft Project will warn you that these changes won't be saved. The normal Gantt Chart view, however, is local and not defined in the Enterprise Global—you can modify it at will. Changes will be saved as part of your local Global.mpt.

9 The new *Hazard* field will be inserted as a column in the Entry Table. Click the dropdown arrow in the *Hazard* cell associated with one of the tasks to see the values you established, as in the following figure:

Figure 404.

Dropdown values for custom Hazard field

A Project Server administrator can make a local field an enterprise field. It's generally considered a best practice to first create a field and make sure it works correctly in a project, and *then* add it to the enterprise global.

10 Re-open the **Custom Fields** dialog box, select the field you just created (Hazard) and click *Add Field to Enterprise.* If you are an administrator, you will see the **Add Field to Enterprise** dialog box, which asks you to confirm or edit the *Field Name* and the *Lookup Table Name.*

Figure 405.

Add Field to Enterprise dialog box

11 In this case, there is no look-up table so the *Lookup Table Name* should be deleted and left empty. Click *OK.* Microsoft Project will confirm the field has been successfully added as an enterprise field to Project Server. Note: Generally only administrators are able to add custom fields to the enterprise.

In addition to custom fields, administrators can create filters, tables, views, and base calendars at the enterprise level by modifying the checked-out enterprise global.

To use any new enterprise global features, changes to the Enterprise Global must be saved and the project must be checked in; you then must exit from and re-start Microsoft Project to refresh the cached enterprise data. It's easy to overlook this feature and think you have not successfully changed the enterprise global when the new field you just created can't be seen!

In contrast to some of the earlier versions Microsoft Project, all types of custom fields are now available for use in portfolio management.

The Organizer and Sharing Custom Objects

Microsoft Project 2016 enables you to share custom objects between projects through the Organizer. The simplest and easiest way to distribute your custom objects to your other project files is to copy the objects from your individual project file to the local Global.mpt file. The Global.mpt is a file that Microsoft Project uses as a template to store a master copy of all your custom objects.

Once you copy objects into the Global.mpt, your custom objects will be available to every one of your existing and future project files; simply applying the format will automatically copy it into the project from the Global.mpt.

Objects	Availability
Views, Tables, Filters, Calendars, Reports, Custom Fields, Groups	Generally, any changes you make to views, tables, filters, calendars, reports, and forms are "local" and only occur in the active project file. When you open a new project file, it only contains the native Microsoft Project defaults for those elements, which are saved in the global file.
Import/export maps	Conversely, any changes you make to import and export maps are global, in that the changes affect the global file and apply to all project files on your computer. When you open a new project file, it contains your customized import and export maps.
Visual Basic modules	Changes you make to Visual Basic modules can be either global or local, according to your preference.
Format settings	When you change format settings (such as bold, italic, color, or bar shape), those settings apply only to the active project file and not to other project files on your computer.

Using the Organizer, you can also manually copy customized objects from one open project to another. For example, if someone sends the Project Server administrator an .mpp file with a new custom table or view, the administrator can easily copy it into the checked-out Enterprise Global (making sure that the name does not conflict with the defaults) to make it available to all enterprise projects.

To access the Organizer:

1 Open a project that is published to Project Server and click the *File* tab to see the following options (*Info* is selected by default):

Figure 406.

Info page

2 Click the *Organizer* button, and from the two available options, select *Organizer*. You will see the **Organizer** dialog box:

Figure 407.

Organizer
dialog box

3 Select the tab that is appropriate for your needs, and use the *Copy*, *Cancel*, *Rename*, and *Delete* buttons to change the objects available in the Global.mpt (to all projects) and the current open file.

4 Alternatively, you can access the **Organizer** dialog box in several other ways, including the following:

❑ From *View:Data* click the *Tables* icon, and from the dropdown list select *More Tables*. In the **More Tables** dialog box, click *Organizer*.

Figure 408.

More Tables
dialog box

❑ From *View:Data* click the *Filters* dropdown arrow and select *More Filters*. In the **More Filters** dialog box, click *Organizer*.

Figure 409.

More Filters
dialog box

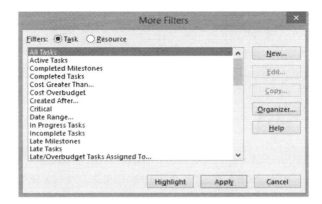

❑ From *View:Task Views* click the *Gantt Chart* dropdown arrow and select *More Views*. In the **More Views** dialog box, click *Organizer*.

Figure 410.

More Views
dialog box

 ❏ From *View:Resource Views* click the *Team Planner* dropdown arrow and select *More Views*. In the **More Views** dialog box, click *Organizer*.

Figure 411.

More Views
dialog box

 5 Close the project.

15.4 Communicating Project Information

Reporting on various aspects of a project is a key project management function.

Microsoft Project 2016 offers a comprehensive set of preconfigured, visually-appealing and informative reports that can be shared with others. This out-of-the-box reporting capability can be further improved by a robust custom report building functionality that is integrated with Microsoft Excel.

To see an overview of the reports-related functions and types of reports available in Microsoft Project 2016, open Microsoft Project and click the *Report* tab:

Figure 412.

Overview of the
Reports tab

In this section, we will first review the various preconfigured reports that are available in Microsoft Project 2016, and then we will discuss how to edit, customize, and share them to meet your unique needs.

Exploring Preconfigured Reports

 🗁 This exercise uses the file **Dashboards.mpp**. Ensure this file is open prior to beginning.

In the *Report* toolbar, preconfigured reports fall into four categories: Dashboards, Resources, Costs, and In Progress.

Note: The image on your screen may differ slightly from the screenshots shared in this exercise, unless you make modifications to the data.

Dashboard Reports

1 From *Report:View Reports* click the *Dashboards* icon to see the available reports in this category.

Figure 413.

Dashboards reports

Dashboard reports provide information over the entire project duration, including summary tasks, critical tasks, project milestones, cost, and schedule information. These reports present data that allows you to quickly assess project status in different areas.

The default reports included in the *Dashboards* dropdown are as follows:

❑ **Burndown report** – Compares planned, completed, and remaining work on a chart that updates automatically as you change project data; this report provides a visual, up-to-date project status. Though these reports are particularly useful in agile project management, they are helpful regardless of project management methodology.

To access a Burndown report, navigate to *Report:View Reports:Dashboards* icon, and select *Burndown* from the dropdown list. Your screen will resemble the following:

Figure 414.

Burndown report

BURNDOWN

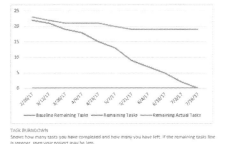

❑ **Cost Overview report** – Shows the current cost status of your project and its top-level tasks; fields available include planned costs, remaining costs, actual costs, cumulative costs, baseline costs, and percentage of completion. This report is especially useful as you work to keep your project within budget.

To access a Cost Overview report, go to *Report:View Reports:Dashboards* icon, and select *Cost Overview*. Following is a sample Cost Overview report:

Figure 415.

Cost Overview report

❑ **Project Overview report** – Shows how much of your project is complete, tasks that are late, and upcoming milestones

To access a Project Overview report, go to *Report:View Reports:Dashboards* icon, and select *Project Overview*. Following is a sample Project Overview report:

Figure 416.

Project Overview report

❑ **Upcoming Tasks report** – By default, shows work that has been accomplished in the current week, the status of other tasks that were/are due this week, and the tasks due to start in the coming week

To access the Upcoming Tasks report, go to *Report:View Reports:Dashboards* icon, and select *Upcoming Tasks.* Your screen will resemble the following:

Figure 417.

Upcoming
Tasks report

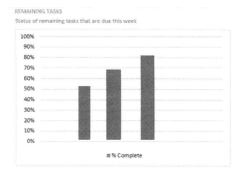

TASKS STARTING SOON
Status of tasks starting in the next week

Name	Resource Names	Start	Finish	Work
Define System Environment	George Brody,Julie Pawlkowski,David Crawford,Joan Higgins,Mike	3/19	4/25	321 hrs

❑ **Work Overview report** – Provides work statistics for all top-level project tasks showing percent complete and what is still to be accomplished; similar to a work burndown report

To access the Upcoming Tasks report, go to *Report:View Reports:Dashboards* icon, and select *Work Overview.* Your screen will resemble the following:

Figure 418.

Work Overview report

Resource Reports

2 From *Report:View Reports* click the *Resources* icon to see the
available reports in this category.

Figure 419.

Resources
reports menu

Resource reports provide details about the work status of all project resources,
as well as more specific resource assignment information.

❏ **Over-allocated Resources report** – Shows the actual and
remaining work for all over-allocated project resources; also includes
a link to the Team Planner view, where you can work to resolve
these over-allocations

To access this report, go to *Report:View Reports:Resources* icon
and select *Over-allocated Resources* from the dropdown list:

Figure 420.

Over-allocated
Resources
report

❑ **Resource Overview report** – View the work status of all project resources to determine how much work is complete and what is still to be finished

To access this report, go to *Report:View Reports:Resources* icon and select *Resource Overview* from the dropdown list:

Figure 421.

Resource
Overview report

Cost Reports

3 From *Report:View Reports* click the *Costs* icon to see the available reports in this category.

Figure 422.

Costs reports
menu

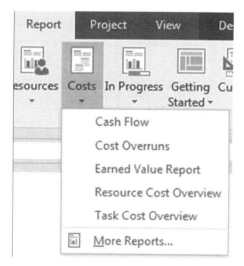

Costs reports provide a full range of cost information, including budgets for all tasks over the entire project duration, tasks and resources that are over budget, earned-value information for all tasks, and costs per task displayed for one-week periods.

❏ **Cash Flow report** – By default, shows the cost (including cumulative cost) of all top-level tasks by quarter; customizable, like most other pre-configured reports; you can display other costs and other time periods.

To access this report, go to the *Costs* icon under *Report:View Reports* and select *Cash Flow* from the dropdown. Your screen will resemble the following:

Figure 423.

Cash Flow report

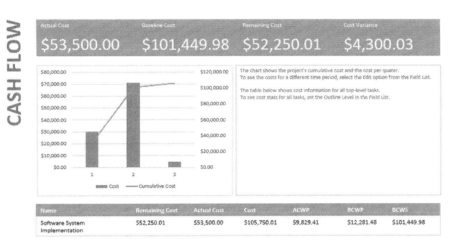

❏ **Cost Overruns report** – Displays the cost variance for all top-level tasks and people assigned to your project; also shows where actuals exceed baseline costs.

To access the Cost Overruns report, go to the *Costs* icon under *Report:View Reports* and select *Cash Flow* from the dropdown. Your screen will resemble the following:

Figure 424.

Cost Overruns report

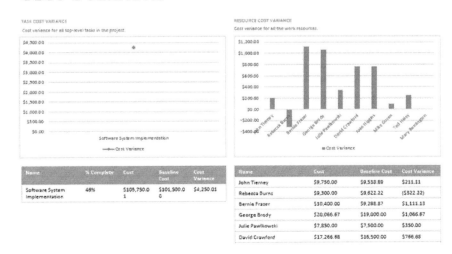

❑ **Earned Value report** – Provides information about earned value, variance, and performance overtime; displays a comparison of costs and schedules to the baseline, which helps you determine if the project is on track

To access the Earned Value report, go to the *Costs* icon under *Report:View Reports* and select *Cash Flow* from the dropdown. Your screen will resemble the following:

Figure 425.

Earned Value report

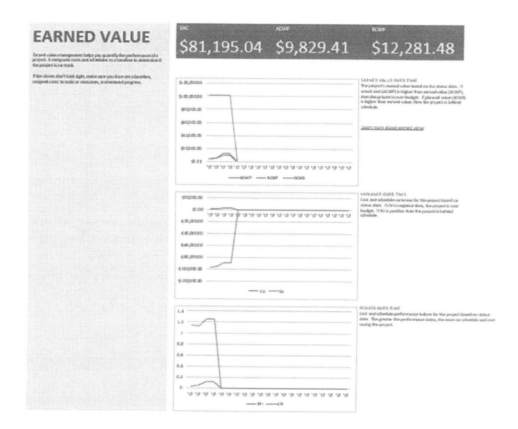

❑ **Resource Cost Overview report** – Shows the cost status of resources (people, material, and cost-types) assigned to your project; cost details appear in a table, and cost distribution information is presented in a chart

To access the Resource Cost Overview report, go to the *Costs* icon under *Report:View Reports* and select *Cash Flow* from the dropdown. Your screen will resemble the following:

Figure 426.

Resource Cost
Overview report

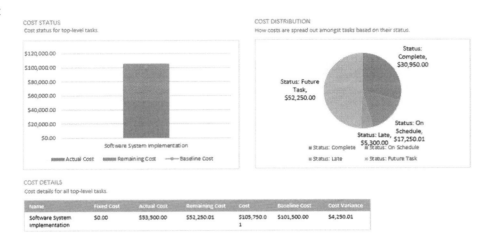

❑ **Task Cost Overview report** – Shows the cost status of your project's top-level tasks; just like the Resource Cost Overview report, cost details appear in a table, and cost distribution information is presented in a chart

To access the Task Cost Overview report, go to the *Costs* icon under *Report:View Reports* and select *Cash Flow* from the dropdown. Your screen will resemble the following:

Figure 427.

Task Cost Overview report

In Progress Reports

4 From *Report:View Reports* click the *In Progress* icon to see the available reports in this category.

Figure 428.

In Progress reports menu

Progress reports provide detailed task information regarding critical, slipping, and late tasks, as well as the status of project milestones.

❑ **Critical Tasks report** – Presents the status of all tasks on the project's critical path

Remember: A delay in a critical path task will cause the schedule to slip.

To access the Critical Tasks report, from *Report:View Reports* click the *In Progress* icon, and from the dropdown list select *Critical Tasks*. Your screen will resemble the following:

Figure 429.

Critical Tasks report

CRITICAL TASKS

A task is critical if there is no room in the schedule for it to slip.
Learn more about managing your project's critical path.

* Status: Complete
* Status: On Schedule
* Status: Late
* Status: Future Task

Name	Start	Finish	% Complete	Remaining Work	Resource Names
Review project plan with team	3/18	4/7	30%	12 hrs	John Tierney,Rebecca Burns,Bernie Frazer
Obtain approval of project plan	4/7	4/12	0%	0 hrs	
Conduct session	5/24	6/2	71%	50 hrs	George Brody,David Crawford,Joan Higgins
Prepare draft document	6/2	6/12	0%	150 hrs	George Brody,David Crawford,Joan Higgins
Determine additional requirements	6/12	6/16	0%	150 hrs	John Tierney,George Brody,Rebecca Burns,David Crawford,Joan Higgins

❑ **Late Tasks report** – Shows all tasks that either started or finished later than their scheduled start and finish dates and that aren't progressing as planned

To access the Late Tasks report, from *Report:View Reports* click the *In Progress* icon, and from the dropdown list select *Late Tasks*. Your screen will resemble the following:

Figure 430.

Late Tasks report

LATE TASKS

Tasks that are late as compared to the status date. A task is late if its finish date has passed or it is not progressing as planned.

Name	Start	Finish	% Complete	Remaining Work	Resource Names
Create Statement of Work	2/26	3/9	90%	4 hrs	John Tierney[75%],Rebecca Burns,Bernie Frazer[63%]

* Status: Complete
* Status: On Schedule
* Status: Late
* Status: Future Task

❑ **Milestone report** – Presents the status of all project milestones, including if they are late, due, or completed

To access this report, from *Report:View Reports* click the *In Progress* icon, and from the dropdown list select *Milestone Report*. Your screen will resemble the following:

Figure 431.

Milestone report

❑ **Slipping Tasks report** – Shows all project tasks that are taking longer to complete than expected (actual finish date is or will be later than baseline finish date)

To access the Slipping Tasks report, from *Report:View Reports* click the *In Progress* icon, and from the dropdown list select *Slipping Tasks*. Your screen will resemble the following:

Figure 432.

Slipping Tasks report

Create a New Report

At times you'll find that the available reports don't meet your organization's exact needs. Microsoft Project 2016 offers several report templates that help you to create your own reports.

📂 This exercise uses the file **Dashboards.mpp**. Ensure this file is open prior to beginning.

1 From *Report:View Reports* click the *New Report* icon to see a dropdown list with all available report templates.

Figure 433.

New report templates: *Blank*, *Chart*, *Table*, and *Comparison*

Creating a Chart Report

2 From the *New Report* dropdown list, select *Chart* to view the Chart template. A **Report Name** dialog box will appear, similar to the following, prompting you to name your new report (it is named "Report 1" by default), as in the following figure:

Figure 434.

Report Name dialog

3 Click *OK* to accept the default entry. Your new report based on the Chart template will appear, similar to the following:

Figure 435.

New Chart report

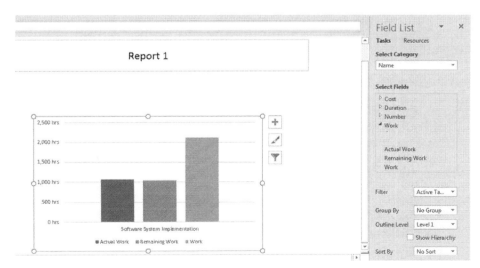

The chart-based report, by default, shows Actual Work, Remaining Work, and Work fields for your project. Use the *Field List* on the right side of the screen to select the fields you want to view and compare in the chart and to further customize the chart to suit your needs. Instruction around report customization is provided later in this section.

Creating a Table Report

4 From *Report:View Reports* click the *New Reports* icon, and from the dropdown list select *Table*. Name your table in the **Report Name** dialog box and click *OK* to see your new report.

Figure 436.

Table report

As you can see, by default this report shows project information that includes the Name, Start, Finish and % Complete fields. By default, this report shows only data at the Project Summary task level (we will cover modifying default settings in the *Customizing Reports* sub-section of this chapter). Just as in the Chart report, you can use the *Field List* on the right side of the screen to customize the table to suit your needs. The *Table Tools* tabs at the top of your screen (*Design* and *Layout*) provide the ability to further customize the table.

Creating a Comparison Report

5 From *Report:View Reports* click the *New Reports* icon, and from the dropdown list select *Comparison*. Name your Comparison report in the **Report Name** dialog box and click *OK* to see your new report.

Figure 437.

Comparison report

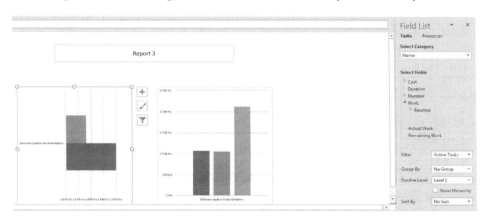

Comparison reports, by default, show two identical Chart-based reports showing Actual Work, Remaining Work, and Work. You can use the *Field List* selections to customize one chart, for the purpose of visually comparing one to the other. We will cover modifying default settings in the *Customizing Reports* sub-section of this chapter.

Creating a Blank New Report

6 The final New Report available is essentially an empty screen, where you can create a report "from scratch." From *Report:View Reports* click the *New Reports* icon, and from the dropdown list select *Blank*. Name your new report in the **Report Name** dialog box and click *OK* to see the foundation for your new report.

Figure 438.

Blank report

Click the *Report Tools* tab functions (shown in the preceding figure) to add images, shapes, charts, tables, and text and to your report.

Note: When you create a custom report, it will appear in the list of available custom reports. To access this list, use the *Custom* icon in *Report:View Reports*.

Figure 439.

Available
custom reports

Customizing Reports

In the preceding section we explored the various preconfigured reports and templates that are included with Microsoft Project 2016. Of course it's likely that you'll want to further customize some of these reports to best meet your organizational needs. Using built-in customization options, you can change the specific data that appears in a report as well as its overall appearance.

Changing the Information and Look of Reports

📁 This exercise uses the file **Dashboards.mpp**. Ensure this file is open prior to beginning.

1 From *Report:View Reports* click the *Dashboards* icon, and from the dropdown list click *Project Overview*. This report (which by default shows how much of your project is complete, tasks that are late, and upcoming milestones) will resemble the following:

Figure 440.

Project
Overview report

2 Click inside the *% Complete* chart in the upper-right portion of your screen and note the Field List sidepane that appears on the right side of your screen. It is within this sidepane that you find the tools to customize the data appearing in the selected report component (chart in this case).

Figure 441.

Field List
sidepane

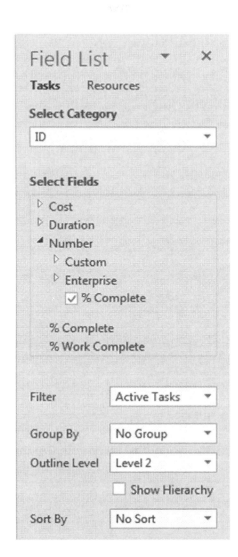

3 When you click on a chart or table, notice that three buttons appear
 to the right of the chart, as follows:

❑ **Chart Elements** [➕]: Click this button to easily add, remove or
 change chart elements, such as the title, key, gridlines, and data
 labels. You will see a list of elements, with a checkbox to the left of
 each. You can use these checkboxes to add (or remove) elements
 to your chart.

Figure 442.

**Chart
Elements** dialog

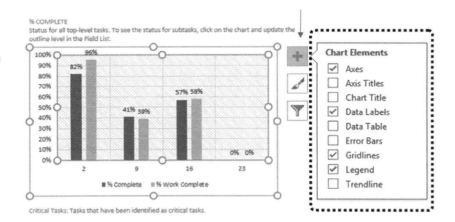

❑ **Chart Styles** [✎]: Click this button for quick access to tools that
 allow you to change the style and color scheme for your chart. By
 default, the *Style* tab is selected. Use the scroll bar to view and
 select alternative chart styles. Select the *Color* tab to alter the chart
 color(s).

Figure 443.

Chart Styles
dialog: *Style* &
Color tabs

❑ **Chart Filters [⛛]**: Click this button for quick access to tools that allow you to customize the data points and names that are visible on your chart.

Figure 444.

Chart Filters dialog

4 When you first clicked on the chart, the Field List sidepane and three additional formatting buttons appeared on your screen. Additionally, two more tabs appear in your toolbar, the *Chart:Design* tab and the *Chart:Format* tab.

Figure 445.

Chart:Design options

Figure 446.

Chart:Format options

Note: Similar toolbars appear when you're working within a table— *Table:Design* and *Table:Format*.

5 Now that we've reviewed the most useful customization tools, let's
 update our chart. Currently the chart reflects only the *% Complete*
 field. In the *Select Fields* section of the Task Field sidepane, uncheck
 the *% Work Complete* checkbox. Your chart will now resemble the
 following:

Figure 447.

Customizing
chart fields

6 Click the *Chart Elements* button (highlighted in the following figure),
 and from the list that appears click *Legend*. A legend will appear on
 your chart, identifying the fields represented.

Figure 448.

Adding a chart
Legend

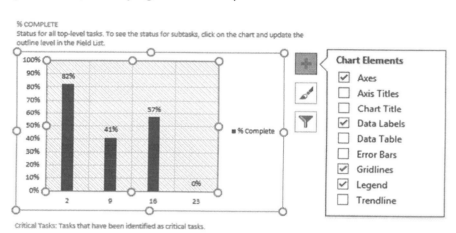

7 By default, this report only shows the status of top-level tasks. To expand the tasks represented, in the Task Field sidepane, use the dropdown arrow in the *Filter* field to select *In progress tasks*. Note the change to your chart:

Figure 449.

Change the
chart data

8 From *Chart Tools:Design*, click one of the available design options to change the style of your chart.

Figure 450.

Chart design

9 Let's change our focus now to the Late Tasks table component of your Project Overview report in the lower-right of your screen. Click your cursor within the table to activate the table customization options. The Field List sidepane will remain visible, and the *Chart Tools:Design/Format* toolbar tab will change to *Table Tools:Design* and *Table Tools:Format*.

10 Select *Constraint Date* in the Field List sidepane to add this field to your table.

Figure 451.

Adding a field to a table

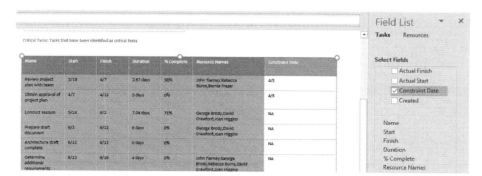

11 Perhaps you'd like this table to reflect the status of all critical tasks, rather than late tasks. In the Task Field sidepane, use the dropdown arrow in the *Filter* field to select *Critical*. Now this table will reflect the status of all critical tasks:

Figure 452.

Critical selected in *Filter* dropdown

12 Unfortunately, the title still says "Late Tasks." Click on *Late Tasks*—it's a text box—and change the text to read "Critical Tasks: Tasks that have been identified as critical tasks."

Note: By default, the Project Overview report displays task information. If you'd prefer to view resource information in the various report components, click the *Reports* link at the top of the Field List sidepane.

13 Save and close your project.

Getting Started

The Getting Started functionality provides some helpful information about how to begin using reports. Its purpose is primarily to provide a high-level tour about existing reporting capabilities.

The *Getting Started* icon, also found in *Report:View Reports*, provides access to some useful functions, including the following:

❑ **Best Practice Analyzer** – Can be used to identify potential issues with your project, such as tasks to which no resources have been assigned

Figure 453.

Best Practices
Analyzer

❑ **Create reports** – An introductory sampling of a dashboard report, covered in more detail earlier in this section

Figure 454.

Create dynamic
reports

❑ **Get started with Project** – Provides an overview of the help topics available as you build your project. As an example, click on the *Organize Tasks* link, and you will be presented with additional help topics to help you build a project plan.

Figure 455.

Get started with
Project

❑ **Organize Tasks** and **Share with Your Team** – Also provide help topics that can assist you as you build a project plan

Figure 456.

Organize Tasks

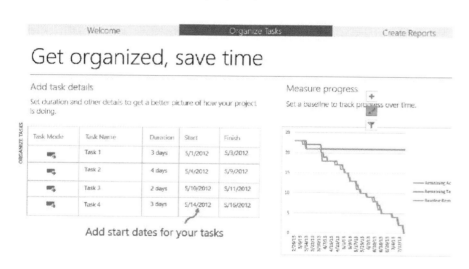

Figure 457.

Share with your team

Note: Every dropdown list in the *Report:View Reports* section of the *Report* toolbar (except *New Report*) provides access to every other available report (pre-configured or custom). Click *More Reports...* in any of these lists to access the **Reports** dialog box, where you can select from any of the available reports.

Figure 458.

Reports dialog box

Sharing Project Information

As we've discussed, Microsoft Project 2016 provides several tools that help you share the project information you've gathered with team members and stakeholders. You can print current report views, save report information as a PDF file, and copy the information and then paste it into other Microsoft Office tools. Custom report templates can also be saved using the Organizer so they are available to others.

Printing a Current Report View

📂 This exercise uses the file **Dashboards.mpp**. Ensure this project is open before beginning.

1 From *Report:View Reports* click the *Dashboard* icon, and from the dropdown list click *Project Overview*. The Project Overview report will appear on your screen.

2 From the *File* menu, click *Print* to view the **Print** dialog box, resembling the following:

Figure 459.

Print dialog box

3 Use the *Printer* dropdown list to select the printer you'd like to use. In the *Settings* section you can define the look of your printed report by selecting the paper size and orientation, and also by determining how much of the report you'd like to print (All, or just a selected page range). Note: As you change settings in the **Print** dialog box, the display on the right provides you with a current preview of your selected options.

4 Click *Print* to print your report.

Capturing Report Information in a PDF File

Report information can also be saved in a PDF format and then shared or printed as needed.

5 Return to your Project Overview report. From the *File* menu, click *Save As* to access the **Save As** dialog box. Navigate to the location where you would like to save the file.

Figure 460.

Save As dialog box

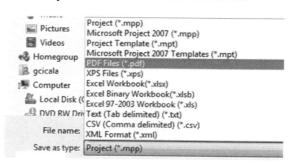

6 In the *Save as type* field, use the dropdown list (as in the preceding figure) to select *PDF Files* and click *Save*. The **Document Export Options** dialog box will appear:

Figure 461.

Document Export Options
dialog box

7 Click *Ok* to accept the default options in this dialog box. A PDF file containing your report information will appear in the location you assigned it to in step 5.

Copying a Report

Microsoft Project 2016 makes it easy for you to copy report information into other Microsoft Office tools.

8 Return again to your Project Overview report. In the *Report Tools* section of the toolbar, click the *Copy Report* icon [⊞] under *Design:Report*. The report data you just copied is stored in the clipboard.

9 Open a new blank document in Microsoft Word (or any other data presentation tool). Place your cursor within the new document, and from *Home:Clipboard* click *Paste* to paste your report data into the Microsoft Word document.

10 Close your project.

Custom Reports and the Organizer

📁 This exercise uses the file **Dashboards_Inst1.mpp**. Ensure this file is open before beginning.

The Organizer allows you to add custom objects (reports, fields, calendars, tables, views, etc.) to your local Global template, where these objects are then available for use across all of your projects. In order to make these objects available on Project Server, contact your Project Server administrator to update the enterprise Global template.

To copy a custom report to your local Global template:

1 From *Report:View Reports* click the *Custom* icon to see the custom reports you created earlier in this section.

Figure 462.

Custom reports

2 From *File:Info* click the *Organizer* icon to see the **Organizer** dialog box.

Figure 463.

Accessing the Organizer

Figure 464.

Organizer dialog box

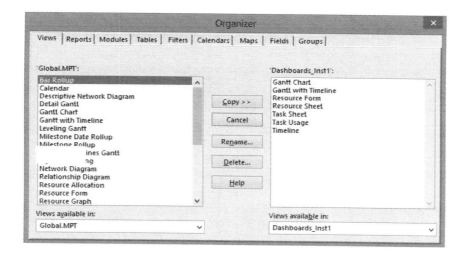

3 Select the *Reports* tab.

Figure 465.

Organizer
dialog box with
Reports tab
selected

The list on the left side of the Organizer shows reports in the Global template, while the list on the right shows reports in the current project.

4 Select *Report 1* (the custom chart report you created) and then click the *Copy* button to move *Report 1* to the Global template. *Report 1* is now available to all of your projects.

5 Click *Close* to close the Organizer, and then close your project.

15.5 Exporting Project Information

In addition to presenting project information within Microsoft Project, Microsoft Project data can be exported into other applications with additional reporting capabilities using the reporting functionality.

Visual Reports

Along with the *Reports* functionality we just reviewed, the *Report* toolbar includes a *Visual Reports* icon. This functionality provides access to Excel and Visio report templates to prepare graphic reports.

In the following exercise, you are in the middle of a project that is scheduled to end on October 1. You were asked to prepare a status report for management as of the end of last week, June 21 (of the current year).

📂 This exercise uses the file **ExportData.mpp**. Be sure this project is open before beginning.

1 From *Report:Export* click the *Visual Reports* [] icon. Your screen will resemble the following:

Figure 466.

Initiating a Visual Report

Notice this dialog box lists the currently available templates on the *All* tab—which appears by default—and shows a sample of the selected report layout in the smaller, right-hand window. You can also create new templates or edit existing ones to define the structure of the report.

2 Select each of the available templates, and you will see a preview of the sample report in the **Create Report** dialog box.

3 With the *All* tab selected, choose the *Baseline Cost Report* and click *View*. Excel builds a local Online Analytical Processing (OLAP) cube file and Excel will open and present your data in an Excel PivotChart or Visio PivotDiagram. Your Microsoft Excel screen will resemble the following:

Figure 467.

Sample Baseline Cost Report

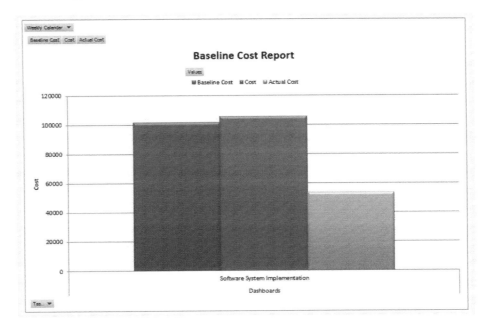

4 Click in the chart to see the PivotChart Fields sidepane, which you can use to adjust the presentation.

Figure 468.

PivotChart Fields sidepane

5 In the PivotChart Fields sidepane, highlight the *Tasks* checkbox and click the adjacent dropdown arrow.

6 In the **Select field:Tasks** dialog box that appears, click the plus sign left of the Project Name to reveal the phases and tasks that comprise the WBS. Clear the task *Build Project plan* by deselecting the check box, as in the following figure:

Figure 469.

Modified Tasks list

7 Click *OK* to remove the empty column in the preceding figure. Your screen will now resemble the following:

Figure 470.

Modified Visual Report view

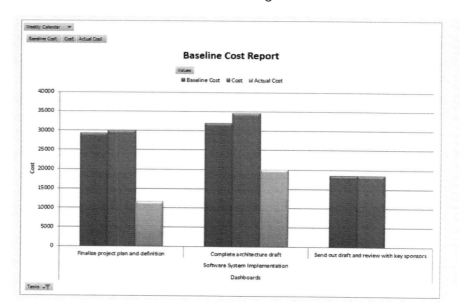

8 At the bottom of the Pivot Chart, click the *Assignment Usage* worksheet tab to see the corresponding tabular data. You also can click the plus sign left of the Project Name to reveal the phases and tasks that comprise the WBS

Figure 471.

Assignment Usage Pivot Table worksheet tab

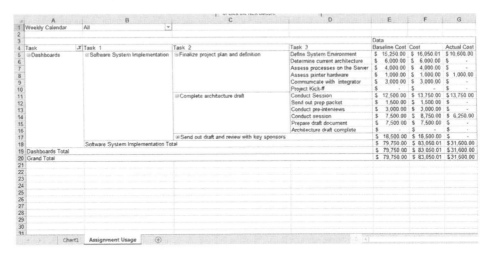

9 Note that you can add currency signs as you can with any Microsoft Excel spreadsheet. Also, if you click on a task name within the chart, such as *Finalize project plan and definition*, a list of available PivotTable fields appears on the right, and the native PivotTable formatting capabilities available in Microsoft Excel are enabled in this worksheet. For more information regarding formatting PivotTables in Excel, please refer to Microsoft Excel online help.

Figure 472.

PivotTable Fields sidepane

10 From the *File* menu in Microsoft Excel, click *Close*. You will be asked if you want to save the Excel document. If you click *Save*, you will save this report as a Microsoft Excel Workbook. Click *Don't Save* and return to Microsoft Project.

11 Again, open the **Visual Reports – Create Report** dialog box (*Report:Export:Visual Reports*), and at the bottom click *Save Data*. You will see the following dialog:

Figure 473.

Save Data dialog
options

Notice that you can save a pivot table with data specific to this project or save an Access database of the data for reporting purposes. You can also modify the contents of the report by using the *Field Picker* tool. There are several different cube types built into the Visual Reports tool. These generally include the types of data in the corresponding Microsoft Project reports and are shown in the following figure:

Figure 474.

Available pivot
table types

12 Choose the Task Usage pivot table type. Then click the *Field Picker* button to see the available and included fields in this cube.

Figure 475.

Field Picker tool

13 Click *Cancel* to return to the **Save Reporting Data** dialog box. Click *Close* to return to the **Visual Reports - Create Report** dialog.

14 Save and close your project.

Note: Some of the visual reports can also be rendered in Microsoft Visio. If you look at the icon next to each report name you will see that the Excel and Vision icons indicate which type of output will be rendered from each visual report.

End of Chapter Quiz Questions

1. Which function enables formatting the Gantt bars and associated text labels on the Gantt Chart?

 []

2. Fill the blank: By comparing a task's baseline to its plan in the _____ _____ view, you can see how a task's actual schedule compares to its original estimate.

3. How can you set the Current Date for a project in Microsoft Project?

 []

4. What are the two ways to change the bar style for a Gantt Chart?

 []

5. How would you insert the column Baseline Start to the left of the Start column in the Entry Table?

 []

6. True or False: Microsoft Project allows you to customize and control almost all aspects of information presentation, including views, formats, and layouts.

7. Fill in the blank: Microsoft Project 2016 _____ calculates the difference between current progress and original estimates.

8. What are the five different variance fields that Microsoft Project automatically calculates, and how are they calculated?

 []

9. How do you get accurate variance data when using % Complete tracking?

10. Fill in the blank: Any time the current estimated values are higher than the baseline values, the resulting variance will be a _____ number. This means that any variance greater than is considered_____.

11. What can you see using the **Project Statistics** dialog?

12. What is a table?

13. What can you do if none of the standard tables meet your needs?

14. What are the most useful views for tasks?

_____ & _____

15. What are the most useful views for resources?

_____ & _____

16. What are the most useful views for assignments?

_____ & _____

17. What does the Task Usage view display?

18. What does the Resource Sheet display?

```

```

19. What does the Resource Usage view display?

```

```

20. How would you show the critical and non-critical tasks, as well as progress against those tasks, using a comprehensive view that shows estimates, actuals and baselines all on the same Gantt Chart?

```

```

21. True or False: There is no table that shows all five types of variance.

22. How to do you display the Variance table?

```

```

23. How can you display cost variances in your project?

```

```

24. How can you display work variances in your project?

25. How can you display schedule variances in your project?

26. Fill in the blank: The Variance table includes the _____ and _____ variance fields.

27. What are filters in Microsoft Project, and when would they be helpful?

┌───┐
│ │
│ │
│ │
│ │
└───┘

28. How would you sort by multiple fields?

┌───┐
│ │
│ │
│ │
└───┘

29. Describe the Group by function:

┌───┐
│ │
│ │
│ │
│ │
└───┘

30. How do you create a new view?

┌───┐
│ │
│ │
│ │
│ │
└───┘

31. What are the two major categories of custom fields and who usually sets them up?

┌───┐
│ │
│ │
│ │
│ │
└───┘

32. What is the simplest and easiest way to share your custom objects to your other project files?

33. What are the four categories of preconfigured reports on the *Report* toolbar?

 _____, _____, _____, & _____.

34. How can you create a new report from a template?

35. What does the Visual Reports function provide?

36. How can you access the visual reports?

Concluding Remarks

The Human Touch

In Section 6.2: *A Caution on Automated Project Management Tools*, we said that "A fool with a tool is a faster fool." It's important to bear in mind, though, that the theory we covered is also insufficient.

The theories referenced serve as generalized best practices for what should work most of the time, under ideal conditions; however, the most common adjective used to describe projects is "unique." There's a reason why project management is done by humans and not by automated robots; it takes an experienced, nuanced human touch to combine the theory and the technology and apply them (or don't, as they see fit) to the unique needs of every project.

The other essentially human qualities that organizations require from their project managers is healthy dose of leadership and judgment. A project manager's grasp of theory can be tested and proven through exams that result in hard-earned certifications, such as PMI's Project Management Professional (PMP). However, when project managers meet resistance, the theory can be put to the test, often to the point of triggering project failure.

Project management is the art and science of continuously re-synching the plan to the new realities in the face of these points of resistance. Project leadership and judgment are the keys to success in the battle to save projects in the real-life situations where there's a strong refusal to accept bad news, organizational politics that are set up for failure, and challenges with an embedded culture that's threatening to send a project off the rails.

This book only covered how to put your project in the best position to succeed, but good project leaders embrace the reality that some projects will fail. Project managers often use this realistic foresight to uncover trouble sooner and take proactive measures to get the project on plan or close enough to plan to save it from failure. However, sometimes it is best for project managers to come to terms with the fact that the project realities have been so far separated from what was initially planned that is it time to declare that it's time for the project to "fail faster."

So as comprehensive as this text is in guiding you to use Microsoft Project 2016 to manage your projects, know that much of the skills transcend what was discussed here. And also know that sometimes even the best of efforts are futile, and the best thing a project manager can do for a project destined to fail is to "face the music" and move on.

Happy trails on your project management journey!

Index

About the Author

Gus Cicala is the president, CEO, and co-founder of Project Assistants, a regularly published author on project management, and an acclaimed speaker. He graduated cum laude from the Wharton Business School and has over thirty years of project management experience and thirty-five years of information technology development and consulting expertise.

In his 21 years since founding Project Assistants, he and his team have served their clients, based on the mission to "Deliver the Future into the Present." Project Assistants fulfills their mission by ensuring the success of their clients' vision working with the PMO's expectation to ensure better, faster, & more cost-effective projects.

Project Assistants support their clients through two primary services offerings. The first is PMO definition, deployment, and adoption, which includes Microsoft Project EPM implementation. The second is project management staffing and full-time placements.

In addition to writing this publication, Gus was a contributing author to the third edition of *Expediting Drug and Biologics Development.* He was also a contributing author on the topic of project leadership for *The Keys to Our Success: Lessons Learned from 25 of Our Best Project Managers.*

Gus' articles on Microsoft Project are routinely published, including in the Microsoft Project Users Group, Macmillan's Que book series: Special Edition: Using Microsoft Project, and Microsoft's own Step-by-Step guides for Microsoft Project. He was a long-standing member of Microsoft's product advisory council and an active member of the Microsoft Partner Research Panel, both of which had a say in the very features, functions, and distribution of Microsoft Project.

In Gus' personal life, he has been married to his lovely wife, Susan, for 37 years and enjoys much of his free time at their Christmas tree farm in Shaftsbury, Vermont. Gus & Susan raised four adult children and now have five grandchildren (so far). Gus owns & flies a Piper Arrow as an instrument rated private pilot. He is the former president and active Board of Directors member of the Limen House, a non-profit organization dedicated to turning around the lives of recovering alcoholics and addicts in Wilmington, Delaware. Gus is also one of the founders of the rapidly growing social entrepreneurship program at Malvern Prep.

 www.linkedin.com/in/guscicala/

 @GusCicala

 www.projectassistants.com
guscicala@projectassistants.com
800-642-9259

Made in the USA
Middletown, DE
19 June 2017